ST. THOMAS AQUINAS

Treatise on Man

ST. THOMAS AQUINAS

Treatise on Man

Translated by

JAMES F. ANDERSON

Professor of Philosophy

Villanova University

PRENTICE-HALL, INC.

Englewood Cliffs, N.J.

For my children

Fourth printing ...... April, 1965

© 1962 by

PRENTICE-HALL, INC.

Englewood Cliffs, N.J.

Library of Congress
Catalog Card No. 62-7450

Printed in the United States of America

93066-C

Table of Contents

Introduction

Although there are hundreds—perhaps thousands—of scientific studies concerned with every detail of man's life—social, economic, psychological, physical, etc.—one question commonly overlooked by researchers in all these fields is: what is man?

In this Treatise, St. Thomas Aquinas proposes to answer that question, and others closely related to it. One might say: "the question is trivial—everyone knows what man is." Unfortunately, this is far from being true. From the earliest times, up to today, men have held widely divergent, and even contradictory, views about the nature of man. For example, he has been thought of as essentially a spirit imprisoned in the flesh—a mind united to a body only accidentally and temporarily. (Platonism, old and new; Origen; Descartes). On the other hand—and these conceptions are typically modern, though not unknown in earlier times—man has been viewed as an animal essentially no different from other animals; or likened to a machine, necessarily producing the acts he does; or even to a chemical compound, reducible some day to a chemical formula.

The basic answer to the question, what is man?, is widely unknown. It is not a trivial question. If we do not know what man essentially is, we shall be in a state of *fundamental* ignorance of everything else about him: man must know at least what he is, if he is to know anything else about himself specifically as a human being. This knowledge is something that we need to have *as men.*

St. Thomas' Treatise on Man occurs in the First Part of his *Theological Summa* (*Summa Theologiae*), which treats of God and the Order of Creation, and which is itself divided into three main parts: (1) God: The Divine Unity (questions 2-26); (2) God: The Trinity of Persons (questions 27-43); (3) God: The Creator and Governor of the Universe (questions 44-119). The Treatise on Man (questions 75-89) falls under this third part, which contains six treatises—on Creation in General, on The Angels, on The Work of the Six Days, on Man, on The First Man, and on The Divine Government.

Since the Treatise on Man occurs in a theological work, it follows the theological order, considering the nature of man in relation to the soul and not in relation to the body except in so far as the body has relation to the soul, as St. Thomas points out in his own Introduction.

Accordingly, St. Thomas considers first the human soul in its essence and its union with the body; secondly, he treats of its powers; thirdly, of its operation. He does not in this treatise, as in his commentary on Aristotle's work, *On The Soul*, follow the philosophical order, ascending from the sensible to the spiritual—from vegetative life, to sense life, to intellectual life. Rather, he here starts with the problem of the soul's spirituality, proceeding then to the problem of its union with the body, to its faculties, and finally, its acts. (The last question of the treatise—question 89, on the Separate Soul's Knowledge—is omitted as not pertaining to the basic subject matter of philosophical psychology as commonly conceived.)

The question immediately arises: if this treatise on man occurs in a *theological* work and follows a *theological* order, then what value has it specifically for *philosophical* instruction? The question is an excellent one, and the answer to it is this: although the *order* followed in this Treatise is theological, the *argumentation* is philosophical: its validity does not rest upon any antecedent theological commitment; St. Thomas proceeds demonstratively from reason. That is why the Treatise on Man is a fitting text to be used in those philosophy courses which are variously named "rational psychology," "philosophical psychology," "the philosophy of man."

Finally, a word about the translation. Not only has a consistent effort been made to render St. Thomas' Latin into English without sacrificing his true meaning—no translator can conscientiously aim at doing less—but also to render it into idiomatic English. This is, to a degree, an impossible undertaking, since there are often no strict equivalents in our ordinary usage for certain Thomistic words and expressions, e.g., *"potentia"* and *"actus," "esse," "ratio," "species," "intentionale," "principium," "phantasma," "corruptio," "differentia," "secundum,"* etc. Nevertheless, this translation of an important segment of St. Thomas' *Summa Theologiae*—the Treatise on Man—is not only substantially accurate but also sufficiently idiomatic, we hope, to be useful to college students, and to interested laymen in general.

Grateful acknowledgment is due the English Dominican translators of the *Summa;* their monumental work has been of great assistance to me.

I am indebted to the editors of the Ottawa-Piana *Summa Theologiae* of St. Thomas Aquinas (1941) for most of the references given in the footnotes.

J. F. A.

On Man, Who Is Spiritual and Bodily in His Substantial Make-up: and First, Concerning What Belongs to the Essence of the Soul

(In Seven Articles)

Having considered the spiritual and the corporeal creature, we must now treat of man, who is spiritual and bodily in his substantial make-up. First we shall consider the nature of man, and secondly his origin.[1] Now the theologian considers the nature of man in relation to the soul but not in relation to the body, except in so far as the body has relation to the soul. That is why the first object of our study will be the soul. And since Dionysius says[2] that three things are found in spiritual substances—essence, power and operation—we shall treat first of what belongs to the essence of the soul; secondly, of what belongs to its power or its potencies;[3] thirdly, of what belongs to its operation.[4]

Concerning the first, two points are to be considered: the nature of the soul in itself, and the union of the soul with the body. Under the first head there are seven points of inquiry.

First Article

IS THE SOUL A BODY?

Objection 1. It seems that the soul is a body. For the soul is the mover of the body. Nor does it move unless moved. First, because nothing, it seems, can move unless it is itself moved, since nothing gives what it has not; e.g., what is not hot does not produce heat; secondly, because if there be anything that moves and is itself not moved, it must be the cause of eternal and uniform movement, as is proved.[5] Now this does not appear to be the case in the movement of an animal, which is caused by the soul. Therefore the soul is a moved mover. But every moved mover is a body. Therefore the soul is a body.

1. Question XC.
2. *On the Celestial Hierarchy* XI, 2.
3. Question LXXVII.
4. Question LXXXIV.
5. Aristotle, *Physics* VIII, 10 (267b3).

1

Objection 2. Moreover, all knowledge is caused by means of a likeness. But there can be no likeness of a body to an incorporeal thing. Therefore, if the soul were not a body, it would be unable to know corporeal things.

Objecion 3. Again, between the mover and the moved there must be some contact. But there is contact only between bodies. Since, therefore, the soul moves the body, it seems that the soul is a body.

On the contrary: Augustine says that the soul "is simple in comparison with the body, inasmuch as it does not occupy space by any bulk." [6]

I answer that: A precondition of inquiry concerning the nature of the soul is the proposition that the soul is the first principle of life in those things in our world which live; for we call living things "animate," and lifeless things, "inanimate." Now life is evidenced chiefly by two activities: knowledge and movement. The ancient philosophers, not being able to rise above their imagination, supposed that the principle of these actions was something bodily; for they asserted that only bodies were real things, and that what is not bodily is nothing.[7] Hence they maintained that the soul is some sort of body. Although the falsity of this opinion can be demonstrated in many ways, we shall make use of only one proof, which indeed shows more universally and certainly that the soul is not a body.

It is manifest that not every source of vital action is a soul, for then the eye would be a soul, since it is a source of vision; and the same could be said of the other instruments of the soul. Rather, it is the *first* source of life which we call the soul. True, a corporeal thing may be a source of life, as the heart is a source of life in an animal. But no such thing can be the *first* source of life. For it is clear that to be a source of life, or to be a living thing, does not belong to a body as a body, since, if that were the case, every body would be a living thing, or a source of life. Therefore a body can be a living thing, or even a source of life, as *a certain kind of* body. Now that it is actually a certain kind of body it owes to some source which is called its "act." Therefore the soul, which is the first source of life, is not a body, but the actuating form of a body; just as heat, which is the source of heating, is not a body, but an actuating form of a body.

Reply Objection 1. Since everything which is moved must be moved by something else, a process which cannot go on indefinitely, we must admit that not every mover is moved. For, since to be moved is to pass from potency to act, the mover gives what it has to the thing moved, in that it causes it to be in act. But it has been shown that there exists a mover which is altogether immovable, and which is not moved either essentially or by accident.[8] And such a mover can cause an eternally uniform move-

6. *On the Trinity* VI, 6.
7. The pre-Socratics are meant.
8. Aristotle, *Physics* VIII, 5 (258b4); 6(258b15); 10(267b3).

ment. There is, however, another kind of mover, which, though not moved essentially, is moved by accident; and for this reason it does not cause a uniform movement. Such a mover is the soul. There is, again, another mover, which is moved through itself, viz., the body. And because the ancient natural philosophers believed that nothing existed except bodies, they maintained that every mover is moved, and that the soul is moved through itself, and is a body.

Reply Objection 2. The likeness of the thing known need not be actually present in the nature of the knower. But given a being which first knows potentially and afterwards knows actually, the likeness of the thing known must not be actually in the nature of the knower, but only potentially; e.g., color is not actually in the pupil of the eye, but only potentially. Hence it is necessary, not that the likeness of corporeal things be actually in the nature of the soul, but that there be a potentiality in the soul for such a likeness. But the ancient naturalists did not know how to distinguish between act and potency. That is why they held that the soul must be a body in order to know all bodies, and that it must be composed of the factors of which all bodies are formed.

Reply Objection 3. There are two kinds of contact, that of *quantity,* and that of *power.* By the former a body can be touched only by a body; by the latter a body can be touched by an incorporeal reality, which moves that body.

Second Article

IS THE HUMAN SOUL SOMETHING SUBSISTENT?

Objection 1. It seems that the human soul is not something subsistent. For that which subsists is said to be "this particular thing." Now the term, "this particular thing," is predicated not of the soul, but of that which is composed of soul and body. Therefore the soul is not something subsistent.

Objection 2. Further, everything subsistent can be said to "operate." But the soul is not said to operate. For, as Aristotle remarks, "to say that the soul feels or understands is like saying that the soul weaves or builds." [9] Therefore the soul is not subsistent.

Objection 3. Then, too, if the soul were something subsistent, it would have some operation apart from the body. But it has no operation apart from the body, not even that of understanding; for the act of understanding does not take place without an image, which cannot exist apart from the body.[10] Therefore the human soul is not something subsistent.

---

9. Aristotle, *On the Soul* I, 4 (408b11).

10. Literally, "phantasm"; i.e., a sense-representation of any sort, and not only a visual image.

On the contrary: Augustine says: "Whoever understands that the nature of the mind is that of a substance and not that of a body, will see that those who maintain the corporeal nature of the mind are led astray because they associate with the mind those things without which they are unable to think of any nature"—viz., images of bodily things.[11] Therefore the human mind is not only incorporeal in its nature, but is also a substance, viz., something subsistent.

I answer that: It must necessarily be granted that the source of intellectual operation, which we call the soul of man, is a principle both incorporeal and subsistent. For it is clear that by means of the intellect man can know the natures of all corporeal things. Now whatever knows certain things cannot have any of them in its own nature, because that which is in it naturally would prevent the knowledge of anything else. Thus we observe that a sick man's tongue, being affected by a feverish and bitter humor, is insensible to anything sweet, and everything seems bitter to it. Therefore, if the intellectual principle contained within itself the nature of any body, it would be unable to know all bodies. Now every body has its own determinate nature. Therefore it is impossible for the intellectual principle to be a body. It is also impossible for it to understand by means of a bodily organ, since the determinate nature of that organ would likewise impede knowledge of all bodies; as when a certain determinate color is not only in the pupil of the eye, but also in a glass vase, the liquid in the vase seems to be of that same color.

Therefore the intellectual principle, which is called the "mind" or the "intellect," has essentially an operation in which the body does not share. Now, only that which subsists in itself can have an operation in itself. For nothing can operate except what is in act. Hence a thing operates according as it is. Thus we say not that heat imparts heat, but that what is hot imparts heat. It therefore follows that the human soul, which is called "intellect" or "mind," is something incorporeal and subsistent.

Reply Objection 1. The expression, "this particular thing," can be taken in two senses: (1) for anything subsistent; (2) for that which subsists and is complete in a specific nature. The former sense excludes the inherence of an accident or of a material form; the latter excludes also the imperfection of the part. Thus a hand can be called "this particular thing" in the first sense, but not in the second. Therefore, since the human soul is a part of the human species, it can be called "this particular thing" in the first sense, as being something subsistent, but not in the second; for in this sense it is the composite of body and soul which is said to be "this particular thing."

Reply Objection 2. Aristotle said those things not in order to express

---

11. *On the Trinity* X, 7.

his own opinion, but the opinion of those who said that to understand is to be moved, as is clear from the context—or it must be said that to operate through itself belongs to what exists through itself. But sometimes a thing can be said to exist through itself if it be not inherent, as an accident or a material form, even though it be a part. Nevertheless, that is said to subsist properly and through itself which is neither inherent in the above sense, nor a part. In this sense, the eye or the hand cannot be said to subsist through itself; nor can it for that reason be said to operate through itself. Hence the operations of the parts are, through each part, attributed to the whole. For we say that man sees with the eye and feels with the hand, and not in the same sense as when we say that what is hot gives heat by its heat; for heat, properly speaking, does not give heat. It can therefore be said that the soul understands just as the eye sees. But it is more correct to say that man understands through the soul.

Reply Objection 3. The body is necessary for the action of the intellect, not as its organ of action, but by reason of the object. For the image is to the intellect what color is to the sight. Neither does such a dependence on the body prove the intellect to be nonsubsistent. Otherwise, it would follow that an animal is nonsubsistent simply because it requires external sensibles for sensation.

Third Article

ARE THE SOULS OF BRUTE ANIMALS SUBSISTENT?

Objection 1. It seems that the souls of brute animals are subsistent. For man is of the same genus as other animals, and, as we have shown, the soul of man is subsistent.[12] Therefore the souls of other animals are subsistent.

Objection 2. Moreover, the relation of the sensory power to sensible objects is like the relation of the intellectual power to intelligible objects. But the intellect, without the body, understands intelligible objects. Therefore the sensory power, without the body, apprehends sensible objects. But the souls of brute animals are sensory in character. Therefore they are subsistent, for the same reason that the human soul, which is intellectual, is subsistent.

Objection 3. Again, the soul of brute animals moves the body. But the body is not a mover, but is moved. Therefore the soul of brute animals has an operation apart from the body.

On the contrary: It is written: "Man alone we believe to have a subsistent soul; whereas the souls of animals are not subsistent." [13]

---

12. Preceding article.
13. Gennadius, *On the Teachings of the Church.* (Not available in English.)

I answer that: The ancient philosophers made no distinction between sense and intellect, and referred both to a corporeal principle, as has been said.[14] Plato, however, distinguished between intellect and sense, but he referred both to a spiritual source, maintaining that sensing, like understanding, belongs to the soul of itself.[15] From this it followed that even the souls of brute animals are subsistent. But Aristotle held that understanding is the only operation of the soul which is performed without a physical organ.[16] On the other hand, sensation, and the operations of the sensory soul following upon it, clearly involve some change in the body; e.g., in the act of vision, the pupil of the eye is affected by the likeness of color; and it is so with the other senses. Hence it is clear that the sensory soul has no operation properly its own, and that every operation of the sensory soul belongs to the composite. Therefore the conclusion is that, since the souls of brute animals have no *per se* operations, they are not subsistent. For the operation of anything follows the way of its being.

Reply Objection 1. Although man is of the same genus as other animals, he is of a different species. Now, difference of species is derived from difference of form; nor does every difference of form necessarily imply a diversity of genus.

Reply Objection 2. The relation of the sensory power to the sensible object is in one way the same as that of the intellectual power to the intelligible object, in so far as each is in potency to its object. But in another way their relations differ, in that the impression of the sensible object on the sense faculty is accompanied with change in the body; so that when the intensity of the object is excessive, the sense is corrupted. This never occurs in the case of the intellect. For an intellect that understands the highest of intelligible objects is more able afterwards to understand those that are lower. If, however, in the process of intellectual activity the body is fatigued, this result is accidental, inasmuch as the intellect requires the operation of the sensory powers in the production of the sense representations.[17]

Reply Objection 3. A motive power is of two kinds. *One,* the appetitive power, which commands motion, and whose operation in the sensory soul is not without the body; for anger, joy, and passions of a like nature, are accompanied by some change in the body. The *other* motive power is that which executes motion in adapting the members for obeying the appetite; and the act of this power does not consist in moving, but in being moved. Whence it is clear that movement is not an act of the sensory soul without the body.

---

14. *Summa Theologiae,* Question L, article 1.

15. *Theaetetus* 184c.

16. *On the Soul* III, 4 (429a24).

17. Literally: "phantasms" which contain the indispensable material from which our abstractive-intellectual knowledge is obtained.

Fourth Article

IS THE SOUL MAN?

Objection 1. It seems that the soul is man. For it is written (*2 Corinthians 4:16*): "Though our outward man is corrupted, yet the inward man is renewed day by day." But that which is within man is the soul. Therefore the soul is the inward man.

Objection 2. Further, the human soul is a substance. But it is not a universal substance. Therefore it is a particular substance. Therefore it is a hypostasis or a person. But it can be only a human person. Therefore the soul is a man, for a human person is a man.

On the contrary: Augustine commends Varro as holding that man "is not the soul alone, nor the body alone, but both soul and body." [18]

I answer that: The assertion, "the soul is a man," can be taken in two senses. First, that man is a soul, though this particular man (Socrates, for instance) is not a soul, but is composed of soul and body. I say this because some held that the form alone belongs to the species, while matter is part of the individual and not of the species. This cannot be true, for to the nature of the species belongs what the definition signifies, and in natural things the definition does not signify the form alone, but both the form and the matter. Hence in natural things the matter is part of the species; not, indeed, signate matter, which is the principle of individuation, but common matter. For just as it belongs to the nature of this particular man to be composed of this soul, of this flesh, and of these bones, so it belongs to the nature of man to be composed of soul, flesh, and bones; for whatever belongs in common to the substance of all the individuals contained under a given species must belong also to the substance of the species.

The phrase, "the soul is a man," may also be understood in this sense, viz., that this soul is this man. Now this could be held if it were supposed that the activity of the sensory soul were proper to it without the body; because in that case all the acts which are attributed to man would belong only to the soul. But each thing is that which performs its own operations, and consequently that is man which performs the acts of a man. But it has been shown above that sensation is not the act of the soul alone.[19] Since, then, sensation is an operation of man, but not his proper operation, it is clear that man is not only a soul, but something composed of soul and body. Plato, through supposing that sensation was proper to the soul, could maintain man to be "a soul making use of a body." [20]

---

18. *On the City of God* XIX, 3.
19. Preceding article.
20. cf. *Alcibiades* 130c.

Reply Objection 1. According to Aristotle,[21] "each thing seems to be chiefly what is most important in it." Thus, what the governor of a state does, the state is said to do. In this way sometimes what is most important in man is said to be man: sometimes it is the intellectual part which, in truth, is called the inward man; and sometimes the sensitive part with the body is called man in the opinion of those who are preoccupied solely with sensible things. And this is called the outward man.

Reply Objection 2. Not every particular substance is a hypostasis or a person, but that which has the complete nature of its species. Hence a hand, or a foot, cannot be called a hypostasis, or a person; nor, likewise, is the soul alone so called, since it is a part of the human species.

Fifth Article

IS THE SOUL COMPOSED OF MATTER AND FORM?

Objection 1. It would seem that the soul is composed of matter and form. For potency is opposed to act.[22] Now all things that are in act participate in the First Act, which is God. It is by participation in God that all things are good, beings, and living things, as is clear from the doctrine of Dionysius. Therefore, all things that are in potency participate in the first potency. But the first potency is primary matter. Therefore, since the human soul is, after a manner, in potency (which appears from the fact that sometimes a man is potentially understanding), it seems that the human soul participates in primary matter, as a part of itself.

Objection 2. Moreover, wherever the properties of matter are found, there matter is. But the properties of matter are found in the soul, viz., to be a subject, and to be changed. For the soul is subject to science and to virtue; and it changes from ignorance to knowledge and from vice to virtue. Therefore there is matter in the soul.

Objection 3. Further, things which have no matter have no cause of their being, as is said.[23] But the soul has a cause of its being, since it is created by God. Therefore the soul has matter.

Objection 4. Further, what has no matter, and is only a form, is a pure act, and is infinite. But this belongs to God alone. Therefore the soul has matter.

On the contrary: Augustine proves that the soul was made neither of corporeal matter, nor of spiritual matter.

I answer that: The soul has no matter. We may consider this question

---

21. *Nichomachean Ethics* IX, 8 (1168b31).

22. *"Actus,"* a word often untranslatable into idiomatic English: it means that which renders actual in any way, or is a principle of actuation, as such. "Act" thus may be said of a form, whether substantial or accidental, of an action, or, finally, of being or existing.

23. Aristotle, *Metaphysics* VII, 6 (1045b4).

in two ways. First, from the notion of a soul in general, for it belongs to the notion of a soul to be the form of a body. Now, either it is a form in its entirety, or by virtue of some part of itself. If in its entirety, then it is impossible that any part of it should be matter, if by matter we understand something purely potential; for a form, as such, is an act, and that which is purely potential cannot be part of an act, since potency is repugnant to act as being its opposite. If, however, it be a form by virtue of a part of itself, then we shall call that part the "soul," and that matter which it actualizes first we shall call the "primary living thing."

Secondly, we may proceed from the specific notion of the human soul, insofar as it is intellectual. For it is evident that whatever is received into something is received according to the mode of the recipient. Now a thing is known in as far as its form is in the knower. But the intellectual soul knows a thing in its nature unqualifiedly; e.g., it knows a stone simply as a stone; and therefore the form of a stone absolutely, as to its proper formal notion, is in the intellectual soul. Consequently, the intellectual soul itself is an absolute form, and not something composed of matter and form. For if the intellectual soul were composed of matter and form, the forms of things would be received into it as individuals, and so it would only know the individual; as is the case with the sense powers, which receive forms in a bodily organ. For matter is the principle by which forms are individuated. It follows, therefore, that the intellectual soul, and every intellectual substance which has knowledge of forms absolutely, is exempt from composition of matter and form.

Reply Objection 1. The First Act is the universal source of all acts, because It is infinite, precontaining all things in its power, as Dionysius says. Therefore It is participated in by things, not as a part of themselves, but by diffusion of Its processions. Now as potency is receptive of act, it must be proportioned to act. But the acts received which proceed from the First Infinite Act, and are participations of it, are diverse; so that there cannot be one potency which receives all acts, in the same way that there is one act from which all participated acts are derived; for then the receptive potency would equal the active potency of the First Act. Now the receptive potency in the intellectual soul is other than the receptive potency of primary matter, as appears from the diversity of the things received by each. For primary matter receives individual forms; whereas the intellect receives absolute forms. Hence the existence of such potency in the intellectual soul does not prove that the soul is composed of matter and form.

Reply Objection 2. To be a subject and to be changed belong to matter by reason of its being in potency. Therefore, just as the potency of the intellect is one thing and the potency of primary matter another, so in each is there a different manner of subjectivity and of change. For the intellect is subject to knowledge, and is changed from ignorance to knowledge, by reason of its being in potency with regard to the intelligible species.

Reply Objection 3. The form causes matter to be, and so does the agent, whence, the agent causes matter to be in so far as it changes it to the actuality of a form. A subsistent form, however, does not owe its being to some formal principle, nor has it a cause changing it from potency to act. So after the words quoted above, Aristotle concludes that "in things composed of matter and form there is no other cause but that which moves from potency to act; while things that have no matter are all truly beings in themselves." 24

Reply Objection 4. Everything participated is compared to the participator as its act. But any created form which is held to subsist through itself, must have being by participation; for even life, or anything of that sort, is a participator of being, as Dionysius says. Now participated being is limited by the capacity of the participator, so that God alone, Who is His own being, is pure act and infinite. But in intellectual substances, there is composition of act and potency, not, indeed, of matter and form, but of form and participated being. That is why some say that they are composed of *that by which* they are and *that which* they are; for the act of being itself is that by which a thing is.25

Sixth Article

IS THE HUMAN SOUL INCORRUPTIBLE?

Objection 1. It would seem that the human soul is corruptible. For things having a like beginning and career seemingly have a like end. But the beginning, by generation, of men is like that of animals, for they are made from the earth. And the process of life is alike in both; because "all things breathe alike, and man hath nothing more than the beast," as it is written (*Ecclesiastes 3:19*). Therefore, as the same text concludes, "the death of man and beast is one, and the condition of both is equal." But the souls of brute animals are perishable. So, too, therefore, is the human soul.

Objection 2. Moreover, whatever is out of nothing can return to nothingness, because the end should correspond to the beginning. But as it is written (*Wisdom 2:2*), "We are born of nothing"; and this is true, not only of the body, but also of the soul. Therefore, as is concluded in the same text, "After this we shall be as if we had not been," even as to our soul.

---

24. *Metaphysics* VII, 6 (1045b21).

25. Throughout this Reply *esse* is translated five times by the word "being" and once, at the end, by the phrase "act of being." The meaning is the same, viz., existential act, or that "act" which *existing* is.

Objection 3. Again, nothing is without its own proper operation. But the operation proper to the soul, which is to understand with a phantasm [or sense representation] cannot be without the body. For the soul understands nothing without a phantasm, and "there is no phantasm without the body," as Aristotle says.[26] Therefore the soul cannot survive the dissolution of the body.

On the contrary: Dionysius says that human souls "owe to divine goodness that they are intellectual, and that they have an incorruptible substantial life." [27]

I answer that: It must be said that the intellectual principle which we call the human soul is incorruptible. For a thing may be corrupted in two ways—through itself and by accident. Now it is impossible for any subsistent being to be generated or corrupted accidentally, i.e., by the generation or corruption of something else. For generation and corruption belong to a thing in the same way that being belongs to it, which is acquired by generation and lost by corruption. Therefore, whatever has being in itself cannot be generated or corrupted except through itself; while things which do not subsist, such as accidents and material forms, are said to acquire being or lose it through the generation or corruption of composites. Now it was shown above that the souls of brutes are not self-subsistent, but only the human soul.[28] Thus the souls of brutes are corrupted, when their bodies are corrupted, while the human soul could not be corrupted unless it were corrupted through itself. This is altogether impossible, not only as regards the human soul, but also as regards anything subsistent that is a form alone. For it is evident that what belongs to a thing by virtue of the thing itself is inseparable from it. But being belongs to a form, which is an "act," by virtue of itself. And thus, matter acquires being in act according as it acquires form; while it is corrupted so far as the form is separated from it. But it is impossible for a form to be separated from itself; and therefore it is impossible for a subsistent form to cease to exist.

Granted even that the soul were composed of matter and form, as some pretend, we should nevertheless have to maintain that it is imperishable. For corruption is found only where there is contrariety, since generation and corruption are from contraries and into contraries. Therefore the heavenly bodies, since they have no matter subject to contrariety, are incorruptible. Now there can be no contrariety in the intellectual soul: it is a receiving subject according to the manner of its being, and those things which it receives are without contrariety. For the notions even of contraries are not themselves contrary; rather, contraries belong to the

---

26. *On the Soul* I, 1 (403a9).
27. *The Divine Names* IV, 2.
28. Article 3.

same science. Therefore it is impossible for the intellectual soul to be corruptible.

Moreover, we may take a sign of this from the fact that everything naturally desires being after its own manner. Now in things that have knowledge, desire follows upon knowledge. The senses indeed do not know being, except under the conditions of *here* and *now,* whereas the intellect apprehends being absolutely, and for all time; so that everything that has an intellect naturally desires always to exist. But a natural desire cannot be in vain. Therefore every intellectual substance is imperishable.

Reply Objection 1. It is in the person of the foolish, that Solomon adduces that argument (*Cf. Wisdom 2:2*). Therefore the saying that man and animals have a like beginning in generation is true of the body; for all animals alike are made of earth. But it is not true of the soul. For while the souls of brutes are produced by some power of the body, the human soul is produced by God. To signify this, it is written of other animals: "Let the earth bring forth the living soul" (*Genesis 1:24*); while of man it is written (*Genesis 2:7*) that "He breathed into his face the breath of life." And so in the last chapter of Ecclesiastes it is concluded: "The dust returns into its earth from whence it was; and the spirit returns to God Who gave it." Again, the process of life is alike as to the body, concerning which it is written (*Ecclesiastes 3:19*): "All things breathe alike," and (*Wisdom 2:2*): "The breath in our nostrils is smoke." But the process is not alike in the case of the soul, for man has understanding whereas animals do not. Hence it is false to say: "Man has nothing more than beasts." Thus death comes to both alike as to the body, but not as to the soul.

Reply Objective 2. As a thing can be said to be created, not by reason of a passive potency, but only by reason of the active potency of the Creator, Who can produce something out of nothing, so when we say that a thing can be reduced to nothing, we do not imply in the creature a potency to non-being, but in the Creator the power of ceasing to bestow being. But a thing is said to be perishable because there is in it a potency to non-being.

Reply Objection 3. To understand with a phantasm is the proper operation of the soul by virtue of its union with the body. After separation from the body, it will have another mode of understanding, similar to other substances separated from bodies, as will appear more clearly later on.[29]

---

29. Question LXXXIX, article 1.

Seventh Article

IS THE SOUL OF THE SAME
SPECIFIC NATURE AS AN ANGEL?

Objection 1. It seems that the soul is the same specifically as an angel. For each thing is ordered to its proper end by the nature of its kind, whence is derived its inclination toward that end. But the end of the soul is the same as that of an angel, viz., eternal beatitude. Therefore they are specifically the same.

Objection 2. Moreover, the ultimate specific difference is pre-eminent, because it completes the nature of the species. But nothing is nobler either in an angel or in a soul than the fact of being intellectual. Therefore the soul and the angel agree in the ultimate specific difference. Therefore they are of the same specific nature.

Objection 3. Again, it seems that the soul does not differ from an angel except in its union with the body. But since the body is outside the essence of the soul, it does not seem to belong to its specific nature. Therefore the soul and an angel are of the same kind.

On the contrary: Things which have different natural operations are of different species. But the natural operations of the soul and of an angel are different, since, as Dionysius says, "Angelic minds have simple and genuine intellects, not gathering their knowledge of divine things from visible things." Subsequently he says the contrary of this about the soul. Therefore the soul and an angel are not of the same species.

I answer that: Origen held that human souls and angels are all of the same specific nature and this because he supposed that in these substances the difference of degree was accidental, resulting from their free choice, as was said above.[30] But this cannot be, because in incorporeal substances there cannot be diversity of number without diversity of kind and inequality of nature. For, since they are not composed of matter and form, but are subsistent forms, it is evident that there must be among them a diversity in kind. For it cannot be understood that a separate form exists except as one of a single kind. Thus, supposing a separate whiteness to exist, it could only be one; since one whiteness does not differ from another except as in this or that subject. But diversity of species is always accompanied by diversity of nature. Thus, in the kinds of colors, one is more perfect than another; and the same applies to other species. For differences which divide a genus are contrary to one another. Contraries, however, are related to one another as the perfect to the imperfect, since the "principle of contrariety is privation and habit," as is said.[31]

---

30. Question XLVII, article 2.
31. Aristotle, *Metaphysics* IX, 4(1055a33).

The same would also follow if the aforesaid substances were composed of matter and form. For if the matter of one be distinct from the matter of another, it is required *either* that the form be the principle of the distinction of matter, so that the matter is diversified because of its rela-tion to diverse forms (in which case there would still result a difference of kind and an inequality of nature); *or else* that the matter is the source of the distinction of forms. But one matter cannot be said to be distinct from another except by a distinction of quantity, which has no place in incorporeal substances, such as an angel and the soul. Hence, it is not possible for the angel and the soul to be of the same specific kind. How it is that there can be many souls of one kind will be shown later.[32]

Reply Objection 1. This argument is concerned with the proximate and natural end. Eternal beatitude, however, is the ultimate and supernatural end.

Reply Objection 2. The ultimate specific difference is pre-eminent because it is the most determinate, in the same way as act is superior to potency. But the intellectual in that mode is not the highest thing, because it is indeterminate and common to many degrees of intellectuality; just as the sensible is common to many degrees of sensible being. Hence, just as all sensible things are not of one kind, so neither are all intellectual beings of one kind.

Reply Objection 3. The body is not of the essence of the soul, but the soul, by its essential nature, is unitable to the body; so that, properly speaking, it is not even the soul, but rather the composite, which belongs in the species. And the very fact that the soul in a certain way requires the body for its operation shows that the soul is endowed with a grade of intellectuality inferior to that of an angel, who is not united to a body.

---

32. Question LXXVI, article 2.

The Union of Body and Soul

(*In Eight Articles*)

First Article

IS THE INTELLECTUAL PRINCIPLE
UNITED TO THE BODY AS ITS FORM?

Objection 1. It seems that the intellectual principle is not united to the body as its form. For Aristotle says that "the intellect is separate," and that "it is not the act of any body." [1] Therefore it is not united to the body as its form.

Objection 2. Moreover, every form is determined according to the nature of the matter of which it is the form; otherwise no conformity would be required between matter and form. Therefore, in view of the fact that every body has a determinate nature, if the intellect were united to the body as its form it would follow that the intellect has a determinate nature; and thus it would not be capable of knowing all things, as is clear from what was said above. [2] This is contrary to the nature of the intellect. Therefore the intellect is not united to the body as its form.

Objection 3. Further, every receptive power which is an "act" of a body, receives a form materially and individually; for what is received is in the receiver according to the mode of the receiver. But the form of the thing understood is not received into the intellect materially and individually, but rather immaterially and universally. Otherwise, the intellect would not be capable of knowing immaterial and universal objects, but only individuals, as with the senses. Therefore the intellect is not united to the body as its form.

Objection 4. Again, power and action have the same subject, for the same subject is what can, and does, act. But intellectual action is not the action of a body, as we have seen. [3] Therefore neither is the intellectual power a power of the body. But a virtue or a power cannot be more abstract or more simple than the essence from which the virtue or power is derived. Therefore, neither is the substance of the intellect the form of a body.

---

1. *On the Soul* III, 4(429b5).
2. Question LXXV, article 2.
3. Question LXXV, article 2.

Objection 5. Also, whatever has being in itself is not united to the body as its form, because a form is that by which a thing exists. Thus the very being of a form does not belong to the form by itself. But the intellectual principle has being in itself and is subsistent, as was said above.[4] Therefore it is not united to the body as its form.

Objection 6. And again, whatever exists in a thing by reason of its nature exists in it always. But to be united to matter belongs to form by reason of its nature, because form is the "act" of matter, not by an accidental quality, but by its own essence; otherwise matter and form would not make a thing substantially one, but only accidentally one. Therefore a form cannot be without its own proper matter. But the intellectual principle, since it is incorruptible, as was shown above, remains separate from the body after the body's dissolution.[5] Therefore the intellectual principle is not united to the body as its form.

On the contrary: According to Aristotle, difference is derived from a thing's form.[6] But the difference which constitutes man is *rational,* which is said of man because of his intellectual principle. Therefore the intellectual principle is the form of man.

I answer that: It must be said that the intellect which is the source of intellectual operation is the form of the human body. For that whereby primarily anything acts is a form of the thing to which the act is attributed; e.g., that by which a body is primarily healed is health, and that by which the soul knows primarily is knowledge. Health, then, is a form of the body, and knowledge is a certain form of the soul. The reason for this is that nothing acts except so far as it is in act. Consequently, a thing acts by that whereby it is in act. Now the first thing by which the body lives is manifestly the soul. And as life is manifested through various activities in different degrees of living things, that whereby we primarily perform each of these vital actions is the soul. For the soul is the primary source of our nourishment, sensation, and local movement; and likewise of our understanding. Therefore this primary source of understanding in us, whether it be called the intellect or the intellectual soul, is the form of the body. This is the demonstration used by Aristotle.[7]

But if anyone says that the intellectual soul is not the form of the body, he must explain how it is that this action of understanding is the action of this particular man; for each one is conscious that it is he himself who understands. Now an action is attributed to anyone in three ways, as is clear from what Aristotle says.[8] For a thing is said to move or act, either

----

4. Question LXXV, article 2.
5. Question LXXV, article 6.
6. *Metaphysics* VII, 2 (1043a19). "Difference" (*differentia*) means a thing's distinguishing characteristic.
7. *On the Soul* II, 2 (414a12).
8. *Physics* V, 1 (224a31).

by virtue of its whole self, e.g., as a physician heals; or by virtue of a part, as a man sees by his eye; or through an accidental quality, as when we say that something that is white builds; because it is accidental to the builder to be white. So when we say that Socrates or Plato understands, this clearly is not attributed to him accidentally, since it is ascribed to him as man and this is to be predicated of him essentially. We must therefore say either that Socrates understands by virtue of his whole self, as Plato maintained, holding that man is an intellectual soul;[9] or that the intellect is a part of Socrates. The first cannot stand, as was shown above, because it is one and the same man who is conscious both that he understands and that he senses.[10] But one cannot sense without a body, and therefore the body must be some part of man. It follows therefore that the intellect by which Socrates understands is a certain part of Socrates, so that it is in some way united to the body of Socrates.

As to this union, the Commentator held that it is through the intelligible species, as having a double subject, viz., the possible intellect, and the images [or sense representations] which are in the bodily organs.[11] Thus, through the intelligible species, the possible intellect is linked to the body of this or that particular man. But this link or union does not sufficiently explain the fact that the act of the intellect is the act of *Socrates*. This can be clearly seen from comparison with the sense power, from which Aristotle proceeds to consider things relating to the intellect. For the relation of images to the intellect is, as he says, like the relation of colors to the sense of sight.[12] Therefore, just as the forms of colors are in the sight, so the forms of sense representations are in the possible intellect. Now of course because the colors, the likenesses of which are in the sight, are on a wall, the action of seeing is not attributed to the wall; for we do not say that the wall sees, but rather that it is seen. Therefore, from the fact that the forms of sense representations are in the possible intellect, it does not follow that Socrates, in whom those images are present, understands, but that he or his sense representations are understood.

Some, however, have tried to maintain that the intellect is united to the body as its mover, and hence that the intellect and body form one thing in such a way that the act of the intellect could be attribued to the whole. This is, however, false for many reasons. First, because the intellect does not move the body except through the appetite, whose movement presupposes the act of the intellect. The reason therefore why Socrates understands is not because he is moved by his intellect, but rather, contrariwise,

---

9. cf. above, Question LXXV, article 4.
10. *ibid.*
11. Averroes, *Commentary on Aristotle's "On the Soul"* (*In De An.*) *III*, comm. 5 (VI, 164v).
12. *On the Soul* III, 7 (431a14).

he is moved by his intellect because he undertsands. Secondly, because, since Socrates is a certain individual in a nature of one essence composed of matter and form, if the intellect be not his form, it follows that it must be outside his essence, and then the intellect is to the whole Socrates as a mover to the thing moved. But understanding is an action that remains in the agent; it does not pass into something else, as with the action of heating. Therefore understanding cannot be attributed to Socrates for the reason that he is moved by his intellect. Thirdly, because the action of a mover is never attributed to the thing moved, except as to an instrument, just as the action of a carpenter is ascribed to a saw. Therefore, if understanding is attributed to Socrates as the action of his mover, it follows that it is attributed to him as to an instrument. This is contrary to the teaching of Aristotle, who holds that understanding is not effected through a bodily instrument.[13] Fourthly, because, although the action of a part be ascribed to the whole, as the action of the eye is attributed to a man, even so it is never ascribed to another part, except perhaps accidentally; for we do not say that the hand sees because the eye sees. Therefore, if the intellect and Socrates are united in the above manner, the action of the intellect cannot be attributed to Socrates. If, however, Socrates be a whole composed of a union of the intellect with whatever else belongs to Socrates, the intellect being united to the other parts of Socrates only as a mover, it follows that Socrates is not one absolutely, and consequently neither a being absolutely, for a thing is a being according as it is one.

There remains, therefore, no other explanation than that given by Aristotle; viz., that this particular man understands because the intellectual principle in him is his form.[14] Thus from the very operation of the intellect it is apparent that the intellectual principle is united to the body as its form.

The same can be clearly shown from the nature of the human species. For the nature of each thing is manifested by its activity. Now the proper operation of man as man is understanding, for it is in this that he surpasses all the other animals. From this Aristotle concludes that the ultimate happiness of man must consist in this operation as properly belonging to him.[15] Man must therefore derive his specific nature from that which is the source of this operation. But the specific nature of each thing is derived from its form. It follows therefore that the intellectual principle is the proper form of man.

But we must consider that the higher a form is, the more it rises above corporeal matter, the less it is immersed in matter, and the more it excels matter by its power and its operation. Hence we observe that the form

---

13. *On the Soul* III, 4 (429a26).
14. *On the Soul* II, 2 (414a12).
15. *Nicomachean Ethics* X, 7 (1177a17).

of a mixed body has an operation not caused by its elemental qualities. And the higher we advance in the order of forms, the more we find that the power of the form excels the elementary matter; as the vegetative soul excels the form of the metal, and the sensible soul excels the vegetative soul. Now the human soul is the highest in the order of forms. Therefore, in its power it excels corporeal matter by the fact that it has an operation and a power in which corporeal matter has no share whatever. This power is called the intellect.

It must be noted, moreover, that if anyone held that the soul is composed of matter and form, it would follow that in no way could the soul be called the form of the body. For since form is an "act," and matter is being only in potency, that which is composed of matter and form cannot in its entirety be the form of another. But if it is a form by virtue of some part of itself, then that part which is the form we call the "soul," and that of which it is the form we call the *"primary living thing,"* as was said above.[16]

Reply Objection 1. As Aristotle observes, the highest natural form, viz., the human soul, to which the consideration of the natural philosopher is directed is indeed separate, but it exists in matter.[17] (This he proves from the theory that man and the sun generate man from matter). It is separate according to its intellectual power, because an intellectual power is not the power of a bodily organ, as the power of seeing is the "act" of the eye; for understanding is an act which cannot be performed by a bodily organ, as can the act of seeing. But it exists in matter in so far as the soul itself, to which this power belongs, is the form of the body, and the term of human generation. And so Aristotle says that "the intellect is separate," because it is not the power of a bodily organ.[18]

From this the answer to the Second and Third objections is clear. For in order that man may be able to understand all things by means of his intellect, and that his intellect may understand all things immaterial and universal, it is sufficient that the intellectual power be not the "act" of the body.

Reply Objection 4. The human soul, by reason of its perfection, is not a form immersed in corporeal matter, or entirely embraced by matter. Therefore there is nothing to prevent some power of the soul from not being the "act" of the body, although the soul is essentially the form of the body.

Reply Objection 5. The soul communicates that being in which it subsists to the corporeal matter, out of which, with the intellectual soul, there results one being; so that the being of the whole composite is also the being of the soul itself. This is not the case with other forms, which

---

16. Question LXXV, article 5.
17. *Physics* II, 2 (194b12).
18. *On the Soul* III, 4 (429b5).

are not subsistent. For this reason the human soul retains its own being after the dissolution of the body, whereas the other forms do not.

Reply Objection 6. To be united to the body belongs to the soul by reason of itself, just as it pertains to a light body by reason of itself to be raised up. And just as a light body remains light when removed from its proper place, retaining meanwhile an aptitude and an inclination for its proper place, so the human soul retains its proper being when separated from the body, having an aptitude and a natural inclination to be united to the body.

Second Article

IS THE INTELLECTUAL PRINCIPLE MULTIPLIED
ACCORDING TO THE NUMBER OF BODIES?

Objection 1. It seems that the intellectual principle is not multiplied in accordance with the number of bodies, but that there is one intellect in all men. For an immaterial substance is not multiplied numerically within one species. But the human soul is an immaterial substance, since it is not composed of matter and form, as was shown above.[19] Therefore there are not many human souls in one species, but all men are of one species. Therefore there is but one intellect in all men.

Objection 2. Moreover, when the cause is removed, the effect is also removed. Therefore, if human souls were multiplied according to the number of bodies, it would seem to follow that if the bodies were removed, the number of souls would not remain, but from all the souls there would be only one remaining. This is heretical, for it would do away with the distinction of rewards and punishments.

Objection 3. Further, if my intellect is distinct from your intellect, my intellect is an individual, and so is yours; for individuals are things which differ in number but agree in one species. Now whatever is received into anything is present in it according to the mode of the receiver. Therefore the forms of things would be received individually into my intellect, and also into yours; this is contrary to the nature of the intellect, which knows universals.

Objection 4. Again, the thing understood is in the intellect which understands. So if my intellect is distinct from yours, what is understood by me must be distinct from what is understood by you; and thus it will be reckoned as something individual, and will be only potentially something understood. Hence the common intention will have to be abstracted from both, since from all things that are diverse something intelligible and common to them may be abstracted. But this is contrary to the nature

---

19. Question LXXV, article 5.

of the intellect, for then the intellect would appear not to be distinct from the imagination. It seems to follow, therefore, that there is one intellect in all men.

Objection 5. Also, when the disciple receives knowledge from the teacher, it cannot be said that the teacher's knowledge begets knowledge in the disciple, because then knowledge too would be an active form, such as heat is—which is clearly false. It seems, therefore, that the same individual knowledge which is in the teacher is communicated to the disciple. This cannot be, unless there is one intellect in both. Seemingly, then, the intellect of the disciple and of the teacher is but one; consequently, the same applies to all men.

Objection 6. And again, Augustine says: "If I were to say that human souls are simply manifold, I should laugh at myself."[20] But the soul seems to be one chiefly in respect to the intellect. Therefore there is one intellect of all men.

On the contrary: Aristotle says that the relation of universal causes to what is universal is like the relation of particular causes to individuals.[21] But it is impossible that a soul, one in species, should belong to animals of diverse species. Therefore it is impossible that one individual intellectual soul should belong to several individuals.

I answer that: It is utterly impossible for one intellect to belong to all men. This is clear if, as Plato maintained, man is the intellect itself. For if Socrates and Plato have one intellect, it would follow that Socrates and Plato are one man, and that they are not distinct from each other, except by something outside the essence of each. The distinction between Socrates and Plato would then not be other than that of a man now wearing a tunic, now a cloak—which is simply absurd.

This is likewise clearly impossible if, following Aristotle's judgment, it is held that the intellect is a part or a power of the soul which is the form of man.[22] For it is impossible for many distinct individuals to have one form, just as it is impossible for them to have one act of being. For the form is the principle of existing.

Again, this is clearly impossible, whatever one may hold as to the manner of the union of the intellect to this or that man. For if there is one principal agent, and two instruments, it can, obviously, be said that there is simply one agent, but several actions; as when one man touches several things with his two hands, there will be one who touches, but two contacts. If, on the contrary, there be one instrument and several principal agents, it is said that there are several agents, but one act; e.g., if many pull a ship by means of a single rope, the pullers will be many, but the pulling will be one. But if there is one principal agent,

---

20. *On the Quantity of the Soul* XXXII.
21. *Physics* II, 3 (195b26).
22. *On the Soul* II, 2 (414a13).

and one instrument, we say that there is one agent and one action; as when the smith strikes with one hammer, there is one striker and one stroke. Now it is clear that no matter how the intellect is united or joined to this or that man, the intellect has the primacy among all the other things which pertain to man; for the sense powers obey the intellect, and are at its service. So if we suppose two men to have two intellects and one sense, e.g., if two men had one eye, there would be two seers, but one seeing. But if the intellect is one, no matter how diverse may be all those things which the intellect uses as instruments, it is in no way possible to say that Socrates and Plato are more than one understanding being. And if we add that understanding, which is the act of the intellect, is not produced by any organ, but by the intellect itself, it will further follow that there is only one agent and one action; in other words, all men are but one understander, and have but one act of understanding, i.e, in respect to one and the same intelligible object.

Now my intellectual action could be distinguished from yours by the diversity of the sense images—for there is one representation of a stone in me, and another in you—if the image itself, according as it is one thing in me and another in you, were a form of the possible intellect. For the same agent produces diverse actions through diverse forms; e.g., through the diverse forms in things in relation to the same eye, there are diverse seeings. But the sense representation itself is not the form of the possible intellect; the intelligible form abstracted from sense representations is that form. Now in one intellect, from diverse representations of the same kind, only one intelligible form is abstracted; as appears in one man, in whom there may be various images of a stone, and yet from all of them only one intelligible form of a stone is abstracted, by which the intellect of that one man, by one operation, understands the nature of a stone, notwithstanding the diversity of representations. Therefore, if there were one intellect for all men, the diversity of sense images in this man and in that could not cause a diversity of intellectual operation in this man and that man, as the Commentator imagines.[23] In conclusion, therefore, it is absolutely impossible and incongruous to posit one intellect for all men.

Reply Objection 1. Although the intellectual soul, like the angel, has no matter from which it is produced, nevertheless it is the form of a certain matter; and in this it is unlike an angel. Therefore, in accordance with the division of matter, there are many souls of one kind; while it is utterly impossible for many angels to be of one kind.

Reply Objection 2. Everything has unity in the same way that it has being, and consequently we must judge of the multiplicity of a thing as we judge of its act of being. Now it is clear that the intellectual soul is,

23. Averroes, *Commentary on Aristotle's "On the Soul"* (*In De An.*) III, comm. 5. (VI, 166v).

according to its own act of being, united to the body as its form. And yet, after the dissolution of the body, the intellectual soul retains its own being. In like manner, the multiplicity of souls is proportionate to the multiplicity of bodies; and yet, after the dissolution of the bodies, the souls remain multiplied in their being.

Reply Objection 3. The individuation of the one understanding, or of the species whereby he understands, does not exclude the understanding of universals. Otherwise, since separate intellects are certain subsistent substances, and consequently individual, they could not understand universals. But it is the materiality of the knower, and of the species through which he knows, that prevents the knowledge of the universal. For just as every action is in accordance with the mode of the form whereby the agent acts (e.g., heating is according to the mode of the heat), so knowledge is according to the mode of the form by which the knower knows. Now the common nature manifestly becomes distinct and multiplied by reason of the individuating principles which come from the matter. Therefore if the form, which is the means of knowledge, is material—i.e., is not abstracted from material conditions—its likeness to the nature of a species or genus will be according to the distinction and multiplication of that nature by means of individuating principles. Thus the knowledge of the nature in its community will be impossible. But if the species be abstracted from the conditions of individual matter, there will be a likeness of the nature without those things which make it distinct and multiplied. And thus there will be knowledge of the universal. Nor does it matter, as to this particular point, whether there be one intellect or many; because, even if there were only one, it would necessarily be an individual intellect, and the form through which it understands, an individual form.

Reply Objection 4. Whether the intellect be one or many, what is understood is one. For what is understood is in the intellect not in itself, but according to its likeness; for "the stone is not in the soul, but its likeness is," as is said.[24] Yet it is the stone which is understood, not the likeness of the stone, except by a reflection of the intellect on itself. Otherwise, the sciences would not be about things, but about intelligible likenesses. Now it is possible for diverse things, according to diverse forms, to be likened to the same thing. And since knowledge is brought about through the assimilation of the knower to the thing known, it follows that the same thing can be known by several knowers; as is evident in regard to the senses; for several see the same color by means of diverse likenesses. In the same way several intellects understand one thing. But there is this difference, according to Aristotle, between the sense and the intellect: a thing is sensibly perceived as it exists extra-mentally in its own particular being; whereas, though the nature of the thing understood

---

24. Aristotle, *On the Soul* III, 8 (431b29).

is outside the soul, its extra-mental mode of being is not that according to which it is known.[25] For the common nature is understood by abstraction from the individuating principles; whereas such is not its manner of existence outside the soul. On the other hand, for Plato the thing understood exists extra-mentally in the same way as it is understood. For Plato supposed that the natures of things exist separate from matter.

Reply Objection 5. One knowledge exists in the disciple and another in the teacher. How it is caused will be shown later.[26]

Reply Objection 6. Augustine means that souls are not simply manifold without their being united in the one nature of the species.

Third Article

BESIDES THE INTELLECTUAL SOUL, ARE THERE OTHER SOULS IN MAN ESSENTIALLY DIFFERENT FROM ONE ANOTHER?

Objection 1. It seems that besides the intellectual soul there are in man other souls essentially different from one another, viz, the sensory soul and the nutritive soul. For the perishable and the imperishable are not substantially one and the same. Rather, the intellectual soul is imperishable, whereas the other souls—the sensory and the nutritive—are perishable, as was shown above.[27] Therefore in man the essence of the intellectual soul, the sensory soul, and the nutritive soul, cannot be the same.

Objection 2. Moreover, if it be said that the sensory soul in man is imperishable, against this is the dictum that the "perishable and the imperishable differ in kind." [28] But the sensory soul in the horse, the lion, and other brute animals, is perishable. If therefore in man it be imperishable, the sensory soul in man and the brute animal will not be generically the same. Now, an "animal" is so called from the fact that it has a sensory soul; and therefore *animal* will not be one genus common to man and other animals—which is incongruous.

Objection 3. Again, the Philosopher says that "the embryo is an animal before it is a man." [29] But this would be impossible if the essence of the sensory soul were the same as that of the intellectual soul; for an animal is such by its sensory soul, while a man is a man by the intellectual soul. Therefore in man the essence of the sensory soul is not the same as the essence of the intellectual soul.

Objection 4. And again, the Philosopher says that "the genus is taken

25. *ibid.,* (432a2).
26. Question CXVII, article 1.
27. Question LXXV, article 6.
28. Aristotle, *Metaphysics* IX, 10 (1059a10).
29. *On the Generation of Animals* II, 3 (736a35).

from the matter, and 'difference' from the form." [30] But *rational*, which
is the "difference" constituting man, is taken from the intellectual soul;
while he is called "animal" by reason of his having a body animated by
a sensory soul. Therefore the intellectual soul is compared to the body
animated by a sensory soul as form to matter. Therefore in man the intellectual soul is not essentially the same as the sensory soul, but presupposes it as a material subject.

On the contrary: It is said: "Nor do we hold that there are two souls
in one man, as James and other Syrians write—one, animal, by which
the body is animated, and which is mingled with the blood; the other,
spiritual, which obeys the reason. Rather, we say that it is one of the same
soul in man which both gives life to the body by being united to it, and
orders itself by its own reason." [31]

I answer that: As Aristotle points out, Plato held that there were several souls in one body, distinct even according to organs. To these souls
he referred the different vital actions, saying that the nutritive power
is in the liver, the appetitive[32] in the heart, and the knowing power in
the brain. This opinion is rejected by Aristotle as regards those parts of
the soul which in their operations make use of physical organs. His
reason is that in those animals which continue to live when they have
been divided, in each part are observed the various activities of the soul,
such as those of sense and appetite. Now this would not be the case if
the various principles of the soul's activities were essentially diverse
in their distribution through the various parts of the body. But with
regard to the intellectual part, Aristotle seems to leave it in doubt whether
it be only logically distinct from the other parts of the soul, or also
locally.

The opinion of Plato could be maintained if, as he held, the soul were
united to the body, not as its form, but as its mover. For nothing incongruous is involved if the same moveable thing be moved by several
movers; and still less if it be moved according to its various parts. If we
suppose, however, that the soul is united to the body as its form, it is simply impossible for several essentially different souls to be in one body. This
can be made clear by three reasons.

In the first place, an animal in which there were several souls would
not be absolutely one. For nothing is absolutely one except through one
form whereby a thing has being; because a thing has both being and
unity from the same source. That is why things which are denominated
by various forms are not absolutely one; e.g, "white-man." If, therefore,
man were living by one form, the vegetative soul, and animal by another

30. *Metaphysics* VII, 2 (1043a5;a19). See note 6, above.
31. Gennadius, *On the Teachings of the Church* XV. (Not available in English.)
32. Literally, "concupiscible."

form, the sensory soul, and man by another form, the intellectual soul,
it would follow that man is not absolutely one. Thus Aristotle argues
against Plato, that if the Idea of an animal is distinct from the Idea of
a biped, then a biped animal is not absolutely one.[33] For this reason,
against those who hold that there are several souls in the body, he asks:
"What contains them?"—i.e., what makes them one? [34] It cannot be said
that they are united by the unity of the body; because it is rather the soul
that contains the body and makes it one, than the reverse.

  Secondly, this is seen to be impossible by considering the mode in which
one thing is predicated of another. For things derived from various forms
are predicated of one another either accidentally—if the forms are not
intrinsically related (as in saying, "something white is sweet")—, or essentially, in the second mode of essential predication, if the forms are intrinsically related to each other because the subject enters into the
definition of the predicate. (Thus a surface is presupposed for color, so
that if we say, "a body with a surface is colored," we have the second
mode of essential predication.) Hence, if there is one form by which a
thing is an animal, and another form by which it is a man, it follows
either that one of these two things could not be predicated of the other,
except accidentally (supposing these two forms not to be intrinsically
related to one another), or that one would be predicated of the other
according to the second mode of essential predication, if one soul be
presupposed to the other. But both of these consequences are clearly
false. For "animal" is predicated of "man" essentially and not accidentally,
and "man" is not part of the definition of "animal," but just the reverse.
Therefore it is necessarily by the same form that a thing is animal and
man. Otherwise, a man would not really be the being which is an animal
so that "animal" could be essentially predicated of "man."

  Thirdly, this is shown to be impossible by the fact that when one
activity of the soul is intense it impedes another; which could never be
the case unless the principle of such actions were essentially one.

  It must therefore be said that the sensory soul, the intellectual soul
and the nutritive soul are in man numerically one and the same soul.
This can easily be understood if one considers the way in which species
and forms are diversified. For the species and forms of things are found
to differ from one another according to degrees of relative perfection;
e.g., in the order of things the animate are more perfect than the inanimate, animals more perfect than plants, and man more perfect than brute
animals. Furthermore, in each of these genera there are various degrees.
For this reason Aristotle compares the species of things to numbers,
which differ in species by the addition or subtraction of unity.[35] He also

---

33. *Metaphysics* VII, 6 (1045a14).
34. *On the Soul* I, 5 (411b6).
35. *Metaphysics* VII, 3 (1043b34).

compares the various souls to the species of figures, one of which contains
another, as a pentagon contains and exceeds a tetragon.[36] Thus the intellectual soul contains virtually[37] whatever belongs to the sensory soul
of brute animals, and to the nutritive soul of plants. Therefore, just
as a surface which is of a pentagonal shape is not tetragonal by one
shape, and pentagonal by another (since a tetragonal shape would be
superfluous as being contained in the pentagonal), so neither is Socrates
a man by one soul, and an animal by another; but by one and the same
soul he is both animal and man.

Reply Objection 1. The sensory soul is imperishable, not by reason of
its being sensory, but by reason of its being intellectual. When, therefore,
a soul is sensory only, it is perishable; but when the intellectual is joined
to the sensory, then the sensory soul is imperishable. For although the sensory does not give imperishability, yet it cannot deprive the intellectual of
its imperishability.

Reply Objection 2. Not forms, but composites, are classified either
generically or specifically. Now man is perishable like other animals.
Therefore the differences, "perishable" and "imperishable," which are
consequent upon the forms involved, do not give rise to a generic difference between man and the other animals.

Reply Objection 3. The embryo has first of all a soul which is merely
sensory, and when this is removed, it is supplanted by a more perfect
soul, which is both sensory and intellectual, as will be shown later.[38]

Reply Objection 4. We must not conclude to a diversity in natural
things on the basis of the diversity of logical notions or intentions which
result from our manner of understanding; for reason can apprehend one
and the same thing in various ways. Therefore since, as we have said,[39]
the intellectual soul contains virtually what belongs to the sensory soul,
and something more, reason can consider separately what belongs to the
power of the sensory soul, as something imperfect and material. And
because it observes that this is something common to man and to other
animals, it forms thence the notion of the genus. On the other hand,
that wherein the intellectual soul exceeds the sensory soul the reason
takes as formal and perfecting; and from this it gathers the specific difference of man.

---

36. *On the Soul* II, 3(414b28).
37. Literally, "in its power."
38. Question CXVIII, article 2, ad 2.
39. Preceding article.

Fourth Article

IN MAN, IS THERE ANOTHER FORM
BESIDES THE INTELLECTUAL SOUL?

Objection 1. It seems that in man there is another form besides the intellectual soul. For Aristotle says that "the soul is the act of a physical body which has life potentially." [40] Therefore the soul is to the body as a form to matter. But the body has a substantial form by which it is a body. Therefore some other substantial form in the body precedes the soul.

Objection 2. Further, man is a self-mover, as every animal is. "Now everything that moves itself is divided into two parts, of which one moves, and the other is moved," as is proved.[41] But the part which moves is the soul. Therefore the other part must be such that it can be moved. But primary matter cannot be moved since it is a being only potentially, while everything that is moved is a body. Therefore in man and in every animal there must be another substantial form, by which the body is constituted.

Objection 3. Then, too, the order of forms is consequent upon their relationship to primary matter; for "priority" and "posteriority" are predicated in respect of some starting-point. Therefore, if there were not in man some other substantial form besides the rational soul, and if the rational soul inhered immediately in primary matter, it would follow that it ranks among the most imperfect forms, which inhere in matter immediately.

Objection 4. Furthermore, the human body is a mixed body. Now mixture does not result from matter alone; for then we should have mere corruption. Therefore the forms of the elements must remain in a mixed body; and these are substantial forms. Therefore in the human body there are other substantial forms besides the intellectual soul.

On the contrary: Of one thing there is one substantial act of being. But the substantial form gives substantial being. Therefore of one thing there is only one substantial form. But the soul is the substantial form of man. Therefore there cannot be in man another substantial form besides the intellectual soul.

I answer that: If it were supposed that the intellectual soul is not united to the body as its form, but only as its mover, as the Platonists maintain, it would necessarily follow that in man there is another substantial form by which the body would be made mobile in its being by the soul. But if the intellectual soul is united to the body as its substantial

---

40. *On the Soul* II, 1 (412a28).
41. Artistotle, *Physics* VIII, 5(257b12).

form, as we have said above,[42] it is impossible for another substantial form besides the intellectual soul to be found in man.

In order to make this evident, bear in mind that the substantial form differs from the accidental form in this, that the accidental form does not make a thing simply to be, but to be such and such, as heat does not make a thing simply to be, but to be hot. Therefore by the presence of the accidental form a thing is not said to come to be or to be generated simply, but to come to be such and such, or to exist in some particular mode. Likewise, when an accidental form is lost, a thing is said to be destroyed not simply, but in a certain respect. The substantial form, however, gives being unqualifiedly, and hence by its coming a thing is said to be generated simply, and by its loss to be destroyed simply. For this reason the ancient natural philosophers, who held that primary matter was some actual being, such as fire, or air, or something of that kind, maintained that nothing is generated simply or destroyed simply, but that "every becoming is nothing but an alteration," as is said.[43] Therefore, if besides the intellectual soul there pre-existed in matter another substantial form by which the subject of the soul were actually existent, it would follow that the soul does not give being simply, and consequently that it is not a substantial form; and so with the advent of the soul there would not be absolute generation, nor with its removal absolute corruption. All of which is clearly false.

It must therefore be said that there is no other substantial form in man besides the intellectual soul; and that just as the soul contains virtually the sensory and nutritive souls, so does it contain virtually all lower forms, and does alone whatever the less perfect forms do in other things. The same is to be said of the sensory soul in brute animals, and of the nutritive soul in plants, and universally of all more perfect forms in relation to the imperfect.

Reply Objection 1. Aristotle does not say that the soul is the act of a body only, but "the act of a physical organic body which has life potentially"; and that this potentiality "does not exclude the soul."[44] Clearly, then, in the being of which the soul is called the "act," the soul itself is included; as when we say that heat is the "act" of what is hot, and light of what is lucid. And this means, not that the lucid is lucid in separation from light, but that it is lucid through light. In like manner, the soul is said to be the "act" of a body, etc., because it is by the soul that the body is a body, and is organic, and has life potentially. But "first act" is said to be in potency in relation to "second act," which is operation. Now such a potentiality of first act to second act does not remove, i.e., does not exclude, the soul.

---

42. Above, article 1.
43. Aristotle, *Physics* I, 4 (187a30).
44. *On the Soul* II, 2(412a27; b 25).

Reply Objection 2. The soul does not move the body by its being, according to which it is united to the body as its form, but by the motive power, whose act presupposes that the body is already actualized by the soul; so that the soul by its motive power is the part which moves; and the animate body is the part moved.

Reply Objection 3. There are in matter diverse degrees of perfection, such as being, living, sensing, and understanding. Now what is added is always more perfect. Therefore that form which gives matter only the first degree of perfection is the most imperfect, while that form which gives the first, second, and third degree and so on, is the most perfect: and yet it is present to matter immediately.

Reply Objection 4. Avicenna held that the substantial forms of the elements remain entire in the mixed body, and that the mixture is made by the contrary qualities of the elements being reduced to an equilibrium. But this is impossible. For the diverse forms of the elements must necessarily be in diverse parts of matter, and for the distinction of the parts we must suppose dimensions, without which matter cannot be divisible. Now matter subject to dimension is not found except in a body. But several distinct bodies cannot be in the same place. Consequently, the elements in the mixed body would be distinct as to position. Hence there would not be a true mixture—which involves the whole, but only a mixture that seems so to the sense, a mixture according to the juxtaposition of very small particles.

Averroes maintained that the forms of elements, by reason of their imperfection, are between accidental and substantial forms, and so can be *more* or *less;* and therefore in the mixture they are modified and reduced to an equilibrium, so that one form emerges from them. But this is even more impossible. For the substantial being of each thing consists in something indivisible; and, we read, every addition and subtraction varies the species, as in numbers.[45] Consequently, it is impossible for any substantial form to receive *more* or *less.* Nor is it less impossible for anything to be a mean between substance and accident.

Therefore it must be said, with Aristotle, that the forms of the elements remain in the mixed body, not actually, but virtually.[46] For the proper qualities of the elements remain, though modified; and in these qualities is the power of the elementary forms. This quality of the mixture is the proper disposition for the substantial form of the mixed body; e.g., the form of a stone, or of any animated thing.

---

45. Aristotle, *Metaphysics* VII, 3(1044a9).
46. *On the Generation of Animals* I, 10(327b22).

Fifth Article

IS THE INTELLECTUAL SOUL
SUITABLY UNITED TO SUCH A BODY?

Objection 1. It would seem that the intellectual soul is not suitably united to such a body. For matter must be proportionate to form. But the intellectual soul is an imperishable form. Therefore it is not fittingly united to a perishable body.

Objection 2. Moreover, the intellectual soul is a completely immaterial form. A proof of this is its operation in which physical matter does not share. But the more subtle a body is, the less matter it has. Therefore the soul should be united to a most subtle body—to fire, for instance—, and not to a mixed body, still less to a terrestrial body.

Objection 3. Again, since the form is the source whence the species is derived, one form cannot produce a variety of species. But the intellectual soul is one form. Therefore, it should not be united to a body which is composed of parts of various species.

Objection 4. And again, a more perfect form should have a more perfect subject. But the intellectual soul is the most perfect of souls. Therefore since the bodies of other animals are naturally provided with a covering—e.g., with hair instead of clothes, and hoofs instead of shoes, and are, moreover, naturally provided with arms, such as claws, teeth, and horns—it seems that the intellectual soul should not have been united to a body which is imperfect, through being deprived of the above means of protection.

On the contrary: Aristotle says that "the soul is the act of a physical organic body having life potentially." [47]

I answer that: Since the form is not for the sake of the matter, but rather the matter for the sake of the form, the reason why the matter is such as it is must be derived from the form; and not conversely. Now the intellectual soul, as we have seen above, holds in the order of nature the lowest place among the intellectual substances. [48] So much so, that it is not naturally endowed with the knowledge of truth, as the angels are, but has to obtain knowledge from individual things by way of the senses, as Dionysius remarks. But nature never fails anyone in what is necessary. That is why the intellectual soul had to be endowed not only with the power of understanding but also with the power of sensing. Now the action of the senses is not performed without a bodily instrument. Therefore the intellectual soul had to be united to a body which could be the fitting organ of sense.

---

47. *On the Soul* II, 1 (412a27; b5).
48. Question LV, article 2.

Now all the other senses are based on the sense of touch. But the organ of touch must be a mediator between contraries, such as hot and cold, wet and dry, and the like, which are objects of the sense of touch; and in this way touch is in potency with regard to contraries, and is able to perceive them. Therefore the more the organ of touch is brought to a state of equable development, the more acute will be the sense of touch. But the intellectual soul has the power of sense in all its completeness, because what belongs to the inferior nature pre-exists more perfectly in the superior, as Dionysius says. Therefore the body to which the intellectual soul is united had to be a mixed body, above others reduced to the most equable constitution. For this reason, among animals man has the better sense of touch. And among men, those who have the better sense of touch have the better intellect. A sign of which is our observation that those who are refined in body are, as Aristotle says, "well endowed in mind."[49]

Reply Objection 1. Perhaps someone might try to avoid this objection by saying that before sin the human body was incorruptible. But such an answer does not seem sufficient, because before sin the human body was immortal, not by nature, but by a gift of divine grace; otherwise its immortality would not be forfeited through sin, as neither was the immortality of the devil.

Therefore the objection must be answered in another way: in matter two conditions are to be found: one which is chosen in order that the matter be suitable to the form; the other which follows necessarily as a result of a previous disposition. The artisan, for instance, chooses iron for the making of a saw, because it is suitable for cutting through hard material; but that the teeth of the saw may become blunt and rusted follows from a necessity imposed by the matter itself. So the intellectual soul requires a body which is harmoniously constituted—a body that is corruptible, nevertheless, by necessity of its matter. But if it be said that God could avoid this necessity, we answer that in the establishment of natural things, the question is not what God can do, but what befits the natures of things, as Augustine remarks. God, however, provided in this case by applying, through the gift of grace, a remedy against death.

Reply Objection 2. A body is not necessary to the intellectual soul by reason of its intellectual operation considered as such, but because of the sensitive power, which requires an organ harmoniously tempered. Therefore the intellectual soul had to be united to such a body, and not to a simple element, or to a mixed body, in which fire was in excess; because otherwise, by reason of the excessive active power of the fire, there could not be an equability of temperament. And this body of an equable temperament has a dignity of its own in being remote from contraries. In this it resembles in a way a heavenly body.

---

49. *On the Soul* II, 9(421a26).

Reply Objection 3. The parts of an animal, such as the eye, hand, flesh, and bones, etc, do not make the species, but the whole does; and therefore, properly speaking, we cannot say that these constitute diverse species, but rather diverse dispositions. This is suitable to the intellectual soul, which, although it be one in its essence, yet because of its perfection, is manifold in its power. Consequently, for its various operations the soul requires various dispositions in the parts of the body to which it is united. For this reason we observe that there is a greater variety of parts in perfect than in imperfect animals; and in these a greater variety than in plants.

Reply Objection 4. The intellectual soul, as comprehending universals, has a power that is open to infinite things. Therefore it cannot be limited by nature to certain fixed natural judgments or even to certain fixed means whether of defense or of clothing, as is the case with other animals, whose souls are endowed with a knowledge and a power for fixed particular things. Instead of all these, man has by nature his reason and his hands, which are the organs of organs, since by their means man can make for himself instruments of an infinite variety, and for any number of purposes.

Sixth Article

IS THE INTELLECTUAL SOUL UNITED TO THE BODY
THROUGH THE MEDIUM OF ACCIDENTAL DISPOSITIONS?

Objection 1. It seems that the intellectual soul is united to the body through the medium of accidental dispositions. For every form resides in its own disposed matter. But dispositions to a form are accidents. Therefore we must presuppose accidents to exist in matter prior to the substantial form; and therefore prior to the soul, since the soul is a substantial form.

Objection 2. Moreover, diverse forms of one species require diverse parts of matter. But diverse parts cannot be understood except in accordance with the division of dimensive quantities. Therefore we must suppose dimensions in matter prior to the substantial forms, of which there are many belonging to one species.

Objection 3. Again, what is spiritual is connected with what is corporeal by virtual contact. But the "virtue" of the soul is its power. Therefore it seems that the soul is united to the body by means of a power, which is an accident.

On the contrary: Accident is posterior to substance, both in the order of time and in the order of reason, as is said.[50] No accidental form, there-

---

50. Aristotle, *Metaphysics* VI, 1(1028a32).

fore, can be understood to exist in matter prior to the soul, which is the substantial form.

I answer that: If the soul were united to the body merely as a mover, there would be nothing to prevent the existence of certain dispositions mediating between the soul and the body; on the contrary, they would be necessary, for on the part of the soul there would be required the power to move the body, and on the part of the body, a certain aptitude to be moved by the soul.

If, however, the intellectual soul is united to the body as the substantial form, as was said above, it is impossible for any accidental disposition to come between the body and the soul, or between any substantial form whatever and its matter.[51] The reason is this: since matter is in potency to all acts in a certain order, what is absolutely first among the acts must be understood as being first in matter. Now the first among all acts is the act of being. Therefore, it is impossible for matter to be apprehended as being hot, or being quantified, before actually being. But matter has being in act through the substantial form, which makes it to *be*, without qualification, as we have said above.[52] Therefore it is impossible for any accidental dispositions to pre-exist in matter before the substantial form, and consequently before the soul.

Reply Objection 1. As appears from what has been already said, the more perfect form virtually contains whatever belongs to the inferior forms; and therefore while remaining one and the same, it perfects matter according to the various degrees of perfection.[53] For the same essential form makes man an actual being, a body, a living being, an animal, and a man. Now it is clear that each genus has its own proper accidents following upon it. Therefore just as matter is apprehended as existent before being understood as corporeal, etc., so those accidents which are proper to being are understood before corporeality. And thus, dispositions are understood in matter before the form, not as regards all its effects, but as regards the posterior effect.

Reply Objection 2. Dimensions of quantity are accidents consequent upon corporeality, which belongs to the whole matter. Hence, once matter is understood as corporeal and measurable, it can be understood as distinct in its various parts, and thus as receptive of different forms according to further degrees of perfection. For although it is essentially the same form which gives to matter the various degrees of perfection, as we have said, yet it is considered as different according to the way that the reason thinks of it.[54]

Reply Objection 3. A spiritual substance, which is united to a body as

---

51. Article 1.
52. Article 4.
53. Articles 3 and 4.
54. Above, article 4.

its mover only, is united to it by power or "virtue." But the intellectual soul is united to the body as a form by its very act of being; but it directs and moves the body by its power and virtue.

Seventh Article

IS THE SOUL UNITED TO THE
ANIMAL BODY BY MEANS OF A BODY?

Objection 1. It seems that the soul is united to the animal body by means of a body. For Augustine says that "the soul administers the body by light, i.e., by fire and air, which are most akin to a spirit." [55] But fire and air are bodies. Therefore the soul is united to the human body by means of a body.

Objection 2. Moreover, a link between things seems to be that entity whose removal involves the cessation of their union. But when breathing ceases, the soul is separated from the body. Therefore the breath, which is a kind of tenuous body, is the means of union between soul and body.

Objection 3. Again, things which are very distant from one another are not united except by something between them. But the intellectual soul is very distant from the body, both because it is incorporeal and because it is incorruptible. Therefore it seems to be united to the body by means of an incorruptible body; and such would be some heavenly light, which would harmonize the elements, and unite them together.

On the contrary: The Philosopher says: "We need not ask if the soul and body are one, just as neither do we ask if wax and its shape are one." [56] But the shape is united to the wax without a body intervening. Therefore also the soul is thus united to the body.

I answer that: If the soul, following the opinion of the Platonists, were united to the body only as a mover, it would be fitting to say that some other bodies intervene between the soul and body of man, or of any animal whatever; for a mover naturally moves what is distant from it by means of something nearer. But if the soul is united to the body as its form, as we have said above, it is impossible for it to be united by means of another body.[57]

The reason for this is that a thing is said to be "one" according as it is also said to be a "being." Now the form, through itself, makes a thing to be in act, since it is itself essentially an "act"; nor does it give being through some intermediary. Hence, the unity of a thing composed of matter and form exists through the form itself, which by reason of its very nature is united to matter as its "act." Nor is there any other cause

---

55. *A Literal Commentary on "Genesis"* VII, 19.
56. *On the Soul* II, 1(412b6).
57. Article 6 and article 1.

of union except the agent, which causes matter to be in act, as is said.[58]

This makes clear the falsity of the opinions of those who maintained the existence of some mediate bodies between the soul and body of man. Of these, certain Platonists said that the intellectual soul has an incorruptible body naturally united to it, from which it is never separated, and by means of which it is united to the corruptible body of man. Others said that the soul is united to the body by means of a corporeal spirit. Others, again, said it is united to the body by means of light, which, they say, is a body and of the nature of the fifth essence; so that the vegetative soul would be united to the body by means of the light of the sidereal heaven, the sensory soul, by means of the light of the crystal heaven, and the intellectual soul by means of the light of the empyrean heaven. Now all this is clearly fictitious and ridiculous. For light is not a body; and the fifth essence does not enter materially into the composition of a mixed body, because it is unchangeable, but does so only virtually; and lastly, because the soul is immediately united to the body as form to matter.

Reply Objection 1. Augustine speaks there of the soul inasmuch as it moves the body. That is why he uses the word "administration." It is true that it moves the grosser parts of the body by the more tenuous parts. And the first instrument of the motive power is a kind of spirit, as the Philosopher says.[59]

Reply Objection 2. The union of soul and body ceases with the cessation of breath, not because this is the means of union, but because of the removal of that disposition by which the body is conditioned for such a union. Nevertheless the breath is a means of moving, as the first instrument of motion.

Reply Objection 3. The soul is indeed very distant from the body, if we consider the condition of each separately; so that if each had a separate being, many means of connection would have to intervene. But inasmuch as the soul is the form of the body, it does not have being apart from the being of the body, but through its own being it is united to the body immediately. This is the case with every form which, if considered as an "act," is very distant from matter—which is a being only in potency.

Eighth Article

IS THE WHOLE SOUL IN EACH PART OF THE BODY?

Objection 1. It seems that the whole soul is not in each part of the body. For the Philosopher says: "It is not necessary for the soul to be in

---

58. Aristotle, *Metaphysics* VII, 6(1045b21).
59. *On the Cause of the Movement of Animals* X (703a9).

each part of the body; it suffices that it be in some principle of the body causing the other parts to live, for each part has a natural movement of its own." [60]

Objection 2. Moreover, the soul is in the body of which it is the "act." But it is the "act" of an organic body. Therefore it exists only in an organic body. But each part of the human body is not an organic body. Therefore the whole soul is not in each part.

Objection 3. Also, it is said that "the relation of a part of the soul to a part of the body, such as the sight to the pupil of the eye, is the same as the relation of the whole soul to the whole body of an animal." [61] If, therefore, the whole soul is in each part of the body, it follows that each part of the body is an animal.

Objection 4. Again, all the powers of the soul are rooted in the essence of the soul. If, therefore, the whole soul be in each part of the body, it follows that all the powers of the soul are in each part of the body; and thus, the sight will be in the ear, and hearing in the eye; which is absurd.

Objection 5. And again, if the whole soul is in each part of the body, each part of the body is immediately dependent on the soul. Thus one part would not depend on another, nor would one part be superior to another; which is clearly untrue. Therefore the soul is not in each part of the body.

On the contrary: Augustine says that "in each body the whole soul is in the whole body and wholly in each part." [62]

I answer that: As we have remarked, if the soul were united to the body merely as its mover, one might say that it is not in each part of the body, but only in one part, through which it would move the others. But since the soul is united to the body as its form, it must necessarily be in the whole body, and in each of its parts. For it is not an accidental form, but the substantial form of the body. Now a substantial form actuates not only the whole, but each part of the whole. For since a whole consists of parts, a form of the whole which does not give being to each of the parts of the body is a form consisting in composition and order, such as the form of a house; and such a form is accidental. But the soul is a substantial form, and therefore it must be the form and the "act," not only of the whole, but also of each part. Therefore, on the withdrawal of the soul, just as we do not speak of an animal or a man unless equivocally (as we speak of a painted "animal" or a stone "animal"), so it is with the hand, the eye, the flesh and bones, as the Philosopher says.[63] This is signalized by the fact that, on the withdrawal of the soul, no part of the body retains its proper function; although that which retains its

60. *op. cit.*, X, (703a34).
61. Aristotle, *On the Soul* II, 1(412b17; b27).
62. *On the Trinity* VI, 6.
63. *On the Soul* II, 1(412b10; b17).

specific nature retains its specific operation. But "act" is in that of which it is the "act." That is why the soul must be in the whole body, and in each part thereof.

That it is entire in each part of the body may be gathered from the following considerations: since a whole is that which is divided into parts, there are three kinds of totality, corresponding to three kinds of division. There is a whole which is divided into quantitative parts, such as a whole line, or a whole body. There is also a whole which is divided into logical and essential parts, as a thing defined is divided into the parts of a definition, and a composite into matter and form. There is, further, a third kind of whole which is potential, divided into parts of power.

The first kind of totality does not apply to forms, except perhaps accidentally; and then only to those forms which have an indifferent relationship to a quantitative whole and its parts. Thus, whiteness, as far as its essence is concerned, is equally disposed to be in the whole surface and in each part of it; so that when the surface is divided, the whiteness is divided by accident. But a form which requires diversity in the parts, such as a soul, and especially the soul of perfect animals, is not equally related to the whole and the parts. Hence it is not divided accidentally, viz., through the division of quantity. Quantitative totality, therefore, cannot be attributed to the soul, either essentially or accidentally. But the second kind of totality, which concerns logical and essential perfection, properly and essentially belongs to forms; and likewise virtual totality, because form is the principle of operation. Therefore if it be asked whether the whole whiteness is in the whole surface and in each part thereof, it is necessary to distinguish. If we mean the quantitative totality which whiteness has accidentally, then the whole whiteness is not in each part of the surface. The same is to be said of totality of power, since the whiteness which is in the whole surface moves the sight more than the whiteness which is in a small part of it. But if we mean totality of species and essence, then the whole whiteness is in each part of the surface.

Since, however, the soul has no quantitative totality, either essentially, or accidentally, as we have seen, it is enough to say that the whole soul is in each part of the body by totality of perfection and of essence, but not by totality of power. For it is not in each part of the body with regard to each of its powers; but with regard to sight, it is in the eye; with regard to hearing, it is in the ear, and so on. We must observe, nevertheless, that since the soul requires a variety of parts, its relation to the whole is not the same as its relation to the parts; for to the whole it is compared primarily and essentially as to its proper and proportionate perfectible subject; but to the parts, secondarily, inasmuch as they are ordained to the whole.

Reply Objection 1. The Philosopher is speaking there of the motive power of the soul.

Reply Objection 2. The soul is the "act" of an organic body, as of its primary and proportionate perfectible subject.

Reply Objection 3. An animal is that which is composed of a soul and a whole body, which is the soul's primary and proportionate perfectible subject. The soul is not thus in a part. Whence it does not follow that a part of an animal is an animal.

Reply Objection 4. Some of the powers of the soul are in it according as it exceeds the entire capacity of the body, viz., the intellect and the will; and hence these powers are not said to be in any part of the body. Other powers are common to soul and body. That is why each of these powers need not be wherever the soul is, but only in that part of the body which is adapted to the operation of such a power.

Reply Objection 5. One part of the body is said to be superior to another because of the various powers of which the parts of the body are the organs. For that part which is the organ of a higher power is a nobler part of the body; as is also that part which serves the same power in a nobler manner.

What Belongs to the Powers of the Soul in General

(In Eight Articles)

We proceed to consider those things which belong to the powers of the soul—first, in general, second, in particular [succeeding Question].

First Article

IS THE ESSENCE OF THE SOUL ITS POWER?

Objection 1. It would seem that the essence of the soul is its power. For Augustine says that "mind, knowledge and love are in the soul substantially, or, what is the same thing, essentially";[1] and that "memory, understanding, and will are one life, one mind, one essence." [2]

Objection 2. Further, the soul is superior to primary matter. But primary matter is its own potency. Much more therefore is the soul its own potency.

Objection 3. Moreover, the substantial form is simpler than the accidental form; a sign of which is that the substantial form is not intensified or lessened, but remains indivisible. But the accidental form is its own power. Much more therefore is that substantial form which is the soul.

Objection 4. Also, we sense by the sense power and we understand by the intellectual power. But "that by which we first sense and understand is the soul," according to the Philosopher.[3] Therefore the soul is its power.

Objection 5. Then, too, whatever does not belong to the essence is an accident. Therefore, if the power of the soul is something else beside its essence, then it is an accident; which is contrary to Augustine, who says that the foregoing [i.e., the trinities mentioned in objection 1] "are not in the soul as in a subject, as color or shape, or any other quality, or quantity, is in a body; for such a thing does not extend beyond the subject in which it is, whereas the mind can love and know other things." [4]

---

1. *On the Trinity* IX, 4.
2. *op. cit.,* X, 11.
3. *On the Soul* II, 2 (414a12).
4. *On the Trinity* IX, 4.

Objection 6. Again, "a simple form cannot be a subject." [5] But the soul is a simple form, since it is not composed of matter and form, as was said above.[6] Therefore the power of the soul cannot be in it as in a subject.

Objection 7. And again, an accident is not the principle of a substantial difference. But *sensory* and *rational* are substantial differences; and they are taken from sense and reason, which are powers of the soul. Therefore the powers of the soul are not accidents; and so it would seem that the power of the soul is its own essence.

On the contrary: Dionysius says that "heavenly spirits are divided into essence, power, and operation." [7] Much more, then, in the soul is the essence distinct from the "virtue" or power.

I answer that: It is impossible to admit that the power of the soul is its essence, although some have maintained it. For the present purpose this may be proved in two ways. First, because, since potency and act divide being and every genus of being, a potency and its act must be referred to the same genus. Therefore, if the "act" be not in the genus of substance, the potency which is said in relation to that act cannot be in the genus of substance. Now the operation of the soul is not in the genus of substance—this belongs to God alone, whose operation is His own substance. Therefore the divine potency or power which is the source of His operation is the divine essence itself. This cannot be true either of the soul or of any creature, as we have said above when speaking of the angels.[8] Secondly, this can also be shown to be impossible in the soul. For the soul by its very essence is an "act." Therefore, if the very essence of the soul were the immediate source of operation, whatever has a soul would always have actual vital actions, as that which has a soul is always an actually living thing. For, as a form, the soul is not an "act" ordained to a further "act"; it is rather the ultimate term of generation. Hence, for it to be in potency to another act does not belong to it according to its essence as a form, but according to its power. So the soul itself, as the subject of its power, is called the "first act," with a further relation to the second "act" [operation]. Now we observe that what has a soul is not always in act with respect to its vital operations. Hence it is also said in the definition of the soul that it is "the act of a body having life *potentially*"; which potentiality, however, "does not exclude the soul." [9] Therefore it follows that the essence of the soul is not its power. For nothing is in potency by reason of an act, as such.

Reply Objection 1. Augustine is speaking of the mind as it knows and loves itself. Thus knowledge and love, as referred to the soul as known

5. Boethius, *On the Trinity* II.
6. Question LXXV, article 5.
7. *On the Celestial Hierarchy* XI, 2.
8. Question LIX, article 2.
9. Aristotle, *On the Soul* II, 1(412a25).

and loved, are substantially or essentially in the soul, for the very substance or essence of the soul is known and loved. We are to understand in the same way what he says in the other passage, viz., that those things are "one life, one mind, one essence." Or, as some aver, this passage is true in the sense in which the potential whole is predicated of its parts, being midway between the universal whole and the integral whole. For the universal whole is in each part according to its entire essence and power, as animal in a man and in a horse; and therefore it is properly predicated of each part. But the integral whole is not in each part, either according to its whole essence, or according to its whole power. Therefore in no way is it predicated of the individual parts. Yet in a way it is predicated, though improperly, of all the parts together; as if we were to say that the wall, roof and foundation are a house. But the potential whole is in each part according to its whole essence, though not according to its whole power. Therefore it can in a way be predicated of each part, but not so properly as the universal whole. In this sense, Augustine says that the memory, understanding and will are the one essence of the soul.

Reply Objection 2. The "act" to which primary matter is in potency is the substantial form. Therefore the potency of matter is nothing else but its essence.

Reply Objection 3. Action belongs to the composite, as does the act of being; for to act belongs to what exists. Now the composite has being substantially through the substantial form; and it operates through the power consequent upon the substantial form. Hence an active accidental form is to the substantial form of the agent (e.g., heat compared to the form of fire) as the power of the soul is to the soul.

Reply Objection 4. That the accidental form is a source of action is due to the substantial form. Therefore the substantial form is the primary source of action, but not the proximate one. In this sense the Philosopher says that "the soul is that whereby we understand and sense."

Reply Objection 5. If we take accident according as it is contradistinguished to substance, then there can be no medium between substance and accident; for they are contradistinguished by affirmation and negation, viz., according to being in a subject, and not being in a subject. In this sense, since the power of the soul is not its essence, it must be an accident. It belongs to the second species of quality.[10] But if we take accident as one of the five predicables,[11] in this sense there is a medium between substance and accident. For all that belongs to the essence of a thing pertains to *substance.* But not everything that is outside the essence can be designated as an *accident* in this sense; but only that which is not caused by the essential principles of the species. For *property* does not

10. In Aristotelian doctrine there are four species of quality: (1) habit and disposition, (2) power and impotency, (3) passion and passible quality, (4) form and figure.
11. Namely, genus, difference, species, property, and accident.

belong to the essence of a thing, but is caused by the essential principles of the species; and hence it is a middle between the essence and accident thus understood. In this sense the powers of the soul may be said to be middles between substance and accident, as being natural properties of the soul. When Augustine says that knowledge and love are not in the soul as accidents in a subject, this must be understood in the sense given above, inasmuch as they concern the soul, not as loving and knowing, but as loved and known. His demonstration proceeds on this basis; for if love were in the soul loved as in a subject, it would follow that an accident transcends its subject, since even other things are loved through the soul.

Reply Objection 6. Although the soul is not composed of matter and form, yet it has an admixture of potency, as was said above; and for this reason it can be the subject of an accident.[12] The statement quoted is verified in God, Who is Pure Act; and it is in treating of this subject that Boethius employs the phrase.

Reply Objection 7. Rational and sensory, as differences, are not taken from the powers of sense and reason, but from the sensory and rational soul itself. But because substantial forms, which in themselves are unknown to us, are known by their accidents, nothing prevents us from sometimes substituting accidents for substantial differences.

Second Article

ARE THERE SEVERAL POWERS OF THE SOUL?

Objection 1. It would seem that there are not several powers of the soul. For the intellectual soul approaches nearest to the likeness of God. But in God there is one simple power. So, too, therefore, in the intellectual soul.

Objection 2. Moreover, the higher a power is, the more unified it is. But the intellectual soul excels all other forms in power. Therefore above all others it has one "virtue" or power.

Objection 3. Also, action belongs to that which exists in act. But by the one essence of the soul, man has actual being in the different degrees of perfection, as we have seen above.[13] Therefore by the one power of the soul he performs operations of diverse grades.

On the contrary: The Philosopher places several powers in the soul.[14]

I answer that: It is necessary to attribute several powers to the soul. In evidence of this truth, bear in mind that, as the Philosopher says, the lowest order of things cannot acquire complete fulfillment, or goodness,

---

12. Question LXXV, article 5, ad 4.
13. Question LXXVI, articles 3 and 4.
14. *On the Soul* II, 3(414a31).

but they acquire, by few movements, a certain partial fulfillment.[15] Those which belong to a higher order acquire complete fulfillment by many movements. Those yet higher acquire complete fulfullment by few movements, and the highest perfection is found in those things which enjoy complete fulfillment without any movement whatever. Thus, he is least of all disposed to health who can only acquire partial health by means of a few remedies. Better disposed is he who can acquire complete health by means of many remedies, and better still, he who can by a few remedies; but best of all is he who has complete health without any remedies. It must therefore be said that things below man achieve certain limited goods, and so have a few determinate operations and powers. But man can achieve a universal and a perfect fulfillment, because he can attain to beatitude. Yet he is in the lowest degree, according to his nature, of those to whom beatitude is possible; and therefore the human soul requires many and various operations and powers. But to angels a smaller variety of powers is sufficient. In God, however, there is no power or action beside His own Essence.

There is yet another reason why the human soul abounds in a variety of powers: it is on the boundary line between spiritual and physical creatures, and therefore the powers of both meet together in the soul.

Reply Objection 1. The intellectual soul approaches to the divine likeness more than do the lower creatures, in its being able to acquire complete fulfillment, although by many and various means; and in this it falls short of creatures superior to it [viz., angels].

Reply Objection 2. A single power is superior [to several powers] if its range is equal, but several powers are superior if they extend to move than the single power.

Reply Objection 3. One thing has one substantial act of being, but may have several operations. So there is one essence in the soul, but several powers.

Third Article

ARE THE POWERS DISTINGUISHED BY THEIR ACTS AND OBJECTS?

Objection 1. It seems that the powers of the soul are not distinguished by acts and objects. For nothing is determined to its specific kind by what is posterior or extrinsic to it. But the act is posterior to the power, and the object is extrinsic to it. Therefore the soul's powers are not specifically distinct by acts and objects.

Objection 2. Moreover, contraries are what differ most from each other. Therefore if the powers are distinguished by their objects, it follows

---

15. *On the Heaven* II, 12(292a22).

that the same power could not have contrary objects. This is clearly false in almost all the powers; for the power of vision extends to white and black, and the power of taste to sweet and bitter.

Objection 3. Again, if the cause be removed, the effect is removed. Hence if the difference of powers came from the difference of objects, the same object would not come under different powers. This is clearly false, for the same thing is known by the cognitive power, and desired by the appetitive.

Objection 4. And again, that which of itself is the cause of anything, is the cause of it in all cases. But various objects which belong to various powers belong also to some one power; as sound and color belong to sight and hearing, which are different powers, yet come under the one power of *common sense.*[16] Therefore the powers are not distinguished according to the difference of their objects.

On the contrary: Things posterior are distinguished in the light of things prior. But the Philosopher says that "acts and operations are logically prior to the powers; and these again are preceded by their opposites." i.e., their objects.[17] Therefore the powers are distinguished according to their acts and objects.

I answer that: Powers as such are ordained to acts. Therefore the nature of a power must be gathered from the act to which it is ordained; and consequently the nature of a power is diversified according as the nature of the act is diversified. Now the nature of an act is diversified according to the various natures of the objects. For every act is either of an active power or of a passive power. Now, the object is to the act of a passive power as the source and the moving cause; for color is the source of vision, inasmuch as it moves the sight. On the other hand, to the act of an active power the object is a term and an end; just as the object of the power of growth is completed quantity, which is the end of growth. Now, from these two things an act receives its specific character, viz., from its source, or from its end or term. For the act of heating differs from the act of cooling in this, that the former proceeds from something hot—which is the active source—to heat; while the latter proceeds from something cold—which is the active source—to cold. Therefore the powers are of necessity distinguished by their acts and objects.

Nevertheless, it must be borne in mind that things which are accidental do not change the species. For since to be colored is accidental to an animal, its species is not changed by a difference of color, but by a difference in that which belongs to the nature of an animal, i.e., by a difference in the sensory soul, which is sometimes found accompanied by reason and sometimes not. Hence *rational* and *irrational* are differences dividing *animal,* constituting its various species. In like manner, therefore, not

---

16. A specific internal unifying sense power, not to be confused with "common sense" in the colloquial meaning of the term.

17. *On the Soul* II, 4(415a18).

just any variety of objects diversifies the powers of the soul, but a difference in that to which the power of its very nature is directed. Thus, the sense power of its very nature is directed to the passive quality which of itself is divided into color, sound, and the like, and therefore there is one sense power with regard to color, viz., sight, and another with regard to sound, viz., hearing. But it is accidental to a passive quality, such as something colored, to be a musician or a grammarian, great or small, a man or a stone. Therefore by reason of such differences the powers of the soul are not distinguished.

Reply Objection 1. Act, though posterior in being to potency, is nevertheless prior to it in intention and in reason, as is the end in relation to the agent. And the object, although extrinsic, is nevertheless the source or the end of the action; and the conditions which are intrinsic to a thing are proportionate to its source and end.

Reply Objection 2. If any power were to have one of two contraries as such for its object, the other contrary would necessarily belong to another power. But the power of the soul does not of itself regard the nature of the contrary, but rather the common aspect of both contraries; just as sight does not of itself regard the nature of whiteness, but rather the nature of color. This is because, of two contraries, one, in a manner, includes the nature of the other, since they are to one another as perfect and imperfect.

Reply Objection 3. Nothing prevents things which coincide in reality from being considered under different aspects; and therefore they can belong to various powers of the soul.

Reply Objection 4. The higher power of itself regards a more universal formality in its object than the lower power; because the higher a power is, to a greater number of things does it extend. Therefore many things are combined in the one formality of the object which the higher power considers of itself; while they differ in the formalities regarded by the lower powers of themselves. Thus it is that various objects belong to various lower powers; which objects, however, are subject to one higher power.

Fourth Article

IS THERE ORDER AMONG THE POWERS OF THE SOUL?

Objection 1. It seems that there is no order among the powers of the soul. For in those things which come under one division, there is no priority and posteriority, but all are naturally simultaneous. But the powers of the soul are contradistinguished from one another. Therefore there is no order among them.

Objection 2. Moreover, the powers of the soul are related to their objects, and to the soul itself. On the part of the soul, there is no order among the powers, because the soul is one. In like manner, there is no order among them in relation to the objects, which are diverse and altogether disparate, as in the case of color and sound. Therefore there is no order among the powers of the soul.

Objection 3. Again, where there is order among powers, the operation of one is found to depend on the operation of another. But the action of one power of the soul does not depend on that of another; for sight can act independently of hearing, and conversely. Therefore there is no order among the powers of the soul.

On the contrary: The Philosopher compares the parts of powers of the soul to figures.[18] But figures have an order among themselves. Therefore the powers of the soul also have order.

I answer that: Since the soul is one, and the powers are many, and since a number of things that proceed from one must proceed in a certain order, there must be order among the powers of the soul. Now there is among them a threefold order, two of these corresponding to the dependence of one power on another, the third deriving from the order of the objects. Now the dependence of one power on another can be taken in two ways: 1) according to the order of nature, in that perfect things are by their nature prior to imperfect things; and 2) according to the order of generation and time, inasmuch as from being imperfect, a thing comes to be perfect. Thus, according to the first kind of order among the powers, the intellectual powers are prior to the sense powers; and consequently they direct them and command them. Likewise the sensory powers are in this order prior to the powers of the nutritive soul.

In the second kind of order, the reverse is true. For the powers of the nutritive soul are prior in generation to the powers of the sensory soul; and therefore they prepare the body for the actions of the sense powers. The same is to be said of the sense powers with regard to the intellectual. But according to the third kind of order, certain sense powers are ordered among themselves, viz., sight, hearing, and smell. For the visible comes naturally first, since it is common to higher and lower bodies. On the other hand, sound is audible in the air, which is naturally prior to the mingling of elements, of which odor is the result.

Reply Objection 1. The species of a given genus are, like numbers and figures, related to one another as prior and posterior, if considered in their being; although they may be said to be simultaneous, according as they receive the predication of the genus common to them.

Reply Objection 2. This order among the powers of the soul is both on the part of the soul (which, though it be one according to its essence, is disposed to various acts in a certain order), and on the part of the objects, and furthermore on the part of the acts, as was said above.

Reply Objection 3. This argument holds good as regards those powers

___

18. *op. cit.*, II, 3(414b20).

among which order of the third kind exists. Those powers, however, among which the two other kinds of order exist, are such that the action of one depends on another.

Fifth Article

ARE ALL THE POWERS OF THE SOUL
IN THE SOUL AS THEIR SUBJECT?

Objection 1. It seems that all the powers of the soul are in the soul as their subject. For as the powers of the body are to the body, so the powers of the soul are to the soul. But the body is the subject of the bodily powers. Therefore the soul is the subject of the powers of the soul.

Objection 2. Moreover, the activities of the powers of the soul are attributed to the body by reason of the soul; because, as is said "the soul is that by which we sense and understand primarily." [19] But the primary sources of the activities of the soul are the powers. Therefore the powers are primarily in the soul.

Objection 3. Again, Augustine says that "the soul senses certain things, not through the body, but in fact without the body, such as fear and the like; and some things it senses through the body." [20] However, if the sense powers were not in the soul alone as their subject, the soul could not sense anything without the body. Therefore the soul is the subject of the sense powers; and for a similar reason, of all the other powers.

On the contrary: The Philosopher says that "sensation belongs neither to the soul, nor to the body, but to the composite." [21] Therefore the sense power is in the composite as its subject. Consequently the soul alone is not the subject of all the powers.

I answer that: The subject of active power is that which is able to act; for every accident denominates its proper subject. Now it is the same being which is able to act, and which does act. Therefore the "subject of power is of necessity the subject of activity," as again the Philosopher says.[22] Now, it is clear from what we have said above that some activities of the soul are performed without a bodily organ, such as understanding and willing. Hence the powers of these activities are in the soul as their subject. But some activities of the soul are performed by means of bodily organs, as seeing by the eye, and hearing by the ear. And so it is with all the other activities of the nutritive and sensory parts of the soul. Therefore the powers which are the sources of these activities have their subject in the composite, and not in the soul alone.

---

19. Aristotle, *op.cit.*, II, 2(414a12).
20. *A Literal Commentary on "Genesis"* XII, 7; 24.
21. *On Sleep* I (454a7).
22. *ibid.*, 454a8.

Reply Objection 1. All the powers are said to belong to the soul, not as their subject, but as their source; because it is through the soul that the composite has the power to perform such activities.

Reply Objection 2. All such powers are in the soul before they are in the composite; not, however, as in their subject, but as in their source.

Reply Objection 3. Plato's opinion was that sensation is an activity proper to the soul, just as understanding is. Now in many things relating to philosophy, Augustine makes use of the opinions of Plato, not asserting them as true, but reporting them. However, as far as the present question is concerned, when it is said that the soul senses some things with the body, and some without the body, this can be taken in two ways. Firstly, the words "with the body" or "without the body" may determine the act of sense according as it proceeds from the one who senses. In this way, the soul senses nothing without the body, because the action of sensation cannot proceed from the soul except by a bodily organ. Secondly, they may be understood as determining the act of sense on the part of the object sensed. And in this way, the soul senses some things with the body, viz., those existing in the body, as when it feels a wound or something of that sort; while it senses some things without the body, viz., those which do not exist in the body but only in the apprehension of the soul, as when it feels sad or joyful on hearing something.

Sixth Article

DO THE POWERS OF THE SOUL FLOW FROM ITS ESSENCE?

Objection 1. It would seem that the powers of the soul do not flow from its essence. For different things do not proceed from one simple thing. But the essence of the soul is one and simple. Since, therefore, the powers of the soul are many and diverse, they cannot proceed from its essence.

Objection 2. Moreover, that from which a thing proceeds is its cause. But the essence of the soul cannot be said to be the cause of the powers, as is clear if one considers the different kinds of causes. Therefore the powers of the soul do not flow from its essence.

Objection 3. Again, "emanation" signifies some sort of movement. But it is proved that nothing is moved by itself except, perhaps, by reason of a part of itself; as an animal is said to be moved by itself, because one part of it moves and another is moved.[23] But the soul is not moved, as has been proved.[24] Therefore the soul does not produce its powers within itself.

On the contrary: The powers of the soul are its natural properties.

23. Aristotle, *Physics* VII, 1(241b24).
24. Aristotle, *On the Soul* I, 4(408a34).

But the subject is the cause of its proper accidents; whence it is also included in the definition of "accident," as is made clear.[25] Therefore the powers of the soul proceed from its essence as from their cause.

I answer that: The substantial and the accidental forms partly agree and partly differ. They agree in this, that each is an "act," and that by each of them something is in some way in act. They differ, however, in two respects. First, because the substantial form makes a thing to be in an unqualified sense; and its subject is only potentially a being; whereas the accidental form does not make a thing to be unqualifiedly, but to be *such,* or so great, or in some particular respect; for its subject is an actual being.[26] Hence it is clear that actuality is found in the substantial form prior to its being found in its subject; and since that which is first in a genus is the cause in that genus, the substantial form causes actual being in its subject. On the other hand, actuality is found in the subject of the accidental form prior to its being found in the accidental form; and therefore the actuality of the accidental form is caused by the actuality of the subject. So the subject, in that it is in potency, is receptive of the accidental form; but in that it is in act, it produces it. This I say of the proper and intrinsic accident; for with regard to the extraneous accident, the subject is receptive only, and such an accident is caused by an extrinsic agent. Secondly, substantial and accidental forms differ, because, since the less primary exists for the sake of the more primary, matter exists for the sake of the substantial form; while, on the contrary, the accidental form exists for the sake of the completeness of the subject.

Now it is clear, from what has been said,[27] that either the subject of the soul's powers is the soul itself alone, which can be the subject of an accident according as it has some potentiality, as was said above,[28] or else this subject is the composite. But the composite exists in act through the soul. Whence it is clear that all the powers of the soul, whether their subject be the soul alone or the composite, flow from the essence of the soul as their source; for it has already been noted that an accident is caused by the subject according as the subject is in act, and is received into it according as it is in potency.

Reply Objection 1. From one simple thing many things can proceed naturally in a certain order; and again, on account of the diversity of the recipients. Thus, from the one essence of the soul many and diverse powers proceed, both because order exists among these powers and also by reason of the diversity of the bodily organs.

---

25. cf. Aristotle, *Metaphysics* VI, 4(1029b30).

26. "Making," or causing, on the part of form, whether substantial or accidental form, is a matter of *formal,* not efficient, causality; e.g., that substantial form which is a rational soul "makes" its possessor rational, even as a ruddy complexion, which is an accidental form, "makes" one appear healthy.

27. Article 5.

28. Question LXXV, article 5, ad 1.

Reply Objection 2. The subject is both the final cause, and in a manner the active cause, of its proper accident. It is also the material cause, inasmuch as it is *receptive* of the accident. From this we may gather that the essence of the soul is the cause of all its powers, as their end, and as their active source; and of some, as receptive of them.

Reply Objection 3. The emanation of proper accidents from their subject is not by way of transmutation, but by a certain natural derivation; just as one thing results naturally from another, as color from light.

Seventh Article

DOES ONE POWER OF THE SOUL ORIGINATE FROM ANOTHER?

Objection 1. It seems that one power of the soul does not originate from another. For if several things originate simultaneously, one of them does not come from another. But all the powers of the soul are created at the same time with the soul. Therefore one of them does not arise from another.

Objection 2. Moreover, the power of the soul originates from the soul as an accident from its subject. But one power of the soul cannot be the subject of another, because nothing is the accident of an accident. Therefore one power does not arise from another.

Objection 3. Again, one opposite does not arise from the other opposite, but everything arises from that which is like it in species. Now the powers of the soul are oppositely divided, as diverse species. Therefore one of them does not proceed from another.

On the contrary: Powers are known through acts. But the act of one power is caused by the act of another power, as the act of the imagination by the act of the senses. Therefore one power of the soul is caused by another.

I answer that: In things which proceed from one thing according to a natural order, just as the first is the cause of all, so that which is nearer to the first is, in a way, the cause of those which are more remote. Now it has been shown above that among the powers of the soul there are several kinds of order.[29] Thus one power of the soul proceeds from the essence of the soul through the mediation of another. But since the essence of the soul is related to the powers both as an active and final cause, and as a receptive cause (either separately by itself, or together with the body), and since the agent and the end are more perfect, while the receptive factor as such is less perfect, it follows that those powers of the soul which precede the others in the order of perfection and nature are the causes of the others after the manner of an end and an active source. For we see that sense is for the sake of intellect, and not con-

---

29. Article 4.

versely. Sense, moreover, is a certain imperfect participation of intellectuality, and therefore, in terms of an order of natural origination, it in a way proceeds from the intellect, as the imperfect from the perfect. But considered as receptive factors, the more imperfect powers are causes in relation to the others. Thus the soul, with respect to the power of sensation which it enjoys, is considered as the subject, and as something material in relation to the intellect. On this account, the more imperfect powers precede the others in the order of generation, for the animal is generated before the man.

Reply Objection 1. As the power of the soul flows from the essence, not by a transmutation, but by a certain natural derivation, and is simultaneous with the soul, so is it the case with one power as regards another.

Reply Objection 2. An accident cannot of itself be the subject of an accident; but one accident is received in a substance prior to another, as quantity prior to quality.[30] In this way, one accident is said to be the subject of another (as surface is of color), inasmuch as a substance receives one accident through the means of another. The same thing may be said of the powers of the soul.

Reply Objection 3. The powers of the soul are opposed to one another as perfect and imperfect; as also are the species of numbers and figures. But this opposition does not prevent the origin of one from another, because imperfect things naturally proceed from perfect things.

Eighth Article

DO ALL THE POWERS REMAIN IN THE SOUL
WHEN SEPARATED FROM THE BODY?

Objection 1. It seems that all the powers of the soul remain in the soul separated from the body. For we read in the book *On the Spirit and the Soul* that "the soul withdraws from the body, taking with itself sense and imagination, reason and intellect and intelligence, concupiscibility and irascibility."[31]

Objection 2. Moreover, the powers of the soul are its natural properties. But properties are always in that to which they belong, and are never separated from it. Therefore the powers of the soul are in it even after death.

Objection 3. Again, the powers even of the sensory soul are not weakened when the body becomes weak; for, as is said, "If an old man were given the eye of a young man, he would see just as well as a young man."[32]

---

30. By an ontological or a natural, not a temporal or a genetic, priority.

31. Pseudo-Augustine (Alcher of Clairvaux), *De spir. et an.* XV. (Not available in English.)

32. Aristotle, *On the Soul* I, 4(408b21).

But weakness is the road to dissolution. Therefore the powers of the soul are not destroyed when the body dies, but remain in the separated soul.

Objection 4. And again, memory is a power of the sensory soul, as the Philosopher proves.[33] But memory remains in the separated soul, for it was said to the rich glutton whose soul was in hell: "Remember that thou didst receive good things during thy lifetime" (*Luke 16:25*). Therefore memory remains in the separated soul; and consequently the other powers of the sensory part of the soul.

Objection 5. Then, too, joy and sorrow are in the concupiscible part of the soul, which is a power of the sensory part. But it is clear that separate souls grieve or rejoice at the pains or rewards which they receive. Therefore the concupiscible power remains in the separate soul.

Objection 6. Furthermore, Augustine says that, "just as the soul, when the body lies senseless, yet not quite dead, sees some things by imaginary vision, so also when by death the soul is wholly separate from the body."[34] But the imagination is a power of the sensory part. Therefore, a power of the sensory part of the soul remains in the separate soul; and consequently all the other powers.

On the contrary: It is said that "man consists of two substances only: the soul with its reason, and the body with its senses."[35] Therefore when the body is dead, the sense powers do not remain.

I answer that: As we have already pointed out, all the powers of the soul belong to the soul alone as their source.[36] But some powers belong to the soul alone as their subject: such as intellect and will. These powers must remain in the soul, after the death of the body. But other powers are in the composite as in their subject. Such is the case with all the powers of the sensory and nutritive parts of the soul. Now accidents cannot remain after the destruction of their subject. Therefore, when the composite is destroyed, such powers do not remain actually; but they remain virtually in the soul, as in their source or root.

So it is false that, as some say, these powers remain in the soul even after the dissolution of the body. It is much more false that, as they also say, the acts of these powers remain in the separate soul; because these powers have no act apart from a bodily organ.

Reply Objection 1. That book has no authority, and so what is there written can be ignored with the same ease as it was asserted. It may be said, nevertheless, that the soul takes with itself these powers, not actually, but virtually.

Reply Objection 2. These powers, which we say do not actually remain

---

33. *On Memory and Reminiscence* 1, (450a12).
34. *A Literal Commentary on "Genesis"* XII, 32.
35. Gennadius, *On the Teachings of the Church* (*De Ecclesiae Dogmatibus*) XXIX. (Not available in English.)
36. Articles 6 and 7.

in the separate soul, are not the properties of the soul alone, but of the composite.

Reply Objection 3. These powers are said not to be weakened when the body becomes weak, because the soul remains immutable, and is the virtual principle of these powers.

Reply Objection 4. The recollection spoken of there is to be taken in the same way as Augustine places memory in the mind; which is not in the way that memory is a part of the sensory soul.[37]

Reply Objection 5. In the separate soul, sorrow and joy are not in the sensory, but in the intellectual appetite, as in the angels.

Reply Objection 6. Augustine in that passage is speaking as inquiring, not as asserting. Therefore he retracted some things which he had said there.[38]

---

37. *On the Trinity* X, 11; XIV, 7.
38. *Retractions* II, 24.

The Powers of the Soul in Particular

(In Four Articles)

We next treat of the powers of the soul in particular. The theologian, however, has only to inquire specifically concerning the intellectual and appetitive powers, in which the virtues reside. And since the knowledge of these powers depends to a certain extent on the other powers, our consideration of the powers of the soul in particular will be divided into three parts: first, we shall consider those powers which are a preamble to intellectuality; secondly, the intellectual powers; thirdly, the appetitive powers.

First Article

ARE THERE FIVE DISTINCT
KINDS OF POWERS IN THE SOUL?

Objection 1. It seems that there are not five distinct kinds of powers in the soul, viz., vegetative, sensory, appetitive, locomotive, and intellectual. For the powers of the soul are called its parts. But only three parts of the soul are commonly assigned, viz., the vegetative, the sensory, and the rational. Therefore there are only three kinds of powers in the soul, and not five.

Objection 2. Moreover, the powers of the soul are the sources of its vital activities. Now a thing is said to "live," in four modes. For the Philosopher states: " 'life' is spoken of in several ways, and even if only one of these is present, the thing is said to 'live' [Thus it is said to 'live'] by intellect and sense, by local movement and rest, and lastly, by movement of decrease and increase due to nourishment." [1] Therefore there are only four kinds of powers of the soul, as the appetitive is excluded.

Objection 3. Again, a special kind of soul ought not to be assigned to that which is common to all the powers. Now desire is common to each power of the soul. For sight desires its appropriate visible object; whence we read (*Ecclesiasticus 40:22*): "The eye desireth favor and beauty, but more than these green sown fields." In like manner, every other power

---

1. *On the Soul* II, 2(413a22).

desires its appropriate object. Therefore the appetitive power should not be made a special kind of power of the soul.

Objection 4. Then, too, the source of movement in animals is sense, or intellect, or appetite, as is said.[2] Therefore the motive power should not be added to the above as a special kind of soul.

On the contrary: The Philosopher says: "The powers are the vegetative, the sensory, the appetitive, the locomotive, and the intellectual."[3]

I answer that: There are five kinds of powers of the soul, as above numbered. Of these, three are called "souls," [4] and four are called "modes of living." [5] The reason of this diversity is that the various souls are distinguished according as the operation of the soul transcends the operation of the bodily nature in various ways; for the whole bodily nature is subject to the soul, and is related to it as its matter and instrument. There exists, therefore, an activity of the soul which so far exceeds the bodily nature that it is not even performed by any bodily organ; and such is the activity of the rational soul. Below this, there is another activity of the soul, which is indeed performed through a bodily organ, but not through a bodily quality, and this is the activity of the sensory soul. For though hot and cold, wet and dry, and other such physical qualities are required for the functioning of the senses, yet they are not required in such a way that the senses operate by means of the power of such qualities; rather, they are required only for the proper disposition of the organ involved. The lowest of the soul's functions is that which is performed by a bodily organ and by the power of a physical quality. Yet this transcends the functioning of the bodily nature;[6] because the movements of bodies are caused by an extrinsic principle, while these vital functions are from an intrinsic factor. For this is common to all the operations of a "soul" (*anima*): every animate thing, in some way, moves itself. Such is the operation of the vegetative soul; for digestion, and what follows, is caused instrumentally by the action of heat, as is said.[7]

Now the powers of the soul are distinguished generically by their objects. For the higher a power is, the more universal is the object to which it extends, as we have said above.[8] But the object of the soul's functioning may be considered in a triple order. For in the soul there is (1) a power whose object is only the body that is united to that soul; and the powers of this genus are called vegetative, for the vegetative power acts only on the body to which the soul is united. There is (2) another genus

---

2. *op. cit.,* III, 10(433a9).
3. *op. cit.,* II, 3(414a31).
4. Namely, the vegetative, the sensory, and the intellectual or rational.
5. i.e., all except the appetitive.
6. i.e., of that which lacks "soul," or is, literally, "inanimate."
7. Aristotle, *op. cit.,* II, 4(416b25).
8. Question LXXVII, article 3, ad 4.

in the powers of the soul which regards a more universal object, viz., every sensible body, and not only the body to which the soul is united. And there is (3) yet another genus in the powers of the soul which regards a still more universal object, viz., not only the sensible body, but universally all being. Therefore it is clear that the latter two genera of the soul's powers[9] have an operation in regard not merely to that which is united to them, but also to something extrinsic. Now, since whatever operates must in some way be united to the object in relation to which it operates, this extrinsic thing, which is the object of the soul's operation, must be related to the soul in a twofold manner. *First,* according as it has a natural aptitude to be united to the soul, and to exist in the soul through its likeness. In this way there are two kinds of powers: (1) the sensory, in regard to the less common object, the sensible body; and (2) the intellectual, in regard to the most common object, universal being. *Secondly,* according as the soul itself has an inclination and tendency to the external thing. And in this way there are again two kinds of powers in the soul: one—the appetitive—according to which the soul is referred to something extrinsic as to an end—which is first in the intention; the other—the locomotive power—according to which the soul is referred to the extrinsic thing as to the term of its operation and movement; for every animal is moved for the purpose of realizing its desires and intentions.

The modes of living, on the other hand, are distinguished according to the degrees of living things. There are some living things in which there exists only vegetative power, as in plants. There are others in which along with the vegetative there exists also the sensory, but not the locomotive power; and such are immobile animals, like shellfish. There are others which, besides this, have locomotive powers, as do the perfect animals,[10] which require many things for their life, and consequently need movement to seek necessaries of life from a distance. And there are some living things which along with these have intellectual power, viz., men. But the appetitive power does not constitute a degree of living things; because "wherever there is sense there is also appetite," as is said.[11]

Thus the first two objections are hereby solved.

Reply Objection 3. Natural appetite is that inclination which each thing has, of its own nature, for something. Hence, by its natural appetite each power desires what is suitable to itself. Animal appetite, however, follows upon the apprehended form. This sort of appetite requires a special power in the soul; apprehension alone does not suffice. For a

---

9. Namely, the sensory and the intellectual.
10. A "perfect" animal is one *complete* in animality, by virtue of having vegetative, sensory, appetitive, and locomotive powers.
11. Aristotle, *On the Soul* II, 3(414b1).

thing is desired according as it exists in its own nature, whereas in the power of apprehension it exists, not according to its own nature, but according to its likeness. So it is clear that sight desires naturally a visible object solely for the purpose of its act, viz., for seeing; whereas the animal by its appetitive power desires the thing seen, not merely for the purpose of seeing it, but also for other purposes. But if the soul did not require the things perceived by the senses, except for the sake of the actions of the senses (i.e., for the purpose of sensing them), there would be no need for a special genus of appetitive powers, since the natural appetite of powers would suffice.

Reply Objection 4. Although sense and appetite are sources of movement in perfect animals, yet sense and appetite, as such, are not sufficient to cause movement, unless another power be added to them; for immobile animals have sense and appetite, and yet they have not the power of motion. Now this motive power is not only in the appetite and sense as commanding the movement, but also in the parts of the body, to make them obey the appetite of the soul which moves them. Of this we have a sign in the fact that when the members are deprived of their natural disposition, they do not move in obedience to the appetite.[12]

Second Article

ARE THE PARTS OF THE VEGETATIVE SOUL FITTINGLY ENUMERATED AS THE NUTRITIVE, GROWTH, AND GENERATIVE?[13]

Objection 1. It seems that the parts of the vegetative soul are not fittingly enumerated as the nutritive, growth, and generative powers. For these are called "natural powers." But the powers of the soul transcend the natural powers. Therefore the above powers should not be classed as powers of the soul.

Objection 2. Moreover, a particular power of the soul should not be assigned to that which is common to living and to non-living things. But generation is common to all things that can come to be and pass away, whether living or not living. Therefore the generative power should not be classed as a power of the soul.

Objection 3. Again, the soul is more powerful than the body. But the body by the same active power gives a thing its specific nature and its due quantity; much more, therefore, does the soul. Hence the augmentative power of the soul is not distinct from the generative power.

Objection 4. And again, every thing is preserved in being by that

---

12. e.g., one cannot walk with paralyzed legs, however great the desire.
13. i.e., the factors providing for nutrition, growth, and reproduction, respectively.

whereby it has being. But the generative power is that whereby a living thing acquires being. Therefore by the same power the living thing is preserved. Now the nutritive power is directed to the preservation of the living thing, for it is "a power which is capable of preserving whatever receives it." [14] Therefore the nutritive power should not be distinguished from the generative power.

On the contrary: The Philosopher says that the operations of this soul are "generation, the use of food, and growth." [15]

I answer that: The vegetative part has three powers. For the vegetative part, as we have said,[16] has for its object the body itself, living by the soul; and for this body a triple operation of the soul is required: one, whereby it acquires being; and to this is directed the generative power, another, whereby the living body acquires its due quantity; and to this is directed the augmentative power; a third, whereby the body of a living thing is preserved in its being and in its due quantity; and to this is directed the nutritive power.

We must, however, recognize a difference among these powers. The powers of nutrition and growth have their effect where they exist, since the body itself united to the soul grows and is preserved by the very growth and nutritive powers which exist in one and the same soul. But the generative power has its effect, not in one and the same body, but in another; for a thing cannot generate itself. Therefore the generative power in a way approaches to the dignity of the sensory soul, which has an operation extending to extrinsic things, although in a more excellent and more universal manner; for that which is highest in an inferior nature approaches to that which is lowest in the higher nature, as is made clear by Dionysius.[17] Therefore, of these three powers, the generative has the greater finality, nobility and perfection; as the Philosopher says, "it belongs to a thing which is already perfect to produce another like unto itself." [18] Furthermore, the generative power is served by the powers of growth and nutrition; and the former power by the latter.

Reply Objection 1. Such powers are called "natural," both because they produce an effect like that of nature, which also gives being, quantity, and preservation (although the above powers accomplish these things in a more perfect way); and because these powers perform their actions instrumentally, through the active and passive qualities, which are the sources of natural actions.

Reply Objection 2. Generation in inanimate things is entirely from an extrinsic source; whereas the generation of living things is effected in a higher way, through something in the living thing itself, which is the

---

14. Aristotle, *On the Soul* II, 4(416b14).
15. *ibid.*, (415a25; b23).
16. Preceding article.
17. *On the Divine Names* VII, 3.
18. Aristotle, *On the Soul* II, 4 (416b24).

semen containing a certain formative principle of the body. Therefore, there must be in the living thing a power that prepares this semen; and this is the generative power.

Reply Objection 3. Since the generation of living things is from a semen, it is necessary that in the beginning an animal of small size be generated. For this reason it must have a power in the soul whereby it is brought to its appropriate size. But the inanimate body is generated ʼfrom determinate matter by an extrinsic agent; and therefore it receives at once its specific nature and its quantity, according to the condition of the matter.

Reply Objection 4. As we have said above, the operation of the vegetative principle is performed by means of heat, the property of which is to consume humidity.[19] Therefore, in order to restore the humidity thus lost, the nutritive power is required, whereby the food is converted into the substance of the body. This is also necessary for the action of the powers of growth and reproduction.

Third Article

ARE THE EXTERIOR SENSES
PROPERLY DISTINGUISHED INTO FIVE KINDS?

Objection 1. It would seem inaccurate to distinguish *five* exterior senses. For sense can know accidents. But there are many kinds of accidents. Therefore, since powers are distinguished by their objects, it seems that the senses are multiplied according to the number of the kinds of accidents.

Objection 2. Moreover, magnitude and shape, and other so-called "common sensibles," are not sensibles by accident, but are contradistinguished from them.[20] Now the diversity of the proper objects diversifies the powers. Since, therefore, magnitude and shape differ more from color than sound does, it seems that there is much more need for another sense power that can grasp magnitude or shape than for that which perceives color or sound.

Objection 3. Again, one sense regards one part of contraries, as sight regards white and black. But the sense of touch grasps several pairs of contraries, such as hot and cold, moist and dry, and the like. Therefore it is not a single sense, but several. There are, then, more than five senses.

Objection 4. And again, a species is not divided against its genus. But

---

19. Preceding article.

20. Aristotle, *op. cit.*, II, 6(418a8). A "common sensible" is an object perceived by several senses, as shape by sight and by touch. An "accidental sensible" is a thing not itself directly sensed but known through objects sensed, as a bird through color and sound. A "proper sensible" is an object perceivable directly by but one sense, as color by sight, or sound by hearing.

taste is a kind of touch. Therefore it should not be classed as a distinct sense from touch.

On the contrary: The Philosopher says: "There is none other besides the five senses." [21]

I answer that: The reason for the distinction and number of the senses has been assigned by some on the basis of the organs, in which one or other of the elements preponderates, such as water, air, or the like. By others it has been assigned to the medium, which is either in conjunction or extrinsic, and is either water or air, or the like. Others have attributed it to the diverse natures of the sensible qualities, according as such quality belongs to a simple body or results from complexity.

But none of these explanations is correct. For the powers are not for the sake of the organs, but the organs for the sake of the powers; and therefore there are not various powers because there are various organs, but on the contrary, nature has provided a variety of organs in order that they might be suitable to the diversity of powers. In the same way nature provided various mediums for the various senses, according to what suited the acts of the powers. Now to be cognizant of the natures of sensible qualities does not pertain to the senses, but to the intellect. The reason for the number and distinction of the exterior senses must therefore be attributed to that which belongs to the senses properly by their own nature. Sense is a passive power, and is naturally affected [22] by the exterior sensible. Hence, the exterior cause of such activation is what is directly perceived by the senses; and the sense powers are diversified according to the diversification of that exterior cause.

Now, this activation is of two kinds, one "natural," the other "spiritual." Natural activation takes place when the form of that which causes it is received, according to its natural being, into the thing activated, as heat is received into the thing heated. But spiritual activation takes place when the form of what causes it is received, according to a spiritual mode of being, into the thing activated, as the form of color is received into the pupil, which does not thereby become colored. Now, for the operation of the senses a spiritual activation is required, whereby the likeness of a sensible form is made present in the sense organ. Otherwise, if a natural activation alone sufficed for the sense's action, all natural bodies would have sensation when they undergo alteration.[22a]

But in some senses we find spiritual activation only, as in sight, while in others we find not only a spiritual but also a natural activation, and this either on the part of the object only, or also on the part of the organ. On the part of the object, we find local natural activation in sound, which

---

21. *op. cit.,* III, 1(424b22).

22. Literally, "immuted," for which there is no idiomatic English equivalent. "Immutation" is an alteration which results in activating a sense power.

22a. Note that "natural" activation is *purely* physical, while "spiritual" activation is as such *cognitive.*

is the object of hearing; for sound is caused by percussion and commotion of the air. We find natural activation by alteration in odor, which is the object of smelling; for in order to give off an odor, a body must be in a measure affected by heat. On the part of the organ, natural activation takes place in touch and taste; for the hand that touches something hot becomes hot, while the tongue is moistened by the humidity of flavors. But the *organs* of smelling and hearing are not affected in their respective operations by any natural activation, except accidentally.

Now sight, which is without natural activation either in its organ or in its object, is the most spiritual, the most perfect, and the most universal of all the senses. After this comes hearing and then smell, which require a natural activation on the part of the object; while local motion is more perfect than, and naturally prior to, the motion of alteration, as is proved.[23] Touch and taste are the most material of all. (Of their distinction we shall speak later on). Hence it is that the three other senses are not exercised through a medium united to them, lest there be a natural activation in their *organ*, as in the case of those two senses.

Reply Objection 1. Not every accident has in itself a power of sense activation, but only qualities of the third species, respecting which there can be alteration.[24] Therefore only such qualities are the objects of the senses, because "the senses are affected by the same things whereby inanimate bodies are affected," as is said.[25]

Reply Objection 2. Size, shape, and the like, which are called "common sensibles," are midway between accidental sensibles and proper sensibles, which are the objects of the senses. For the proper sensibles first, and of their very nature, activate the senses, since they are qualities that cause alterations. But the common sensibles are all reducible to quantity: as to *size* and *number*, it is clear that they are species of quantity; *shape* is a quality, since the nature of shape consists in fixing the bounds of magnitude; *movement* and *rest* are sensed according as the subject is affected in one or more ways in the magnitude of the subject or of its local distance, as in the movement of growth or of locomotion, or again, according as it is affected in some sensible qualities, as in the movement of alteration. And thus to sense movement and rest is, in a way, to sense one thing and many. Now quantity is the proximate subject of the qualities that cause alteration, as surface is of color. Therefore the common sensibles do not move the senses first and of their own nature, but by reason of sensible quality; as the surface by reason of color. Yet they are not accidental sensibles, for they produce a certain diversity in the activation of the senses. For sense is activated differently by a large and by a small surface—even whiteness itself is said to be "great" or "small," and therefore is divided according to its proper subject.

23. Aristotle, *Physics* VIII, 7(260a28).
24. viz., passion and passive quality.
25. Aristotle, *op. cit.*, VII, 2(244b12).

Reply Objection 3. As the Philosopher seems to say, the sense of touch is generically one, but is divided into several specific senses, and for this reason it extends to various pairs of contraries.[26] These senses, however, are not separate from one another in their organ, but are diffused throughout the whole body, so that their distinction is not evident. But taste, which perceives the sweet and the bitter, accompanies touch in the tongue, but not in the whole body; so it is easily distinguished from touch. It can also be said that all those contrarieties agree, each in some proximate genus, and all in a common genus, which is the common and formal object of touch. Such a common genus is, however, unnamed, just as the proximate genus of hot and cold is unnamed.

Reply Objection 4. The sense of taste, according to a saying of the Philosopher, is a kind of touch existing only in the tongue.[27] It is not distinct from touch in general, but only from the species of touch distributed throughout the body. But if touch is only one sense, by reason of the common formality of its object, it must be said that taste is distinguished from touch by reason of a different kind of activation. For touch involves a natural, and not only a spiritual, alteration in its organ, by reason of the quality which is its proper object. But the organ of taste is not necessarily affected by a natural activation according to the quality which is its proper object, so that the tongue itself becomes sweet or bitter, but according to the quality which is a preamble to flavor, and on which it is based. This quality is moisture, the object of touch.

Fourth Article

ARE THE INTERIOR SENSES APPROPRIATELY CLASSIFIED?

Objection 1. It would seem that the interior senses are not appropriately classified. For the common is not divided against the proper. Therefore the "common sense" should not be numbered among the interior sense powers, in addition to the proper exterior senses.

Objection 2. Moreover, there is no need to assign an interior power of perception when the proper and exterior sense suffices. But the proper and exterior senses suffice for us to judge of sensible things; for each sense judges of its proper object. Likewise, they seem to suffice for the perception of their own actions; for since the action of the sense is a kind of intermediary between the power and its object, it seems the power of sight must be much more able to perceive its own vision, as being nearer to it, than its object, color; and so it is with the other senses. Hence for this purpose there is no need to assign an interior power, called the "common sense."

Objection 3. Again, according to the Philosopher, "the imagination and

26. *On the Soul* II, 11(422b17).
27. *op. cit.*, II, 9(421a18); 11(423a17).

the memory are passions of the primary faculty of sense-perception." [28] But "passion" is not divided against its subject. Therefore memory and imagination should not be assigned as powers distinct from sense.

Objection 4. And again, the intellect depends on the senses less than any power of the sensory part of the soul. But the intellect knows nothing except through sense data. That is why it is said that "those who lack one sense lack one kind of knowledge." [29] Much less, then, should we assign to the sensory part of the soul a power, called the "estimative power," to account for the perception of representations which the sense does not perceive.

Objection 5. Then, too, the action of the "cogitative power," which consists in comparing, uniting and dividing, and the action of the "memorative power," which consists in the use of a kind of syllogism for the sake of inquiry, are not less distant from the actions of the "estimative" and "memorative" powers, than the action of the estimative is from the action of the imagination. Therefore either we must add the cogitative and reminiscitive powers to the estimative and memorative powers, or the estimative and memorative powers should not be made distinct from the imagination.

Objection 6. Furthermore, Augustine describes three kinds of vision: *corporeal,* which is an action of the sense; *spiritual,* which is an action of the imagination or phantasy; and *intellectual,* which is an action of the intellect.[30] Therefore there is no interior power between the sense and intellect, besides the imagination.

On the contrary: Avicenna assigns five interior sense powers: *common sense, phantasy, imagination, the estimative,* and *the memorative.*[31]

I answer that: As nature does not fail in necessary things, there must be as many actions of the sensory soul as may suffice for the life of a complete animal. If any of these actions cannot be reduced to one and the same source, they must be assigned to diverse powers; since a power of the soul is nothing else than the proximate principle of the soul's operation.

Now it must be noted that for the life of a complete animal, the animal should apprehend a thing not only at the actual time of sensation, but also when it is absent. Otherwise, since animal motion and action follow upon perception, an animal would not be moved to seek something absent; the contrary of which is especially apparent in the case of complete animals, whose movement is progressive, impelled as they are toward something apprehended and absent. Therefore, through the sensory soul an animal must not only receive the forms of sensible things, when it is presently activated by them, but it must also retain and preserve them.

---

28. *On Memory and Reminiscence* I (450a10).
29. Aristotle, *Posterior Analytics* I, 18(81a38).
30. *A Literal Commentary on "Genesis"* XII, 6; 7; 24.
31. *On the Soul (De Anima),* I, 5(5rb); IV, 1 (17va). (Not available in English.)

Now the acts of receiving and retaining are, in bodily things, traced back to diverse sources; for moist things are well fitted to receive, but they retain with difficulty, while it is the reverse with dry things. Therefore, since the sense power is the act of a bodily organ, it follows that the power which receives the forms of sensible things must be distinct from the power which preserves them.

Again, it must be noted that if an animal were moved only by things pleasing and disagreeable to the senses, there would be no need to attribute to it anything besides the apprehension of those forms which the senses perceive, and in which it takes pleasure or from which it shrinks. But the animal needs to seek or to avoid certain things, not only because they are pleasing or displeasing to the senses, but also because of other advantages and uses, or disadvantages. Thus, the sheep runs away when it sees a wolf, not because of its unseemly color or shape, but as from a natural enemy. So, too, a bird gathers together straws, not because they are pleasant to the sense, but because they are useful for building its nest. Animals, therefore, need to perceive such aspects,[32] which the exterior sense does not perceive. Now some distinct factor is necessary for this, since the perception of sensible forms is caused by an activation on the part of sensible things—which is not the case with the perception of the aforesaid aspects.

Consequently, to account for the reception of sensible forms there are the *proper sense* and the *common sense*. (Of their distinction we shall speak later). But to account for the retention and preservation of these forms, there is the *phantasy,* or the *imagination,* which is a kind of storehouse of forms received through the senses. And for the apprehension of aspects which are not received through the senses, there is the *estimative power;* and for their preservation, the *memorative power,* which is a storehouse of such aspects. An indication of this is the fact that memory in animals arises from some such aspect—e.g., that something is harmful or beneficial. And the very character of something as past, which memory observes, is to be reckoned among these aspects.

Now, it must be noted that as to sensible forms there is no difference between man and other animals; for they are similarly affected by external sensibles. But there is a difference as to the above aspects; for other animals perceive these aspects only by some sort of natural instinct, while man perceives them by means of a certain comparison. Therefore the power which in other animals is called the "natural estimative power" in man is called the "cogitative power," which by some sort of comparison discovers these aspects. Therefore it is also called the "particular reason," to which medical men assign a particular organ, viz., the middle part of the head; for it compares individual notions, just as the "intellectual reason" compares universal notions. As to the memora-

32. Literally, "intentions"—in a very broad sense, "meanings," or "significances."

tive power, man has not only *memory,* as other animals have, in the sudden recollection of the past, but also *reminiscence,* by seeking syllogistically, as it were, for a recollection of the past by the application of individual notions. Avicenna, however, assigns between the estimative and the imaginative power a fifth power, which combines and divides imaginary forms; as when from the imaginary form of gold, and the imaginary form of a mountain, we compose the one form of a golden mountain, which we have never seen. But this operation is not to be found in animals other than man, in whom the imaginative power suffices for this purpose. Averroes also attributes this action to the imagination, in his book *On Sense and the Sensible.* So there is no need to assign more than four interior powers of the sensory part of the soul, viz., the common sense, the imagination, and the estimative and memorative powers.

Reply Objection 1. The interior sense is called "common" not by predication, as if it were a genus, but as the common root and source of the exterior senses.

Reply Objection 2. The proper sense judges of the proper sensible by distinguishing it from other things which come under the same sense; e.g., by distinguishing white from black or green. But neither sight nor taste can distinguish white from sweet, because what distinguishes between two things must know both. Hence, the distinguishing judgment must be assigned to the "common sense." To it, as to a common term, all sense perceptions must be referred, and by it, again, all the "intentions" of the senses are perceived; as when someone sees that he sees. For this cannot be done by the proper sense, which knows only the form of the sensible by which it is affected. In this activation the action of sight is accomplished, and from it follows another activation in the 'common sense' which perceives the act of seeing.

Reply Objection 3. Just as one power arises from the soul by means of another, as we have seen above, so likewise the soul is the subject of one power through another.[33] In this way the imagination and the memory are called "passions" of the primary faculty of sense-perception.

Reply Objection 4. Although the operation of the intellect has its origin in the senses, yet, in the thing apprehended through the senses, the intellect knows many things which the senses cannot perceive. The estimative power functions in like manner, though in a less perfect way.

Reply Objection 5. The cogitative and memorative powers in man owe their excellence not to that which is proper to the sensitive part, but to a certain affinity and proximity to the universal reason, which, in a way, overflows into them. Therefore they are not distinct powers, but the same, yet more perfect than in other animals.

Reply Objection 6. Augustine calls that vision "spiritual" which is effected by the images of bodies in the absence of bodies. Clearly, therefore, it is common to all interior apprehensions.

---

33. Question LXXVII, article 7.

The Intellectual Powers

(In Thirteen Articles)

First Article

IS THE INTELLECT A POWER OF THE SOUL?

Objection 1. It seems that the intellect is not a power of the soul, but the essence of the soul. For the intellect seems to be the same as the mind. Now the mind is not a power of the soul, but the essence; for Augustine says: "Mind and spirit are not names of relations, but denominate the essence." [1] Therefore the intellect is the essence of the soul.

Objection 2. Moreover, diverse kinds of the soul's powers are not united in some one power, but only in the essence of the soul. Now the appetitive and the intellective are diverse kinds of the soul's powers, as the Philosopher says;[2] but they are united in the mind, for Augustine places the intelligence and will in the mind.[3] Therefore the mind and intellect of man is the very essence of the soul, and not a power of it.

Objection 3. Again, according to Gregory, "man understands with the angels." But angels are called "minds" and "intellects." Therefore the mind and intellect of man is not a power of the soul, but the soul itself.

Objection 4. And again, a substance is intellective by the fact that it is immaterial. But the soul is immaterial by its essence. Therefore it seems that the soul must be intellective by its essence.

On the contrary: The Philosopher assigns the intellect as a power of the soul.[4]

I answer that: In accordance with what has been already shown, it is necessary to say that the intellect is a power of the soul, and not the very essence of the soul.[5] For the essence of that which operates is then alone the immediate principle of operation, when the act of operation itself is its act of being; for as power is related to operation as to its "act," so is essence related to the act of being. But in God alone is His act of understanding the same as His very act of Being. Hence, in God alone is His intellect His essence; in all other intellectual beings, the intellect is a power.

---

1. *On the Trinity* IX, 2.
2. *On the Soul* II, 3(414a31).
3. *op. cit.*, X, 11.
4. *On the Soul* II, 3(414a32).
5. Question LIV, article 3; Question LXXVII, article 1.

Reply Objection 1. Sense is sometimes taken for the power, and sometimes for the sensory soul; for the sensory soul takes its name from its principal power, which is sense. And in like manner the intellectual soul is sometimes called "intellect," as from its principal power; and thus it is said that the "intellect is a substance." [6] And it is in this sense also that Augustine says that the mind is a nature or an essence.

Reply Objection 2. The appetitive and intellectual powers are diverse kinds of powers in the soul, by reason of the diverse natures of their objects. But the appetitive power agrees partly with the intellectual power, and partly with the sensory as regards its mode of operation either through a bodily organ or without it; for appetite follows upon apprehension. It is in this way that Augustine puts the will in the "mind"; and the Philosopher, in the "reason."

Reply Objection 3. In the angels there is no other power besides the intellect and the will, which follows the intellect. This is the reason why an angel is called a "mind" or an "intellect," because his whole power consists in this. But the soul has many other powers, such as the sensory and nutritive powers, and therefore the comparison fails.

Reply Objection 4. The immateriality of a created intelligent substance is not its intellect; but rather through its immateriality it has the power of understanding. Therefore it follows, not that the intellect is the substance of the soul, but that it is its "virtue" and power.

Second Article

IS THE INTELLECT A PASSIVE POWER?

Objection 1. It seems that the intellect is not a passive power. For everything is passive by its matter, and acts by its form. But the intellective power results from the immateriality of the intelligent substance. Therefore it seems that the intellect is not a passive power.

Objection 2. Further, the intellective power is imperishable, as was stated above.[7] But, as is said, "if the intellect is passive, it is corruptible." [8] Therefore the intellective power is not passive.

Objection 3. Further, *the agent is nobler than the patient,* as Augustine and Aristotle say. But all the powers of the vegetative part of the soul are active, and yet they are the lowest among the powers of the soul. Much more, therefore, are all the intellectual powers, which are the highest, active in character.

On the contrary: The Philosopher says that "to understand is in a way to be passive." [9]

6. Aristotle, *op. cit.,* I, 4(408b18).
7. Question LXXV, article 6.
8. Aristotle, *On the Soul* III, 5(430a24).
9. *op. cit.,* III, 4(429b24).

I answer that: To be "passive" may be taken in three ways. Firstly, in its most strict sense, when from a thing is taken something which belongs to it either by its nature, or by its proper inclination; as when water loses coolness by heating, and as when a man becomes ill or sad. Secondly, less strictly, a thing is said to be "passive" when something, whether suitable or unsuitable, is taken away from it; in this way not only he who is ill is said to be "passive," but also he who is healed; not only he who is sad, but also he who is joyful; or howsoever he may be altered or moved. Thirdly, in a wide sense a thing is said to be "passive" from the very fact that what is in potency to something receives that to which it was in potency, without being deprived of anything; and in this way whatever passes from potency to act may be said to be "passive," even when it is perfected. It is thus that for us to understand is to be "passive." This is clear from the following reason. For the intellect, as was said above, has an operation extending to universal being.[10] It can therefore be determined whether an intellect is in act or in potency by considering the nature of the relation of the intellect to universal being. For there is an intellect whose relation to universal being is that of the "act" of all being; and such is the divine intellect, which is the essence of God, in which, originally and virtually, all being pre-exists as in its first cause. Therefore the divine intellect is not in potency, but is pure act. But no created intellect can be "act" in relation to the whole universal being; for then it would have to be an infinite being. Therefore no created intellect, by reason of its very being, is the "act" of all things intelligible; but it is compared to these intelligible things as potency to act.

Now, potency has a double relation to act. There is a potency which is always perfected by its act. Such, we say, is the case with the matter of the heavenly bodies. And there is another potency which is not always in act, but proceeds from potency to act; as we observe in things which come into being and pass away. Hence the angelic intellect is always in act as regards those things which it can understand, by reason of its proximity to the first intellect, which is pure act, as was said above.[11] But the human intellect, which is the lowest in the order of intellects and most remote from the perfection of the divine intellect, is in potency with regard to things intelligible, and is at first "like a clean tablet on which nothing is written," as the Philosopher says.[12] This is made clear from the fact that at first we are only in potency towards understanding, and afterwards we are made to understand actually. And so it is evident that with us to understand is in a way to be passive, taking passivity in the third sense. And consequently the intellect is a passive power.

Reply Objection 1. This objection is verified of passivity in the first

---

10. Question LXXVIII, article 1.
11. Question LVIII, article 1.
12. *op. cit.*, III, 4(430a1).

and second senses, which belong to primary matter. But in the third sense, passivity is in anything which is brought from potency to act.

Reply Objection 2. "Passive intellect" is the name given by some to the sense appetite, in which are the passions of the soul; which appetite is also called "rational by participation," because it obeys reason. Others give the name of "passive intellect" to the cogitative power, which is called the "particular reason." And in each case "passive" may be taken in the two first senses, since this so-called "intellect" is the act of a bodily organ. But the intellect which is in potency to things intelligible, and which for this reason Aristotle calls the "possible intellect," is not passive except in the third sense; for it is not an act of a bodily organ.[13] Hence it is imperishable.

Reply Objection 3. The agent is nobler than the patient, if the activity and the passivity are referred to the same thing; but not always, if they refer to different things. Now the intellect is a passive power in regard to the whole universal being, while the vegetative power is active in regard to some particular thing, viz., the body as united to the soul. Therefore nothing prevents such a passive power being nobler than such an active one.

Third Article

IS THERE AN AGENT INTELLECT?

Objection 1. It seems that there is no agent intellect. For as the senses are to things sensible, so is the intellect to things intelligible. But because sense is in potency to things sensible, there is not said to be an agent sense, but only a passive one. Therefore, since our intellect is in potency to things intelligible, it seems that we cannot say that there is an agent intellect, but only a passive one.

Objection 2. Moreover, if it be said that even in the senses there is something active, such as light—on the contrary, light is required for sight, in that it makes the medium to be actually luminous; for color of its own nature moves the luminous medium. But in the operation of the intellect there is no appointed medium that has to be brought into act. Therefore there is no necessity for an agent intellect.

Objection 3. Again, the likeness of the agent is received into the patient according to the condition of the patient. But the possible intellect is an immaterial power. Therefore its immateriality suffices for forms to be received into it immaterially. Now a form is intelligible in act from the very fact that it is immaterial. Therefore there is no need for an agent intellect to make forms actually intelligible.

On the contrary: The Philosopher says: "As in every nature, so in the

---

13. *op. cit.,* III, 4(429a22).

soul, there is something by which it becomes all things, and something by which it makes all things." [14] Therefore we must admit an agent intellect.

I answer that: According to the opinion of Plato, there is no need for an agent intellect in order to make things actually intelligible, but perhaps in order to provide intellectual light to the intellect, as will be explained later.[15] For Plato supposed that the forms of natural things subsisted apart from matter, and consequently that they are intelligible; for a thing is actually intelligible from the very fact that it is immaterial. And he called such forms "species" or "ideas." By participation in these, he said that even physical matter was formed, in order that individuals might be naturally established in their proper genera and species, and also that our intellects were formed by such participation in order to have knowledge of the genera and species of things. But since Aristotle did not hold that the forms of natural things exist apart from matter, and since forms existing in matter are not actually intelligible, it follows that the natures or forms of the sensible things which we understand are not actually intelligible.[16] Now nothing is brought from potency to act except by something in act; e.g., the sense power is actuated by that which is actually sensible. We must therefore attribute to the intellect a power to make things intelligible in act, through the abstraction of intelligible forms from material conditions. And such is the necessity for positing an agent intellect.

Reply Objection 1. Sensible things are found actually existing outside the soul; and hence there is no need for an agent sense. Therefore it is clear that in the nutritive part of the soul all the powers are active, whereas in the sensory part of the soul all are passive; but in the intellective part, there is something active and something passive.

Reply Objection 2. There are two opinions as to the effect of light. For some say that light is required for sight, in order to make colors actually visible. And according to this, the agent intellect is required for understanding in like manner and for the same reason as light is required for seeing. But in the opinion of others, light is required for sight, not for the colors to become actually visible, but in order that the medium may become actually luminous, as the Commentator [Averroes] says.[17] And according to this, Aristotle's comparison of the agent intellect to light is verified in this, that as it is required for understanding, so is light required for seeing; but not for the same reason.[18]

Reply Objection 3. If the agent pre-exists, it may well happen that its

---

14. *op. cit.,* III, 5(430a10).
15. Article 4; question LXXXIV, article 6.
16. *Metaphysics,* II, 4(999b18); VII, 3(1043b19).
17. *Commentary on Aristotle's "On the Soul",* II, comm. 67 (VI, 140r). (Not available in English.)
18. *On the Soul* III, 5(430a15).

likeness is received variously into different things, because of their different dispositions. But if the agent does not pre-exist, the disposition of the recipient has nothing to do with the matter. Now the intelligible in act is not something existing in nature, if by "nature" we mean the nature of sensible things, which do not subsist without matter. And therefore in order to understand them, the immaterial nature of the possible intellect would not suffice but for the presence of the agent intellect, which makes things actually intelligible by way of abstraction.

Fourth Article

IS THE AGENT INTELLECT SOMETHING IN THE SOUL?

Objection 1. It seems that the agent intellect is not somthing in our soul. For the effect of the agent intellect is to give light for the purpose of understanding. But this is done by something higher than the soul, according to *John 1:9,* "He was the true light that enlighteneth every man coming into this world." Therefore the agent intellect is not something in our soul.

Objection 2. Moreover, the Philosopher says of the agent intellect that "it does not sometimes understand and sometimes not understand." [19] But our soul does not always understand, but somtimes it understands, and sometimes it does not understand. Therefore the agent intellect is not something in our soul.

Objection 3. Again, agent and patient suffice for action. If, therefore, the possible intellect, which is a passive power, is something belonging to the soul, and also the agent intellect, which is an active power, it follows that man would always be able to understand when he wished—which is clearly false. Therefore the agent intellect is not something in our soul.

Objection 4. And again, the Philosopher says that "the agent intellect is a substance in actual being." [20] But nothing can be in potency and in act with regard to the same thing. If, then, the possible intellect, which is in potency to all things intelligible, is something in our soul, it seems impossible for the agent intellect to be also something in our soul.

Objection 5. Then, too, if the agent intellect is something in our soul, it must be a power. For it is neither a "passion" nor a "habit," [21] since neither of these have the nature of agents in regard to what the soul receives; rather, "passion" is the very action of the passive power, while

---

19. *op. cit.,* III, 5(430a22).
20. *op. cit.,* III, 5(430a18).
21. *"Habitus,"* a stable disposition *perfecting* a power of the soul, has no precise equivalent in idiomatic English.

'habit' is something which results from acts. Now every power flows from the essence of the soul. It would therefore follow that the agent intellect flows from the essence of the soul. And thus it would not be in the soul by way of participation from some higher intellect; which is unfitting. Therefore the agent intellect is not something in our soul.

On the contrary: The Philosopher says that "it is necessary for these differences," viz., the possible and agent intellect, "to be in the soul." [22]

I answer that: The agent intellect, of which the Philosopher speaks, is something in the soul. In order to make this evident, bear in mind that above the intellective soul of man there is a superior intellect, from which the soul acquires the power of understanding. For what is such by participation, and what is movable, and what is imperfect, always requires the pre-existence of something essentially such, immovable and perfect. Now the human soul is said to be "intellective" by reason of a participation in intellectual power, a sign of which is that it is not wholly intellectual but only in part. Moreover, it attains to the understanding of truth by reasoning with a certain discursiveness and movement. Even more, it has an imperfect understanding, both because it does not understand everything, and because, in these things which it does understand, it passes from potency to act. Hence there must be some higher intellect, by which the soul is helped to understand.

Therefore some held [23] that this intellect, substantially separate, is the agent intellect, which by lighting up the sense images, as it were, makes them to be actually intelligible. But even supposing the existence of such a separate agent intellect, it would still be necessary to attribute to the human soul some power participating in that superior intellect, by which power the human soul makes things to be actually intelligible. Such is also the case in other perfect natural things, among which, besides the universal active causes, each one is endowed with its proper powers derived from those universal agents. For the sun alone does not generate man, but in man himself there is the power of begetting man; and in like manner with other complete animals. Now among these sublunary things nothing is more perfect than the human soul. Therefore it must be said that there is in the soul a power derived from a higher intellect, whereby it is able to illumine the sense representations.

And we know this by experience, since we perceive that we abstract universal forms from their particular conditions; which is to make them actually intelligible. Now no action belongs to anything except through some principle formally inherent in it, as we have said above, of the possible intellect.[24] Therefore the power which is the principle of this

---

22. *op. cit.*, III, 5(430a13).
23. Avicenna and his followers.
24. Question LXXVI, article 1.

action must be something in the soul. For this reason Aristotle compared the agent intellect to light,[25] which is something received into the air, while Plato compared the separate intellect, whose light touches the soul, to the sun, as Themistius says.[26]

But the separate intellect, according to the teaching of our Faith, is God Himself, Who is the soul's Creator, and only beatitude; as will be shown later.[27] Therefore the human soul derives its intellectual light from Him, according to *Psalms 4:7*: "The light of Thy countenance, O Lord, is signed upon us."

Reply Objection 1. That true light illuminates as a universal cause, from which the human soul derives a particular power, as we have explained.

Reply Objection 2. The Philosopher is speaking not of the agent intellect, but of the intellect in act; of which he had already said: "Knowledge in act is the same as the thing."[28] Or, if we refer those words to the agent intellect then they are said because it is not owing to the agent intellect that sometimes we do, and sometimes we do not understand, but to the intellect which is in potency.

Reply Objection 3. If the relation of the agent intellect to the possible intellect were that of an active object to a power (e.g., of the visible in act to the sight), it would follow that we could understand all things instantly, since the agent intellect is that which makes them all in act.[29] But the agent intellect is not an object, rather is it that whereby the objects are made to be in act; and for this, besides the presence of the agent intellect, there must be sense representations, as well as a good disposition of the sensory powers, and practice in this sort of operation. For from one thing understood, other things come to be understood, as from terms, propositions, and from first principles, conclusions. From this point of view, it matters not whether the agent intellect is something belonging to the soul, or something separate from the soul.

Reply Objection 4. The intellectual soul is indeed actually immaterial, but it is in potency to the determinate forms of things. On the contrary, phantasms are actual likenesses of certain forms, but they are immaterial potentially. Therefore nothing prevents one and the same soul, inasmuch as it is actually immaterial, from having a power by which it makes things actually immaterial, by abstraction from the conditions of individual matter (this power is called the "agent intellect"), and another power, receptive of such forms, which is called the "possible intellect" by reason of its being in potency to such forms.

---

25. *On the Soul* III, 5(430a15).
26. cf. Plato, *Republic* VI (508B).
27. Question XC, article 3; I-II, question 3, article 7.
28. *op. cit.*, III, 5(430a19).
29. i.e., all potential intelligibles.

Reply Objection 5. Since the essence of the soul is immaterial, created by the supreme intellect, nothing prevents the power which it derives from the supreme intellect, and whereby it abstracts from matter, from proceeding from the essence of the soul, in the same way as its other powers.

Fifth Article

IS THE AGENT INTELLECT ONE IN ALL MEN?

Objection 1. It seems that there is one agent intellect in all. For what is separate from the body is not multiplied according to the number of bodies. But the agent intellect is separate, as is said.[30] Therefore it is not multiplied in the multitude of human bodies, but is one for all men.

Objection 2. Moreover, the agent intellect is the cause of the universal, which is one in many. But that which is the cause of unity is still more itself one. Therefore the agent intellect is the same in all.

Objection 3. Again, all men agree in the primary conceptions of the intellect. But to these they assent by the agent intellect. Therefore all are united in one agent intellect.

On the contrary: The Philosopher says that "the agent intellect is as a light." [31] But light is not the same in the various illuminated things. Therefore the same agent intellect is not in different men.

I answer that: The truth about this question depends on what we have already said.[32] For if the agent intellect were not something belonging to the soul, but were some separate substance, there would be one agent intellect for all men. And this is what they mean who hold that there is one agent intellect for all. But if the agent intellect is something belonging to the soul, as one of its powers, we are bound to say that there are as many agent intellects as there are souls, which are multiplied according to the number of men, as we have said above.[33] For it is impossible that one and the same power belong to various substances.

Reply Objection 1. The Philosopher proves that the agent intellect is separate by the fact that the possible intellect is separate; because, as he says, "the agent is more noble than the patient." [34] Now the possible intellect is said to be "separate" because it is not the act of any bodily organ. And in this sense the agent intellect is also called "separate"; but not as a separate substance.

Reply Objection 2. The agent intellect is the cause of the universal,

---

30. Aristotle, *ibid.*, (430a17).
31. *ibid.*, (430a15).
32. Preceding article.
33. Question LXXVI, article 2.
34. *On the Soul* III, 5(430a18).

by abstracting it from matter. But for this purpose it need not be one in all intelligent beings though it must be one in relation to all those things from which it abstracts the universal, with respect to which things the universal is one. And this befits the agent intellect in that it is immaterial.

Reply Objection 3. All things which are of one species enjoy in common the action which accompanies the nature of the species, and consequently the power which is the source of such action; but not in such a way that the power be identical in all. Now to know the primary intelligibles[35] is an action belonging to the human species. Therefore all men enjoy in common the power which is the ground [36] of this action; and this power is the agent intellect. But there is no need for it to be identical in all; although it must be derived by all from one source. And thus the possession by all men in common of the primary intelligibles proves the unity of the separate intellect,[37] which Plato compares to the sun, but not the unity of the agent intellect, which Aristotle compares to light.

Sixth Article

IS MEMORY IN THE
INTELLECTUAL PART OF THE SOUL?

Objection 1. It seems that memory is not in the intellectual part of the soul. For Augustine says that "to the higher part of the soul belong those things which are not common to man and beast." [38] But memory is common to man and beast, for he says that "beasts can sense corporeal things through the senses of the body, and commit them to memory." [39] Therefore memory does not belong to the intellectual part of the soul.

Objection 2. Moreover, memory is of the past. But "past" is said of something according to a fixed time. Memory, therefore, knows a thing under the condition of a fixed time; which involves knowledge under the conditions of *here* and *now*. But this is not the province of the intellect, but of the sense. Therefore memory is not in the intellective part of the soul, but only in the sensory part.

Objection 3. Again, in the memory are preserved the likenesses of those things of which we are not actually thinking. But this cannot happen in the intellect, because the intellect is actuated by the fact that the intelligible form is received into it. Now for the intellect to be in act is

---

35. e.g., that what is, is, and what is not, is not.
36. By preparing, through abstraction, for the actual knowing of them by the possible intellect.
37. viz., the divine intellect.
38. *On the Trinity* XII, 2; 8.
39. *op. cit.,* XII, 2.

for it to be actually understanding; and therefore the intellect actually knows all things whose forms it possesses. Therefore the memory is not in the intellective part of the soul.

On the contrary: Augustine says that "memory, understanding, and will are one mind." [40]

I answer that: Since it is of the nature of the memory to preserve the forms of those things which are not apprehended actually, we must first consider whether the intelligible forms can thus be preserved in the intellect. For Avicenna held that this was impossible.[41] He admitted that this could happen in the sensory part, as to some powers, in that they are acts of bodily organs wherein certain forms may be preserved without actual apprehension. But in the intellect, which has no bodily organ, nothing but what is intelligible exists. Hence every thing of which the likeness exists in the intellect must be actually understood. Therefore, according to him, as soon as we cease to understand something actually, the form of that thing ceases to be in our intellect, and if we wish to understand that thing anew, we must turn to the agent intellect, which he held to be a separate substance, in order that the intelligible forms may thence flow again into our possible intellect. And from the practice and repetition of turning to the agent intellect there is formed, according to him, a certain aptitude in the possible intellect for turning itself to the agent intellect; which aptitude he called "the *habitus* of science." According, therefore, to this supposition, nothing is preserved in the intellective part of the soul that is not actually understood; and hence it would not be possible to admit memory in the intellectual part of the soul.

But this opinion is clearly opposed to the teaching of Aristotle. For he says: "when the possible intellect is identified with each thing as knowing it, it is said to be in act"; "this happens when it can operate through itself; and, even then, it is in potency, but not in the same way as before learning and discovering." [42] Now the possible intellect is said to become each thing through receiving the intelligible form of each thing. To the fact, therefore, that it receives the forms of intelligible things it owes its being able to operate when it wills, but not so that it be always operating; for even then it is in potency in a certain sense, though otherwise than before the act of understanding. It is in potency in the sense that whoever has habitual knowledge is in potency to actual thinking.

The foregoing opinion is also opposed to reason. For what is received into something is received according to the condition of the recipient. But the intellect is of a more stable nature, and is more immovable, than

40. *op. cit.,* X, 11.
41. *On the Soul* V, 6(26rb). (Not available in English.)
42. *On the Soul* III, 4(429b5).

physical matter. If, therefore, such matter holds the forms which it receives, not only while it actually does something through them, but also after ceasing to act through them, much more does the intellect receive the intelligible forms unchangeably and lastingly, whether it receive them from things sensible, or from some superior intellect.

Thus, therefore, if we take memory only for the power of retaining forms, we must say that it is in the intellective part of the soul. But if in the notion of memory we include its object as something past, then the memory is not in the soul's intellective, but only in its sensory part, which apprehends individual things. For the past, as past, since it signifies being under a condition of fixed time, is something individual.

Reply Objection 1. Memory, if considered as retentive of forms, is not common to us and other animals. For forms are not retained in the sensory part of the soul only, but rather in the body and soul united, since the memorative power is the act of some organ. But the intellect in itself is retentive of forms, without the association of any bodily organ. Therefore the Philosopher says that "the soul is the seat of the forms, not the whole soul, but the intellect." [43]

Reply Objection 2. The condition of pastness may be referred to two things, viz., to the object known, and to the act of knowledge. These two are found together in the sensitive part, which apprehends something from the fact of its being affected by a present sensible object. Therefore, at one and the same time an animal remembers that he sensed before in the past, and that he sensed some past sensible thing. But as concerns the soul's intellective part, the past is accidental, and is not in itself a part of the object of the intellect. For the intellect understands man as man; and to man, as man, it is accidental that he exist in the present, past, or future. But on the part of the act, the condition of being past, even as such, may be understood to be in the intellect, as well as in the senses. For our soul's act of understanding is an individual act, existing in this or that time, so that a man is said to understand now, or yesterday, or tomorrow. And this is not incompatible with intellectuality, for such an act of understanding, though something individual, is yet an immaterial act, as we have said above of the intellect.[44] And therefore, just as the intellect understands itself, though it be itself an individual intellect, so also it understands its act of understanding, which is an individual act, in the past, present, or future. In this way, then, the notion of memory, in so far as it regards past events, is preserved in the intellect, according as it understands that it previously understood; but not in the sense that it understands the past as it is *here* and *now*.

Reply Objection 3. The intelligible form is sometimes in the intellect only in potency, and then the intellect is said to be "in potency." Some-

---

43. *ibid.,* (429a27).
44. Question LXXV, article 2.

times the intelligible form is in the intellect according to the ultimate completion of the act, and then the intellect understands in act. And sometimes the intelligible form is in a middle state, between potency and act; and then we have habitual knowledge. In this last way the intellect retains the form, even when it does not understand in act.

Seventh Article

IS THE INTELLECTUAL MEMORY

A POWER DISTINCT FROM THE INTELLECT?

Objection 1. It seems that the intellectual memory is distinct from the intellect. For Augustine assigns to the mind memory, understanding and will.[45] But it is clear that the memory is a distinct power from the will. Therefore it is also distinct from the intellect.

Objection 2. Moreover, the principle of distinction among the powers in the soul's sensory part is the same as in its intellective part. But memory in the sensory part is distinct from sense, as we have said.[46] Therefore memory in the intellective part is distinct from the intellect.

Objection 3. Again, according to Augustine, memory, understanding and will are equal to one another, and one flows from the other.[47] But this could not be if memory and intellect were the same power. Therefore they are not the same power.

On the contrary: From its nature the memory is the treasury or storehouse of forms. But the Philosopher attributes this to the intellect, as we have said. Therefore, in the intellectual part of the soul, memory is not a power distinct from the intellect.

I answer that: As has been said above, the powers of the soul are distinguished according to the different character of their objects, for each power is defined in reference to that thing to which is its object.[48] It has also been said above that if any power is directed by its nature to an object according to the common aspect of the object, that power will not be differentiated according to the individual differences under that object; just as the power of sight, in relation to its object under the common aspect of color, is not differentiated by differences of black and white. Now the intellect is related to its object under the common aspect of being, since the possible intellect is that by which we become all things. Therefore the possible intellect is not differentiated by any difference of being. Nevertheless there is a distinction between the power

---

45. *On the Trinity* X, 11.
46. Question LXXVIII, article 4.
47. *op. cit.*, X, 11; XI, 7.
48. Question LXXVII, article 3.

of the agent intellect and of that of the possible intellect; because as regards the same object, the active power, which makes the object to be in
act, must be distinct from the passive power, which is moved by the
object existing in act. Thus the active power is compared to its object
as a being in act to a being in potency; whereas the passive power, on
the contrary, is compared to its object as a being in potency to a being
in act.

Therefore there can be no other difference of powers in the intellect
but that of possible and agent. Hence it is clear that memory is not a
distinct power from the intellect, for it belongs to the nature of a passive
power to retain as well as to receive.

Reply Objection 1. Although it is said [49] that memory, intellect, and
will are three powers, this is not in accordance with the intention of
Augustine, who says expressly that "if we take memory, intelligence, and
will as always present in the soul, whether we actually attend to them or
not, they seem to pertain to the memory only.[50] And by intelligence I
mean that by which we understand when actually thinking; and by will
I mean that love or affection which unites the child and its parents."
Therefore it is clear that Augustine does not take the above three for
three powers; but by "memory" he understands the soul's habit of retention, by "intelligence," the act of the intellect, and by "will," the act of
the will.

Reply Objection 2. Past and present can differentiate the sensory
powers, but not the intellectual powers, for the reason given above.[51]

Reply Objection 3. Intelligence arises from memory, as act from *habitus;* and in this way it is equal to it, but not as a power to a power.

Eighth Article

IS THE REASON A DISTINCT POWER FROM THE INTELLECT?

Objection 1. It seems that the reason is a distinct power from the intellect. For it is stated in the book, *On the Spirit and the Soul* that
"when we wish to rise from lower things to higher, first the sense comes
to our aid, then imagination, then reason, then the intellect." [52] Therefore the reason is distinct from the intellect, just as imagination is from
sense.

Objection 2. Moreover, Boethius says that "intellect is compared to
reason as eternity to time." [53] But it does not belong to the same power

49. Peter Lombard, *Sentences* I, iii, 2(I, 35).
50. *On the Trinity* XIV, 7.
51. Preceding article.
52. Pseudo-Augustine (Alcher of Clairvaux) *On the Spirit and the Soul (De Spir. et.
An.)* XI. (Not available in English.)
53. *The Consolation of Philosophy* IV, prose 6.

to be in eternity and to be in time. Therefore reason and intellect are not the same power.

Objection 3. Again, man has intellect in common with the angels, and sense in common with the brutes. But reason, which is proper to man and by which he is called a "rational animal," is a power distinct from sense. Therefore it is equally true to say that it is distinct from the intellect, which properly belongs to the angels and which enables them to be called "intellectual."

On the contrary: Augustine says that "that in which man excels irrational animals is reason, or mind, or intelligence, or whatever appropriate name we like to give it." [54] Therefore "reason," "intellect," and "mind" are one power.

I answer that: Reason and intellect in man cannot be distinct powers. We shall understand this clearly if we consider their respective acts. For to understand is to apprehend intelligible truth as such, and to reason is to advance from one thing understood to another, so as to know an intelligible truth. And therefore the angels, who possess a perfect knowledge of intelligible truth according to the mode of their nature, have no need to advance from one thing to another; they rather apprehend the truth of things simply and without discursiveness, as Dionysius says.[55] But man arrives at the knowledge of intelligible truth by advancing from one thing to another; and therefore he is called "rational." [56] Reasoning, therefore, is compared to understanding as movement is to rest, or acquisition to possession; of which one belongs to the perfect, the other to the imperfect. And since movement always proceeds from something immobile, and ends in something at rest, hence it is that human reasoning, in the order of inquiry and discovery, proceeds from certain things simply understood, viz., the first principles; and, again, in the order of judgment returns by analysis to first principles, in the light of which it examines what it has found. Now it is clear that rest and movement are not to be referred to different powers, but to one and the same, even in natural things, since by the very same nature a thing is moved towards a certain place, and rests in that place. Much more, therefore, by the same power do we understand and reason. And so it is clear that in man reason and intellect are the some power.

Reply Objection 1. That enumeration is made according to the order of actions, not according to the distinction of powers. Moreover, that book is not of great authority, as we have said.[57]

Reply Objection 2. The answer is clear from what has been said. For

---

54. *A Literal Commentary on "Genesis"* III, 20.
55. *On the Divine Names* VII, 2.
56. *ibid.*
57. Question LXXVII, article 8.

eternity is compared to time as the immobile to mobile. And that is why Boethius compared the intellect to eternity, and reason to time.

Reply Objection 3. Other animals are so much lower than man that they cannot attain to the knowledge of truth, which reason seeks. But man attains, although imperfectly, to the knowledge of intelligible truth, which the angels know. Therefore, the knowing power in the angels is not of a different kind from the knowing power in the human reason, but is compared to it as the perfect to the imperfect.

Ninth Article

ARE THE HIGHER AND LOWER REASON DISTINCT POWERS?

Objection 1. It would seem that the higher and lower reason are distinct powers. For Augustine says that "the image of the Trinity is in the higher part of the reason, and not in the lower." [58] But the parts of the soul are its powers. Therefore the higher and lower reason are two powers.

Objection 2. Moreover, nothing flows from itself. Now the lower reason flows from the higher, and is ruled and directed by it. Therefore the higher reason is another power from the lower.

Objection 3. Again the Philosopher says that the scientific part of the soul, by which the soul knows necessary things, is another principle and another part from the conjecturing and ratiocinating part by which it knows contingent things.[59] And he proves this from the principle that "for those things which are generically different, generically different parts of the soul are ordained." [60] Now the contingent and the necessary are generically different, as are the perishable and the imperishable. Since, therefore, *necessary* is the same as *eternal,* and *temporal* the same as *contingent,* it seems that what the Philosopher calls the "scientific part" must be the same as the higher reason, which, according to Augustine "is intent on the consideration and consultation of things eternal"; and that what the Philosopher calls the "ratiocinating" or "conjecturing" part is the same as the lower reason, which, according to Augustine, "is intent on the ordering of temporal things." [61] Therefore the higher reason is another power than the lower.

Objection 4. And again, Damascene says that "opinion rises from imagination; and then the mind, by judging of the truth or error of the opinion, discovers the truth. Hence *mens* [mind] is derived from *metiendo* [measuring]. And therefore the intellect regards those things which are

---

58. *On the Trinity* XII, 4.
59. *Nichomachean Ethics* VI, 1 (1139a6).
60. *ibid.,* (1139a8).
61. *op. cit.,* XII, 7.

already subject to judgment and true decision." [62] So, then, the opinionative power, which is the lower reason, is distinct from mind and intellect, which we may understand to be the higher reason.

On the contrary: Augustine says that "the higher and lower reason are distinct only by their functions." [63] Therefore they are not two powers.

I answer that: The higher and lower reason, as they are understood by Augustine, can in no wise be two powers of the soul. Does he not say that "the higher reason is that which is intent on the contemplation and consultation of things eternal"? In other words, in "contemplation" it sees them in themselves, and in "consultation" it takes its rules of action from them. But he calls the lower reason that which "is intent on the ordering of temporal things." Now these two—viz., temporal and eternal things—are related to our knowledge in this way, that the one is the means of knowing the other. For in the order of discovery, we come through temporal things to the knowledge of things eternal, according to the words of the Apostle (*Romans 1:20*): "The invisible things of God are clearly seen, being understood by the things that are made." But in the order of judgment, from eternal things already known, we judge of temporal things, and according to the laws of eternal things we order temporal things.

However, it may happen that the medium and what is attained thereby belong to different habits; as the first indemonstrable principles belong to the "habit of intellect," whereas the conclusions which we draw from them belong to the "habit of science." And so it is that from the principles of geometry we may draw conclusions in another science, e.g., optics. But it is to one and the same power of reason that both medium and term belong. For the act of the reason is a kind of movement from one thing to another. But the same movable thing passes through the medium and reaches the end. Therefore the higher and lower reasons are one and the same power, being distinguished, according to Augustine, by the functions of their actions, and in respect of their various habits. For wisdom is attributed to the higher reason, science to the lower.

Reply Objection 1. We can speak of "parts," according to whatever way in which a thing is divided. Hence, so far as reason is divided according to its various acts, the higher and lower reason are called "parts"; but not because they are different powers.

Reply Objection 2. The lower reason is said to "flow" from the higher, or to be "ruled" by it, in so far as the principles used by the lower reason are drawn from and directed by the principles of the higher reason.

Reply Objection 3. The "scientific part," of which the Philosopher speaks, is not the same as the higher reason; for necessary truths are found

---

62. *On the Orthodox Faith* (*De Fide Orth.*) II, 22. (Not available in English.)
63. *On the Trinity* XII, 4.

even among temporal things, of which natural philosophy[64] and mathematics treat. And the "conjecturing" and "ratiocinating" part is more limited than the lower reason, for it regards only contingent things. Neither must it be said without qualification that the power by which the intellect knows necessary things is distinct from the power by which it knows contingent things, because it knows both under the same objective aspect, viz., that of being and truth. Hence necessary things, which have perfect[65] being in truth, it knows perfectly, since it penetrates to their very essence, from which it demonstrates their proper accidents. On the other hand, it knows contingent things imperfectly, since they have only imperfect being and truth. Now *perfect* and *imperfect* in action do not vary the power, but they vary the actions as to the mode of acting; and consequently they vary the principles of the actions and the habits themselves. That is why the Philosopher posits two parts of the soul, viz., the "scientific" and the "ratiocinative," not because they are two powers, but because they are distinct according to diverse aptitudes for receiving diverse habits (concerning whose diversity he there intends to inquire). For *contingent* and *necessary,* though differing according to their proper genera, nevertheless agree in the common aspect of being, which is the object of the intellect, and to which they are diversely related as *perfect* and *imperfect.*

Reply Objection 4. That distinction given by Damascene concerns diversity of acts, not of powers. For "opinion" signifies an act of the intellect which leans to one side of a contradiction, though in fear of the other. While to "judge" or "measure" [*mensurare*] is an act of the intellect applying fixed principles to the examination of propositions. From this is taken the word *mens* (mind). Lastly, to understand is to adhere to the formed judgment with approval.

Tenth Article

IS INTELLIGENCE A POWER DISTINCT FROM INTELLECT?

Objection 1. It would seem that the intelligence is another power than the intellect. For it is said that "when we wish to rise from lower to higher things, first the sense comes to our aid, then imagination, then reason, then intellect, and afterwards intelligence." [66] But imagination and sense are distinct powers. Therefore intellect and intelligence are also distinct.

---

64. Literally, "natural science," including what is now called "the philosophy of nature."

65. *"Perfectum*—literally, finished, completed, brought to an end. "Perfect" knowledge means terminal or definitive knowledge, not exhaustive knowledge.

66. Pseudo-Augustine (Alcher of Clairvaux) *On the Spirit and the Soul* (*De Spir. et An.*) XI.

Objection 2. Moreover, Boethius says that "sense considers man in one way, imagination in another, reason in another, intelligence in another." [67] But intellect is the same power as reason. Therefore intelligence seems to be a distinct power from intellect, just as reason is a distinct power from imagination and sense.

Objection 3. Again, "actions come before powers," as the Philosopher says.[68] But intelligence is an act separate from the others which are attributed to the intellect. For Damascene says that "the first movement is called 'intelligence.' But that intelligence which is about a certain thing is called 'intention'; that which remains and conforms the soul to that which is understood is called 'invention,' and invention when it remains where it is, examining and judging of itself, is called '*phronesis*' (i.e., wisdom), and *phronesis,* when expended, makes 'thought,' i.e., orderly internal speech; from which, they say, comes speech expressed by the tongue." [69] Therefore it seems that intelligence is some special power.

On the contrary: The Philosopher says that "intelligence is of indivisible things in which there is nothing false." [70] But the knowledge of these things belongs to the intellect. Therefore intelligence is not another power than the intellect.

I answer that: This term "intelligence" properly signifies the very act of the intellect, which is to understand. However, in some works translated from the Arabic, the separate substances, which we designate as "angels," are called "intelligences," and perhaps for the reason that such substances are always actually understanding. But in works translated from the Greek, they are called "intellects" or "minds." Thus intelligence is distinct from intellect, not as power is from power, but as act is from power. And such a division is recognized even by philosophers.[71] For sometimes they posit four intellects, viz., the "agent intellect," the "possible intellect," the "habitual intellect," and the "acquired intellect." Of which four, the agent and possible intellects are different powers; just as in all things the active power is distinct from the passive. But the three which are not the agent intellect are distinguished as three states of the possible intellect, which is sometimes in potency only, and thus it is called "possible"; sometimes it is in first act, which is knowledge, and thus it is called the "habitual intellect";[72] and sometimes it is in second act, which is the exercise of knowledge,[73] and thus it is called the "intellect in act," or the "acquired intellect."

Reply Objection 1. If this authority be accepted, "intelligence," there

---

67. *The Consolation of Philosophy* V, prose 4.
68. *On the Soul* II, 4(415a18).
69. *On the Orthodox Faith (De Fide Orth.)*, II, 22. (Not available in English.)
70. *op. cit.,* III, 6(430a26).
71. cf. Avicenna, *On the Soul (De An.)*, I, 5(5vb). (Not available in English.)
72. Because it possesses intelligible forms, but is not actually considering them.
73. Literally, the act: "to consider."

means the act of the intellect. And thus it is divided against intellect as act against power.

Reply Objection 2. Boethius takes "intelligence" as meaning that act of the intellect which transcends the act of the reason. That is why he says that "reason belongs only to the human race, as intelligence alone belongs to God." [74] For it is proper to God to understand all things without any investigation.

Reply Objection 3. All those acts which Damascene enumerates belong to one power, viz., the intellectual power. For this power first apprehends something unqualifiedly, and this act is called "intelligence." Secondly, it directs what it apprehends to the knowledge of something else, or to some operation, and this is called "intention." And when it goes on in search of what it intends, it is called "invention." When, in the light of something known as certain, it examines what it has found, it is said to "know," or to be "wise"; and this pertains to *phronesis* or wisdom. For "it belongs to the wise man to judge," as is said.[75] And when once it has obtained something as certain, through having been examined, it thinks about the means of making it known to others; and this is the "ordering of interior speech," from which external speech proceeds. For, not every difference of acts diversifies powers, but only that which cannot be reduced to one and the same source, as was said above.[76]

Eleventh Article

ARE THE SPECULATIVE AND

PRACTICAL INTELLECTS DISTINCT POWERS?

Objection 1. It seems that the speculative and practical intellects are distinct powers. For the "apprehensive" power and the "motive" power are different kinds of powers, as is made clear.[77] But the speculative intellect is merely an apprehensive power; while the practical intellect is a motive power. Therefore they are distinct powers.

Objection 2. Moreover, diversity in the intelligible nature of the object differentiates the power. But the object of the speculative intellect is truth, and of the practical, good; which differ in intelligible nature. Therefore the speculative and practical intellects are distinct powers.

Objection 3. Again, in the intellective part of the soul, the practical intellect is compared to the speculative, as the estimative is compared to the imaginative power in its sensory part. But the estimative differs

74. *op. cit.,* V, prose 5.
75. Aristotle, *Metaphysics* I, 2(982a18).
76. Question LXXVIII, article 4.
77. Aristotle, *On the Soul* II, 3(414a31).

from the imaginative as power from power, as was said above.[78] Therefore so does the speculative intellect differ from the practical.

On the contrary: There is the dictum that "the speculative intellect
by extension becomes practical." [79] But one power is not changed into
another. Therefore the speculative and practical intellects are not distinct powers.

I answer that: The speculative and practical intellects are not distinct
powers. The reason for this is, as was said above, that what is accidental
to the nature of the object of a power does not differentiate that power.[80]
For it is accidental to a colored thing to be a man, or to be great or small.
Hence all such things are apprehended by the same power of sight. Now,
to a thing apprehended by the intellect, it is accidental whether it be
directed to operation or not. But it is according to this that the speculative and practical intellects differ. For it is the speculative intellect which
directs what it apprehends, not to operation, but to the sole consideration
of truth; while the practical intellect is that which directs what it apprehends to operation. And this is what the Philosopher says, viz., that "the
speculative differs from the practical in its end." [81] Thus each is named
from its end: the one speculative, the other practical, i.e., operative.

Reply Objection 1. The practical intellect is a motive power, not as
executing movement, but as directing toward it; and this belongs to it
according to its way of knowing.

Reply Objection 2. Truth and goodness include one another. For truth
is a certain good; otherwise it would not be desirable. And goodness is a
certain truth; otherwise it would not be intelligible. Therefore, just as
the object of the appetite may be the true, under the aspect of a good
(as when some one desires to know the truth), so the object of the practical intellect is the good directed to operation, under the aspect of truth.
For the practical intellect has as its object the knowledge of truth, even
as the speculative intellect does, but it directs the known truth to operation.

Reply Objection 3. Many differences differentiate the sense powers
which do not differentiate the intellectual powers, as was said above.[82]

---

78. Question LXXVIII, article 4.
79. Aristotle, *op. cit.*, III, 10(433a14).
80. Question LXXVII, article 3.
81. *op. cit.*, III, 10(433a14).
82. Article 7, ad 2; question LXXVII, article 3.

Twelfth Article

IS *SYNDERESIS* [83] A SPECIAL POWER
OF THE SOUL DISTINCT FROM THE OTHERS?

Objection 1. It seems that *synderesis* is a special power, distinct from the others. For those things which fall under one division seem to be of the same genus. But in the *Gloss* of Jerome on *Ezechiel 1:6, synderesis* is divided against the irascible, the concupiscible, and the rational, which are powers. Therefore *synderesis* is a power.

Objection 2. Moreover, opposites are of the same genus. But *synderesis* and sensuality seem to be opposed to one another, because *synderesis* always inclines to good, while sensuality always inclines to evil. (That is why it is signified by the serpent, as Augustine explains). It seems, therefore, that *synderesis* is a power just as sensuality is.

Objection 3. Again, Augustine says that "in the natural power of judgment there are certain rules and seeds of virtue, both true and unchangeable." [84] But this is what we call *"synderesis."* Since, therefore, the unchangeable rules which guide our judgment belong to the superior reason, as Augustine says, it seems that *synderesis* is the same as reason, and thus is a power.

On the contrary: According to the Philosopher, "rational powers are related to opposites." [85] But *synderesis* does not regard opposites, but inclines to good only. Therefore *synderesis* is not a power. For if it were a power, it would be a rational power, since it is not found in brute animals.

I answer that: Synderesis is not a power, but a habit. However, some have held that it is a power higher than reason, while others have said that it is reason itself, not as reason, but as a nature. In order to make this question clear, we must consider, in line with what was said above,[86] that man's act of reasoning, since it is a kind of movement, proceeds from the understanding of certain things (viz., those which are naturally known without any investigation on the part of reason) as from a fixed starting-point; it also terminates in the understanding, in that by means of those naturally known principles[87] we judge of those things which we have discovered by reasoning. Now clearly, just as the speculative reason reasons about speculative matters, so the practical reason reasons about practical matters. Therefore we must be naturally endowed with not only

---

83. The natural "habit," or firm disposition, of the practical intellect whereby it is known that good is to be done and evil avoided.
84. *On Free Will (De Lib. Arb.)* II, 10.
85. *Metaphysics* VIII, 2(1046b5).
86. Article 8.
87. e.g., that a thing cannot be and not be at the same time and in the same respect.

speculative principles, but also practical principles. Now the first speculative principles bestowed on us by nature do not belong to a special power, but a special habit, which is called "the understanding of principles," as is made clear.[88] Hence, the first practical principles, bestowed on us by nature, do not belong to a special power, but to a special natural habit, which we call *"synderesis."* That is why *synderesis* is said to "incline to good," and to "murmur at evil," in that through first principles we proceed to discover, and to judge of what we have discovered. It is therefore clear that *synderesis* is not a power, but a natural habit.

Reply Objection 1. The division given by Jerome has to do with a diversity of acts, and not of powers. Now diverse acts can belong to one power.

Reply Objection 2. The opposition of sensuality to *synderesis* is an opposition of acts, and not of the different species of one genus.

Reply Objection 3. Such unchangeable notions are the first practical principles, concerning which no one errs; and they are attributed to reason as to a power, and to *synderesis* as to a habit. Therefore we judge naturally both by our reason and by *synderesis.*

Thirteenth Article

IS CONSCIENCE A POWER?

Objection 1. It seems that conscience is a power; for Origen says that "conscience is a correcting and guiding spirit accompanying the soul, by which it is led away from evil and made to cling to good." [89] But in the soul, "spirit" designates a power—either the mind itself, according to the text (*Ephesians 4:13*), "Be ye renewed in the spirit of your mind"— or the imagination, so that imaginary vision is called "spiritual," as Augustine remarks. Therefore conscience is a power.

Objection 2. Moreover, nothing is a subject of sin, except a power of the soul. But conscience is a subject of sin; for it is said of some "that their mind and conscience are defiled." (*Titus 1:15*). Therefore it seems that conscience is a power.

Objection 3. Again, conscience must of necessity be either an act, a habit, or a power. But it is not an act, for then it would not always exist in man. Nor is it a habit, for it would not be one thing but many, since we are directed in our actions by many cognitive habits. Therefore conscience is a power.

On the contrary: Conscience can be put aside, but a power cannot be put aside. Therefore conscience is not a power.

I answer that: Properly speaking, conscience is not a power but an

---

88. Aristotle, *Nichomachean Ethics* VI, 6(1141a7).
89. *On St. Paul's Epistle to the Romans* II, 15.

act. This is evident both from the very name and from those things which in the common way of speaking are attributed to "conscience." For conscience, in the essential meaning of the term, implies the relation of knowledge to something; for *"conscientia"* means *"cum alio scientia"* [knowledge with, or applied to, another]. But the application of knowledge to something is done by some act. Therefore from this explanation of the name it is clear that conscience is an act.

The same is manifest from the things which are attributed to conscience. For conscience is said to "witness," to "bind," to "incite," and also to "accuse," "torment," or "rebuke." And all these follow the application of knowledge or science to what we do. This application is made in three ways. In one way, through our recognizing that we have done or have not done something: "Thy conscience knoweth that thou has often spoken evil of others" (*Ecclesiastes 7:23*); and according to this, conscience is said to "witness." In another way, in that through our conscience we judge that something should be done or not done; and in this sense, conscience is said to "incite" or to "bind." In the third way, in that by conscience we judge that something done is well done or ill done, and in this sense conscience is said to "excuse," "accuse," or "torment." Now it is clear that all these things follow the actual application of knowledge to what we do. Therefore, properly speaking, "conscience" designates an act. But since a habit is the source of an act, sometimes the name "conscience" is given first to the natural habit, viz., *synderesis.* Thus Jerome calls *synderesis* "conscience"; Basil calls the natural power of judgment "conscience"; and Damascene says that conscience is the "law of our intellect." For it is customary for causes and effects to be called after one another.

Reply Objection 1. Conscience is called a "spirit," so far as spirit is the same as mind, because conscience is a certain pronouncement of the mind.

Reply Objection 2. Defilement is said to be in the conscience, not as in a subject, but as the thing known is in knowledge, viz., in so far as someone knows that he is defiled.

Reply Objection 3. Although an act does not always remain in itself, yet it always remains in its cause, which is a power and a habit. Now all the habits by which conscience is formed, although many, nevertheless have their efficacy from one primary source, the habit of first principles, which is called *"synderesis."* Hence there is a special reason why this "habit" is sometimes called "conscience," as was said above.[90]

---

90. Article 12.

The Appetitive Powers in General

(In Two Articles)

First Article

IS THE APPETITE A SPECIAL POWER OF THE SOUL?

Objection 1. It seems that the appetite is not a special power of the soul. For no power of the soul is to be assigned to things that are common to living and to non-living beings. But appetite is common to both, since, as is said, "all desire good."[1] Therefore the appetite is not a special power of the soul.

Objection 2. Moreover, powers are differentiated by their objects. But what we desire is the same as what we know. Therefore the appetitive power must not be distinct from the apprehensive power.

Objection 3. Again, the common is not contradistinguished from the proper. But each power of the soul desires some particular desirable thing, viz., its own suitable object. Therefore, respecting that object which is the desirable in general, there is no need to assign some particular power distinct from the others, and called the "appetitive power."

On the contrary: The Philosopher distinguishes the appetitive from the other powers.[2] Damascene also distinguishes the appetitive from the cognitive powers.[3]

I answer that: It is necessary to attribute an appetitive power to the soul. To make this evident, we must consider that some inclination follows every form; e.g., fire, by its form, is inclined to rise, and to generate its like. Now the form has a higher mode of existence in things having knowledge than in those that lack it. For in the latter, the form determines each thing only to its own being, i.e., to the being which is natural to each one. This natural form, therefore, is followed by a natural inclination, which is called the "natural appetite." But in things having knowledge, each one is determined to its own natural being by its natural form, which, nevertheless, is receptive of the forms of other things. Thus sense receives the forms of all sensible things, and the intellect, of all intelligible things. The soul of man is therefore in a way all things by

---

1. Aristotle, *Nichomachean Ethics*, I, 1(1094a3).
2. *On the Soul* II, 3(414a31).
3. *On the Orthodox Faith (De Fide Orth.)*, II, 22. (Not available in English.)

sense and intellect, so that things having knowledge approach, in a way, to a likeness to God, "in Whom all things pre-exist," as Dionysius says.[4]

Therefore, just as in those beings that have knowledge forms exist in a higher manner and above the manner of natural forms, so there must be in them an inclination, called "natural appetite," surpassing the natural inclination in them. And this superior inclination belongs to the appetitive power of the soul, through which the animal is able to desire what it apprehends, and not only that to which it is inclined by its natural form. It is therefore necessary to attribute an appetitive power to the soul.

Reply Objection 1. Appetite is found in things which have knowledge, above the common manner in which it is found in all things, as was said above. Therefore it is necessary, in the light of this fact, to ascribe to the soul a particular power.

Reply Objection 2. What is known and what is desired are the same in reality, but differ in aspect; for a thing is apprehended as something *sensible* or *intelligible,* whereas it is desired as *suitable* or *good.* Now it is diversity of aspect in the objects, and not material diversity, which necessitates a diversity of powers.

Reply Objection 3. Each power of the soul is a form or nature, and has a natural inclination to something. Hence each power desires, by natural appetite, that object which is suitable to itself. Above this natural appetite is the animal appetite, which follows upon cognition, and by which something is desired, not as suitable to this or that power (such as sight for seeing, or sound for hearing), but as suitable absolutely to the animal.

Second Article

ARE THE SENSORY AND

INTELLECTIVE APPETITES DISTINCT POWERS?

Objection 1. It seems that the sensory and intellective appetites are not distinct powers. For powers are not differentiated by accidental differences, as was said above.[5] But it is accidental to the appetible object whether it be apprehended by sense or by intellect. Therefore the sensory and the intellective appetites are not distinct powers.

Objection 2. Moreover, intellectual knowledge is of universals, and is thereby distinguished from sense knowledge, which is of singulars.[6] But there is no place for this distinction in the appetitive part of the soul. For since the appetite is a movement of the soul toward singular

---

4. *The Divine Names* V, 5.
5. Question LXXVII, article 3.
6. All "singulars" are "individuals," yet not all "individuals" are "singulars," but only those which are composed of matter and form. Thus angels are "individuals," but not "singulars"; and God is supremely individual, but not "singular."

things, every act of the appetite seems to be toward such a thing. Therefore intellectual appetite is not distinguished from sense appetite.

Objection 3. Again, just as the appetitive power is classed as sub-
ordinate to the cognitive power, so too is the motive power. But the
motive power which in man follows upon intellect is not distinct from
the motive power which in animals follows upon sense. Likewise, then,
neither is there distinction in the soul's appetitive part.

On the contrary: The Philosopher distinguishes a double appetite,
and says that the higher appetite moves the lower.[7]

I answer that: It must be said that intellectual appetite is a distinct
power from sense appetite. For the appetitive power is a passive power,
which is naturally moved by the thing apprehended. Therefore, as is
said, "the apprehended appetible object is a mover which is not moved,
while the appetite is a moved mover." [8] Now things passive and movable
are differentiated according to the distinction of the corresponding
active and motive principles, for the motive factor must be proportionate
to the movable, and the active to the passive. And, the passive power
itself owes its very nature to its relationship to its active principle. Therefore, since what is apprehended by the intellect and what is apprehended
by sense are generically different, it follows that intellectual appetite is
distinct from sense appetite.

Reply Objection 1. It is not accidental to the thing desired to be apprehended by sense or by intellect; rather, this belongs to it by its nature.[9]
For the appetible object does not move the appetite except as it is apprehended. Thus differences in the thing apprehended are essential
differences in the appetible object. Hence the appetitive powers are
distinguished according to the distinctive character of the things apprehended, as by their proper objects.

Reply Objection 2. The intellectual appetite, though it bears upon
things that are singular in their extra-mental existence, yet it does so
according to some universal aspect; as when it desires something because
it is good. Thus the Philosopher says that hatred can be of a universal, as
when "we hate every kind of thief." [10] In the same way, by the intellectual
appetite we may desire immaterial goods, which are not apprehended by
sense, such as knowledge, virtues, and the like.

Reply Objection 3. As is said a universal opinion does not move except
by means of a particular opinion.[11] Similarly the higher appetite moves
by means of the lower. Hence there are not two distinct motive powers
following upon intellect and sense.

---

7. *On the Soul* III, 9(432b5); 10(433a23); 11(434a12).
8. *op. cit.,* III, 10(433b16).
9. There are some appetible objects which are by nature imperceivable by the senses
—e.g., God and angels; others are by nature thus perceivable, as are all material things.
10. *Rhetoric* II, 4(1382a5).
11. Aristotle, *On the Soul* III, 11(434a16).

The Power of Sensuality

(In Three Articles)

IS SENSUALITY ONLY APPETITIVE?

Objection 1. It seems that sensuality is not only appetitive, but also cognitive. For Augustine says that "the sensual movement of the soul which is directed to the bodily senses is common to us and beasts." [1] But the bodily senses belong to the cognitive powers. Therefore sensuality is a cognitive power.

Objection 2. Moreover, things which fall under one division seem to be of one genus. But Augustine contradistinguishes sensuality from the higher and lower reason, which pertain to cognition. Therefore sensuality also is cognitive.

Objective 3. Again, in man's temptations sensuality stands in the place of the serpent. But in the temptation of our first parents, the serpent presented himself as one giving information and proposing sin—things which belong to the cognitive power. Therefore sensuality is a cognitive power.

On the contrary: Sensuality is defined as "the appetite of things belonging to the body." [2]

I answer that: The term "sensuality" seems to be taken from the sensual movement, of which Augustine speaks, just as the name of a power is taken from its act—e.g., "sight" from seeing. Now the sensual movement is an appetite following upon sense cognition. For the act of the cognitive power is not so properly called a "movement" as the act of the appetite; since the operation of the cognitive power is fulfilled in the very fact that the thing known is in the knower, while the operation of the appetitive power is fulfilled through the desirer being inclined toward the desirable thing. That is why the operation of the cognitive power is likened to rest; whereas the operation of the appetitive power is rather likened to movement. Therefore by "sensual movement" we understand the operation of the appetitive power. Thus "sensuality" is the name of the sense appetite.

---

1. *On the Trinity* XII, 12.
2. Peter Lombard, *Sentences* II, xxiv, 4(I, 421).

Reply Objection 1. By saying that the sensual movement of the soul "is directed to the bodily senses," Augustine does not mean that the bodily senses are included in sensuality, but rather that the movement of sensuality is a certain inclination to the bodily senses, since we desire things which are apprehended through the bodily senses. And thus the bodily senses pertain to sensuality, so to speak, as forerunners.

Reply Objection 2. Sensuality is contradistinguished from the higher and lower reason, as having in common with them the act of movement; for the cognitive power, to which belong the higher and lower reason, is a motive power, as is appetite, to which sensuality pertains.

Reply Objection 3. The serpent not only showed and proposed sin, but also incited to the commission of sin. And in this, sensuality is signified by the serpent.

Second Article

IS THE SENSE APPETITE DIVIDED INTO
THE IRASCIBLE AND CONCUPISCIBLE AS DISTINCT POWERS?

Objection 1. It seems that the sense appetite is not divided into the irascible and concupiscible as distinct powers. For the same power of the soul regards both sides of a contrariety, as sight regards both black and white, as is said.[3] But suitable and harmful are contraries. Since, then, the concupiscible power regards what is suitable, while the irascible is concerned with what is harmful, it seems that the irascible and the concupiscible are the same power in the soul.

Objection 2. Moreover, the sense appetite regards only what is suitable according to the senses. But such is the object of the concupiscible power. Therefore there is no sense appetite differing from the concupiscible power.

Objection 3. Again, hatred is in the irascible part of the soul. For Jerome says on *Matthew 13:33:* "We ought to have the hatred of vice in the irascible power." But hatred, being contrary to love, is in the concupiscible part. Therefore the concupiscible and irascible are the same powers.

On the contrary: Gregory of Nyssa and Damascene assign two parts to the sense appetite, the irascible, and the concupiscible.

I answer that: The sense appetite is one generic power, and is called "sensuality"; but it is divided into two powers, which are species of the sense appetite, viz., the irascible and the concupiscible.

In order to make this clear, we must consider that in natural, perishable things there is needed an inclination not only to the acquisition of what

---

3. Aristotle, *On the Soul* II, 11(422b23).

is suitable and to the avoiding of what is harmful, but also to resistance against corruptive and contrary forces which are a hindrance to the acquisition of what is suitable, and are productive of harm. For example, fire has a natural inclination, not only to rise from a lower place, which is unsuitable to it, toward a higher place, which is suitable, but also to resist whatever destroys or hinders its action. Therefore, since the sense appetite is an inclination following upon sense cognition (just as natural appetite is an inclination consequent to the natural form), there must be in the sensory part of the soul two appetitive powers: one, through which the soul is inclined simply to seek what is suitable, according to the senses, and to fly from what is hurtful, and this is called the "concupiscible"; and another, whereby an animal resists the attacks that hinder what is suitable, and inflict harm, and this is called the "irascible"—whose object therefore is said to be something "arduous," because its tendency is to overcome and rise above obstacles.

Now these two inclinations are not to be reduced to one principle. For sometimes the soul busies itself with unpleasant things, against the inclination of the concupiscible appetite, in order that, following the impulse of the irascible appetite, it may fight against obstacles. And so even the passions of the irascible appetite are seen to counteract the passions of the concupiscible appetite; since concupiscence, on being aroused, diminishes anger, and anger, being aroused, very often diminishes concupiscence. This is clear also from the fact that the irascible appetite is, as it were, the champion and defender of the concupiscible appetite, in rising up against what hinders the acquisition of the suitable things which the concupiscible appetite desires, or against what inflicts harm, from which the concupiscible appetite flies. And for this reason all the passions of the irascible appetite arise from the passions of the concupiscible appetite, and terminate in them; e.g., anger arises from sadness, and, having wrought vengeance, terminates in joy. For this reason also the quarrels of animals are about things concupiscible, viz., food and sex, as is said.[4]

Reply Objection 1. The concupiscible power regards both what is suitable and what is unsuitable. But the object of the irascible power is to resist the attack of the unsuitable.

Reply Objection 2. Just as in the cognitive powers of the sensory part of the soul there is an estimative power, which perceives those things which do not impress the senses, as was said above,[5] so also in the sense appetite there is an appetitive power which regards something as suitable, not because it pleases the senses, but because it is useful to the animal for self-defense. And this is the irascible power.

Reply Objection 3. Hatred in itself belongs to the concupiscible appe-

4. Aristotle, *The History of Animals (Hist. Anim.)* VIII, 1(589a2).
5. Question LXXVIII, article 2.

tite, but by reason of the strife which arises from hatred it may belong to the irascible appetite.

Third Article

DO THE IRASCIBLE AND
CONCUPISCIBLE APPETITES OBEY REASON?

Objection 1. It seems that the irascible and concupiscible appetites do not obey reason. For these two are parts of sensuality. But sensuality does not obey reason; which is why it is signified by the serpent, as Augustine says.[6] Therefore the irascible and concupiscible appetites do not obey reason.

Objection 2. Moreover, what obeys a certain thing does not resist it. But the irascible and concupiscible appetites resist reason, according to the Apostles (*Romans 7:23*): "I see another law in my members fighting against the law of my mind." Therefore the irascible and concupiscible appetites do not obey reason.

Objection 3. Again, as the appetitive power is inferior to the rational part of the soul, so also is the sensory power. But the sensory part of the soul, does not obey reason, for we neither hear nor see just when we wish. Therefore, in like manner, neither do the powers of the sense appetite, the irascible and concupiscible, obey reason.

On the contrary: Damascene says that "the part of the soul which is obedient and amenable to reason is divided into concupiscence and anger." [7]

I answer that: In two ways do the irascible and concupiscible powers obey the higher part, in which are the intellect or reason, and the will: first, as to the reason, and secondly, as to the will. They obey the reason in their own acts, because in other animals the sense appetite is naturally moved by the estimative power; e.g., a sheep, esteeming the wolf as an enemy, is afraid. In man the esimative power, as was said above,[8] is replaced by the cogitative power, which is called by some the "particular reason," because it compares individual notions. Hence in man the sense appetite is naturally moved by this particular reason. But this same particular reason is in man naturally guided and moved according to his power of universal rationality; and that is why in syllogisms particular conclusions are drawn from universal propositions. Clearly, therefore, this universal reasoning power directs the sense appetite, which is divided into the concupiscible and the irascible, and this appetite obeys it. But

---

6. *On the Trinity* XII, 12; 13.
7. *On the Orthodox Faith*, II, 12. (Not available in English.)
8. Question LXXVIII, article 4.

because to draw particular conclusions from universal principles is not the work of the intellect, *as such*,[9] but of the reason, so it is that the irascible and concupiscible appetites are said to obey the *reason* rather than the intellect. Anyone can experience this in himself; for by applying certain universal considerations, anger or fear or the like may be lessened or increased.

The sense appetite is also subject to the will as to the execution [of action], which is accomplished through the motive power. For in other animals movement follows at once the concupiscible and irascible appetites. Thus the sheep, fearing the wolf, flies at once, because it has no superior counteracting appetite. On the contrary, man is not moved at once according to the irascible and concupiscible appetites; but he awaits the command of the will, which is the superior appetite. For wherever there is order among a number of motive powers, the second moves only by virtue of the first; and so the lower appetite is not sufficient to cause movement, unless the higher appetite consents. And this is what the Philosopher says, viz., that "the higher appetite moves the lower appetite, as the higher sphere moves the lower." [10] In this way, therefore, the irascible and concupiscible appetites are subject to reason.

Reply Objection 1. Sensuality is signified by the serpent in what is proper to it as a sensory power. But the irascible and concupiscible powers denominate the sense appetite rather on the part of the act, to which they are led by the reason, as has been said.[11]

Reply Objection 2. As the Philosopher says: "We observe in an animal a despotic and a politic principle; for the soul dominates the body by a despotic rule, but the intellect dominates the appetite by a politic and royal rule." [12] For that rule is called "despotic" whereby a man rules his slaves, who have not the means to resist in any way the orders of the one that commands them, since they have nothing of their own. But that rule is called "politic" and "royal" by which a man rules over free subjects, who, though subject to the government of the ruler, have nevertheless something of their own, by reason of which they can resist the orders of him who commands. And so the soul is said to rule the body by a despotic rule, because the members of the body cannot in any way resist the sway of the soul, but at the soul's command both hand and foot, and whatever member is naturally moved by voluntary movement, are at once moved. But the intellect or reason is said to govern the irascible and concupiscible appetites by a "politic" rule because the sense appetite has something of its own, by virtue of which it can resist the command of reason. For the sense appetite is naturally moved, not only by the esti-

---

9. Whose act is intellection, or intuition.
10. *On the Soul* III, 11(434a12).
11. Articles 1 and 2, above.
12. *Politics* I, 2(1254b2).

mative power in other animals, and in man by the cogitative power which the universal reason guides, but also by the imagination and the sense. This accounts for our experience of the fact that the irascible and concupiscible powers do resist reason, when we sense or imagine something pleasant, which reason forbids, or unpleasant, which reason commands. Therefore, simply because the irascible and concupiscible appetites resist reason in something, it does not follow that they do not obey it.

Reply Objection 3. The exterior senses require for their acts exterior sensible things by which they are activated, and whose presence does not lie in the power of the reason. But the interior powers, both appetitive and cognitive, do not require exterior things. Therefore they are subject to the command of reason, which can not only incite or pacify the affections of the appetitive power, but can also form the images of the imagination.

The Will

(In Five Articles)

DOES THE WILL DESIRE SOMETHING NECESSARILY?

Objection 1. It seems that the will desires nothing necessarily. For Augustine says that "if anything is necessary, it is not voluntary." [1] But whatever the will desires is voluntary. Therefore nothing that the will desires is desired necessarily.

Objection 2. Moreover, "the rational powers," according to the Philosopher, "extend to opposite things." [2] But the will is a rational power, because, as he says, "the will is in the reason." [3] Therefore the will extends to opposite things, and hence is determined to nothing of necessity.

Objection 3. Again, by the will we are masters of our own actions. But we are not masters of that which is of necessity. Therefore the act of the will cannot be necessitated.

On the contrary: Augustine says that "all desire happiness with one will." [4] Now if this were not necessary, but contingent, there would at least be a few exceptions. Therefore the will desires something of necessity.

I answer that: The word "necessity" is used in many ways. For that which must be is necessary. Now a thing's necessity may derive from an intrinsic principle—either material, as when we say that everything composed of contraries necessarily perishes, or formal, as when we say that it is necessary for the three angles of a triangle to be equal to two right angles. And this is (1) "natural" and "absolute" necessity. In another way, a thing's necessity may derive from something extrinsic, viz., either the end or the agent. The necessity is from the end when without it the end is not to be attained or so well attained; in this sense, food is said to be "necessary" for life, and a horse for a journey. This is called (2) "the necessity of the end," and sometimes also "utility." The necessity is from

---

1. *On the City of God* V, 10.
2. *Metaphysics* VIII, 2(1046b5).
3. *On the Soul* III, 9(432b5).
4. *On the Trinity* XIII, 4.

the agent when someone is forced by an agent so that he is unable to do the contrary. This is called (3) the "necessity of coercion."

Now this necessity of coercion is altogether repugnant to will. For we call "violent" that which is against the inclination of a thing. But the very movement of the will is an inclination to something. Therefore, just as a thing is called "natural" because it is according to the inclination of the nature, so a thing is called "voluntary," because it is according to the inclination of the will. Therefore, just as it is impossible for a thing to be at the same time violent and natural, so it is impossible for a thing to be simply coerced, or violent—and voluntary.

But the necessity of the end is not repugnant to will when the end cannot be attained except in one way. Thus from the decision to cross the sea there arises in the will the necessity to desire a ship.[5]

Similarly, neither is natural necessity repugnant to the will. Indeed, just as the intellect of necessity adheres to first principles, so the will must of necessity adhere to the last end, which is happiness. For, as is said, the end is in practical matters what the principle is in speculative matters.[6] For what befits a thing naturally and immutably must be the root and principle of all else pertaining thereto, since the nature of a thing is the first in everything, and every movement arises from something immutable.

Reply Objection 1. The words of Augustine are to be understood as applying to necessity of coercion. But natural necessity "does not take away the liberty of the will," as he himself says in the same place.

Reply Objection 2. The will, so far as it desires a thing naturally, corresponds rather to the intellection of natural principles than to the reason, which extends to contraries. Hence, in this respect, it is rather an intellectual than a rational power.[7]

Reply Objection 3. We are masters of our own actions by reason of our being able to choose this or that. But choice regards not the end, but the means to the end, as is said.[8] Consequently, the desire of the ultimate end is not among those actions of which we are masters.

---

5. There were, of course, no other means of ocean travel in St. Thomas' day.

6. Aristotle, *Physics* II, 9(200a21).

7. See above, question LXXIX, article 8.

8. Aristotle, *Nichomachean Ethics,* III, 2(111b27). Properly speaking, we "will" ends; we "choose" means. See below, question LXXXIII, article 4.

Second Article

DOES THE WILL DESIRE

NECESSARILY WHATEVER IT DESIRES?

Objection 1. It seems that the will desires necessarily all that it desires. For Dionysius says that "evil is outside the scope of the will." [9] Therefore the will tends necessarily to the good which is proposed to it.

Objection 2. Moreover, the object of the will is compared to the will as the mover to the movable thing. But the movement of the movable necessarily follows from the mover. Therefore it seems that the will's object moves it necessarily.

Objection 3. Again, just as the thing apprehended by sense is the object of sense appetite, so the thing apprehended by the intellect is the object of intellectual appetite, which is called "will." But what is apprehended by the sense moves the sense appetite necessarily, for Augustine says that "animals are moved by things seen." [10] Therefore it seems that whatever is apprehended by the intellect moves the will of necessity.

On the contrary: Augustine says that "it is the will by which we sin and live well." [11] Thus the will extends to opposites. Therefore it does not will necessarily whatever it wills.

I answer that: The will does not will of necessity whatever it wills. In order to make this evident we must consider that, just as the intellect naturally and necessarily adheres to first principles, so the will adheres to the last end, as was said already.[12] Now there are some intelligible objects which have no necessary connection with first principles—e.g., contingent propositions, the denial of which does not involve a denial of first principles; and to such objects the intellect does not assent of necessity. But there are some propositions which have a necessary connection with first principles, viz., demonstrable conclusions, a denial of which involves a denial of first principles; and to these the intellect assents necessarily, upon knowing demonstratively the necessary connection of these conclusions with the principles. But it does not assent necessarily until, through the demonstration, it recognizes the necessity of such a connection.

It is the same with the will. For there are certain particular goods which do not have a necessary connection with happiness, since without them it is possible for one to be happy; and to such goods the will does not adhere of necessity. But there are some things which do have a necessary connection with happiness, viz., those whereby man adheres to God, in Whom alone true happiness lies. Nevertheless, until, through the cer-

---

9. *The Divine Names* IV, 32.
10. *A Literal Commentary on "Genesis"* IX, 14.
11. *Retractions* I, 9; *The City of God* V 10.
12. Preceding article.

tainty that results from seeing God, the necessity of such a connection be shown, the will does not adhere to God necessarily, not to those things which are of God. But the will of one who sees God in His essence necessarily adheres to God, just as now we will necessarily to be happy. It is therefore clear that the will does not will necessarily everything it wills.

Reply Objection 1. The will can tend to nothing except under the aspect of good. But because good is of many kinds, the will is not of necessity determined to one.

Reply Objection 2. The mover necessarily causes movement in the movable thing only when the power of the mover exceeds the movable thing in such a way that its entire capacity is subject to the mover. But since the capacity of the will is for the universal and perfect good, it is not subjected to any particular good; and therefore it is not necessarily moved by it.

Reply Objection 3. The sense power does not relate different things to one another, as reason does; but it apprehends simply some single thing. Therefore, in respect of that single thing, it moves the sense appetite in a determinate way. But the reason is a power that relates many things to one another. Therefore the intellectual appetite, i.e., the will, can be moved by several things, but not of necessity by one thing.

Third Article

IS THE WILL A HIGHER POWER THAN THE INTELLECT?

Objection 1. It seems that the will is a higher power than the intellect. For the object of the will is the good and the end. But the end is the first and highest cause. Therefore the will is the first and highest power.

Objection 2. Moreover, in the order of physical things the imperfect precedes the perfect. And this also appears in the powers of the soul; for sense precedes intellect, which is higher. Now the act of the will, according to a natural order, follows the act of the intellect. Therefore the will is a more noble and perfect power than the intellect.

Objection 3. Again, habits are proportioned to their powers, as perfections to what they make perfect. But the habit which perfects the will, viz., charity, is more noble than the habits which perfect the intellect; for it is written (*1 Corinthians 13:2*): "If I should know all mysteries, and if I should have all faith, and have not charity, I am nothing." Therefore the will is a higher power than the intellect.

On the contrary: The Philosopher holds that the intellect is the highest power of the soul.[13]

I answer that: The superiority of one thing over another can be con-

---

13. *Nichomachean Ethics*, X, 7(1177a20).

sidered in two ways: absolutely and relatively.[14] Now a thing is considered such and such absolutely when viewed as it is in itself; but
relatively, when viewed in relation to something else. If therefore the
intellect and will be considered in themselves, then the intellect is seen
to be the higher power; and this is clear if we compare their respective
objects to one another. For the object of the intellect is more simple
and more absolute than the object of the will. For the object of the intellect is the very notion[15] of the appetible good; and the appetible good,
the notion of which is in the intellect, is the object of the will. Now the
more simple and the more abstract a thing is, the nobler and higher it
is in itself; and therefore the object of the intellect is higher than the
object of the will. Since, then, the proper nature of a power is according
to its order to its object, it follows that the intellect, in itself and absolutely, is higher and nobler than the will.

But relatively, and through comparison with something else, we find
that the will is sometimes higher than the intellect; and this happens
when the object of the will resides in something higher than that of the
intellect. Thus I might say that hearing is relatively nobler than sight,
in that something wherein sound is present is superior to something in
which there is color, though color is superior to and simpler than sound.
For, as was said above,[16] the act of the intellect is accomplished through
the likeness of the thing understood being in the one who understands;
while the act of the will is accomplished through the will being inclined
to the thing itself as existing in itself. And that is why the Philosopher
says that "good and evil," which are objects of the will, "are in things,"
but "truth and error," which are objects of the intellect, "are in the
mind." [17] When, therefore, the thing wherein good is present is superior
to the soul itself, in which the understood likeness resides, then, by com
parison with such a thing, the will is higher than the intellect. But when
the thing which is good is inferior to the soul, then, even in comparison
with that thing, the intellect is higher than the will. So it is that the
love of God is better than the knowledge of God;[18] but, on the contrary,
the knowledge of corporeal things is better than the love of them.
Absolutely, however, the intellect is superior to the will.

Reply Objection 1. The notion of cause is perceived by comparing
one thing to another, and in such a comparison the notion of good is
found to be more primary. But truth is more absolute in its signification,
and extends to the notion of good itself. Thus, the good is something

14. Or: *simply,* and *in some respect.*
15. Literally, "reason," i.e., intelligible essence.
16. Question XVI, article 1; question XXVII, article 4.
17. *Metaphysics* V, 4(1027b25).
18. St. Thomas is speaking in the context of this life, where God is immediately
loved, but is not immediately known. In the beatific vision, God is at once perfectly
loved and perfectly known.

true. But, again, the true is something good in that the intellect is a given reality, and truth is its end. And among other ends this is the most excellent; just as is the intellect among the other powers.

Reply Objection 2. What precedes in the order of generation and time is less perfect, for in one and the same thing potency temporally precedes act, and imperfection precedes perfection. But that which is prior simply and in the order of nature is more perfect; for thus act is prior to potency. And in this way the intellect is prior to the will, as the motive power to the movable thing, and as the active to the passive; for it is the apprehended good that moves the will.

Reply Objection 3. This argument is verified of the will as compared with what is above the soul. For charity is the virtue by which we love God.

Fourth Article

DOES THE WILL MOVE THE INTELLECT?

Objection 1. It seems that the will does not move the intellect. For what moves is superior and prior to what is moved, because what moves is an agent, and "the agent is nobler than the patient," as Augustine and Aristotle point out.[19] But the intellect is superior and prior to the will, as was said above.[20] Therefore the will does not move the intellect.

Objection 2. Moreover, what moves is not moved by what is moved, except perhaps accidentally. But the intellect moves the will, because the good apprehended by the intellect moves without being moved; whereas the appetite is a moved mover. Therefore the intellect is not moved by the will.

Objection 3. Again, we can will nothing but what we understand. If, therefore, in order to understand, the will moves by willing to understand, that act of the will must be preceded by another act of the intellect, and this act of the intellect by another act of the will, and so on indefinitely—which is impossible. Therefore the will does not move the intellect.

On the contrary: Damascene says: "It is in our power to learn an art or not, as we will." [21] But a thing is in our power by the will, and we learn an art by the intellect. Therefore the will moves the intellect.

I answer that: A thing is said to "move" in two ways: First, as an end, as when we say that the end "moves" the agent. In this way the intellect moves the will, because the understood good is the object of the will, and moves it as an end. Secondly, a thing is said to "move" as an agent,

19. *On the Soul* III, 5(430a18).
20. Preceding article.
21 *On the Orthodox Faith,* II, 26. (Not available in English.)

as what alters moves what is altered, and what impels moves what is impelled. In this way the will moves the intellect, and all the powers of the soul, as Anselm remarks. The reason is, because wherever there is order among a number of active powers, that power which regards the universal end moves the powers which refer to particular ends. And this occurs both in nature and in political things. For the heaven, which acts for the universal preservation of things that come into being and pass away, moves all lower bodies, each of which acts for the preservation of its own species or of the individual. So, too, a king, who aims at the common good of the whole kingdom, by his rule moves all the governors of cities, each of whom rules over his own particular city. Now the object of the will is the good and the end in general,[22] whereas each power is directed to some suitable good proper to it, as sight is directed to the perception of color, and the intellect to the knowledge of truth. Therefore the will as an agent moves all the powers of the soul to their respective acts, except the natural powers of the vegetative part of the soul, which are not subject to our choice.

Reply Objection 1. The intellect may be considered in two ways: (1) as cognitive of universal being and truth, and (2) as a reality and a particular power having a determinate act. Similarly the will may be considered in two ways: (1) according to the common nature of its object, i.e., as appetitive of universal good; and (2) as a determinate power of the soul having a determinate act. If, therefore, the intellect and will be compared with one another according to the universality of their respective objects, then, as was said above, the intellect is absolutely higher and nobler than the will.[23] If, however, we take the intellect in relation to the common nature of its object and the will as a determinate power, then again the intellect is higher and nobler than the will, because under the notion of being and truth is contained both the will itself, its act, and its object. Thus the intellect understands the will, its act, and its object, just as it understands other species of things, as stone or wood, which are contained under the common notion of being and truth. But if we consider the will in relation to the common nature of its object, which is the good, and the intellect as a reality and a special power, then the intellect itself, its act, and its object, which is the true, each of which is some species of good, are contained under the common notion of good. And in this way the will is higher than the intellect, and can move it. From this it is clear why these powers include one another in their acts; because the intellect understands that the will wills, and the will wills the intellect to understand. In like manner, the good is contained under the true, inasmuch as it is an understood truth, and the true under the good, inasmuch as it is a desired good.

---

22. Literally, "in common"; i.e., taken universally.
23. Preceding article.

Reply Objection 2. The intellect moves the will in one sense, and the will moves the intellect in another, as we have said above.

Reply Objection 3. There is no need to go on indefinitely, but we must stop at the intellect as preceding all the rest. For every movement of the will must be preceded by knowledge, whereas not every act of knowledge is preceded by an act of the will. But the source of considering and understanding is an intellectual principle higher than our intellect, viz., God; as Aristotle also says, explaining in this way that there is no need to proceed indefinitely.[24]

Fifth Article

SHOULD WE DISTINGUISH IRASCIBLE AND
CONCUPISCIBLE FACTORS IN THE SUPERIOR APPETITE?

Objection 1. It seems that we ought to distinguish irascible and concupiscible factors in the superior appetite, which is the will. For the concupiscible power is so-called from *concupiscere* [to desire], and the irascible part from *irasci* [to be angry]. But there is a concupiscence which cannot belong to the sensory appetite, but only to the intellectual, which is the will; e.g., the concupiscence of wisdom, of which it is said (*Wisdom 6:21*): "The concupiscence of wisdom bringeth to the eternal kingdom." There is also a certain anger which cannot belong to the sensory appetite, but only to the intellectual; as when our anger is directed against vice. And so, Jerome commenting on *Matthew 8:33*, warns us "to have the hatred of vice in the irascible part." [25] Therefore we should distinguish irascible and concupiscible parts in the intellectual soul as well as in the sensory.

Objection 2. Moreover, as is commonly said, charity is in the concupiscible, and hope in the irascible part of the soul. But they cannot be in the sense appetite, because their objects are not sensible, but intelligible. Therefore we must assign an irascible and a concupiscible power to the intellectual part of the soul.

Objection 3. Again, it is said in the book, *On the Spirit and the Soul*,[26] that "the soul has these powers," viz., the irascible, concupiscible and rational, "before it is united to the body." But no power of the soul's sensory part belongs to the soul alone, but to the soul and body united, as was said above.[27] Therefore the irascible and concupiscible powers are in the will, which is the intellectual appetite.

---

24. *Eudemian Ethics* VII, 14(1248a26).
25. Commentary on Matthew 8:33.
26. Pseudo-Augustine (Alcher of Clairvaux) *On the Spirit and the Soul (De Spir. et An.)* XVI. (Not available in English.)
27. Question LXXVII, articles 5 and 8.

On the contrary: Gregory of Nyssa says that the "irrational" part of the soul is divided into the desiring and the irascible, and Damascene says the same.[28] And the Philosopher says: "the will is in the reason, while in the irrational part of the soul are concupiscence and anger, or desire and spirit." [29]

I answer that: The irascible and concupiscible are not parts of the intellectual appetite, which is called the will. For, as was said above, a power which is directed to an object according to some common notion is not differentiated by special differences which are contained under that common notion.[30] Thus, because sight is related to what is visible under the common notion of something colored, the visual power is not multiplied according to the different kinds of color. If, however, there were a power ordered to the white as white, and not as something colored, it would be distinct from a power whose object was the black as black.

Now the sense appetite is not directed to the common notion of the good, because neither do the senses apprehend the universal. Therefore the parts of the sensory appetite are differentiated according to the different aspects of particular goods. For the concupiscible factor is concerned with its own proper sort of good, which is something pleasant to the senses and suitable to nature; whereas the irascible factor regards that aspect of goodness whereby the harmful is repelled and combatted. But the will is directed to the good according to the common notion of good, and therefore in the will, which is the intellectual appetite, there is no differentiation of appetitive powers, so that there would be in the intellectual appetite an irascible power distinct from a concupiscible power. Even so, neither on the part of the intellect are the cognitive powers multiplied, although they are multiplied so far as the senses are concerned.

Reply Objection 1. Love, concupiscence, and the like can be understood in two ways. Sometimes they are taken as passions, i.e., as arising with a certain commotion of spirit. And thus they are commonly understood, and in this sense they are only in the sense appetite. In another sense, however, they are simple affections without passion or commotion of spirit, and thus they are acts of the will. And in this sense, too, they are attributed to the angels and to God. But if taken in this sense, they do not belong to different powers, but only to one power, which is called the will.

Reply Objection 2. The will itself may be said to be "irascible," insofar as it wills to repel evil, not from any sudden movement of passion, but from a judgment of the reason. And in the same way the will may be said to be "concupiscible" because of its desire for good. And thus in

---

28. *On the Orthodox Faith* XII. (Not available in English.)
29. *On the Soul* III, 11(432b5).
30. Question LIX, article 4; question LXXIX, article 7.

the irascible and concupiscible [parts of the soul] are charity and hope, i.e., in the will as ordered to such acts.

And in this way, too, we may understand the words quoted from the book, *On the Spirit and the Soul,* viz., that the irascible and concupiscible powers are in the soul "before it is united to the body" (as long as we understand priority of nature, and not of time); although there is no need to place trust in what that book says.

Thus the answer to the third objection is clear.

Free Choice

(*In Four Articles*)

First Article

DOES MAN HAVE FREE CHOICE?

Objection 1. It seems that man has not free choice. For whoever has free choice does what he wills. But man does not what he wills, for it is written (*Romans 7:19*): "For the good which I will I do not, but the evil which I will not, that I do." Therefore man has not free choice.

Objection 2. Moreover, whoever has free choice has in his power to will or not to will, to do or not to do. But this is not in man's power, for it is written (*Romans 9:16*): "It is not of him that willeth"—viz., to will—"nor of him that runneth"—viz., to run. Therefore man has not free choice.

Objection 3. Again, he is free who is his own master, as is said.[1] Therefore what is moved by another is not free. But God moves the will; for it is written (*Proverbs 21:1*): "The heart of the king is in the hand of the Lord; whithersoever He will He shall turn it," and (*Philippians 2:13*): "It is God Who worketh in you both to will and to accomplish." Therefore man has not free choice.

Objection 4. And again, whoever has free choice is master of his own actions. But man is not master of his own actions, for it is written (*Jeremias 10:23*): "The way of a man is not his, neither is it in a man to walk." Therefore man has not free choice.

Objection 5. Then, too, the Philosopher says: "According as each one is, such does the end seem to him." [2] But it is not in our power to be such as we are, for this comes to us from nature. Therefore it is natural to us to follow some particular end, and therefore we are not free in so doing.

On the contrary: It is written (*Ecclesiasticus 15:14*): "God made man from the beginning, and left him in the hand of his own counsel"; and the *Gloss* adds: "That is, in the liberty of choice."

I answer that: Man has free choice, or otherwise counsels, exhortations, commands, prohibitions, rewards and punishments would be in

---

1. Aristotle, *Metaphysics* I, 2(982b26).
2. *Nichomachean Ethics*, III, 5(1114a32).

vain. In order to make this evident, we must consider that some things
act without judgment, as a stone moves downwards; and in like manner
all things which lack knowledge. And some act from judgment, but not
a free judgment; as with brute animals. For the sheep, seeing the wolf,
judges it a thing to be shunned, from a natural and not a free judgment;
because it judges, not from deliberation, but from natural instinct. And
the same thing is to be said of any judgment in brute animals. But man
acts from judgment, because by this cognitive power he judges that
something should be avoided or sought. But because this judgment, in
the case of some particular act, is not from a natural instinct, but from
some act of comparison in the reason, therefore he acts from free judgment and retains the power of being inclined to various alternatives.
For reason in contingent matters may follow opposite courses, as we
see in dialectical syllogisms and rhetorical arguments. Now particular
operations are contingent, and therefore in such matters the judgment
of reason may follow opposite courses, and is not determined to one. And
from the very fact that man is rational, it is necessary that he have free
choice.

Reply Objection 1. As was said above, the sense appetite, though it
obeys the reason, yet in a given case it can resist by desiring what the
reason forbids.[3] This is therefore the good which man does not when
he wishes, viz., "not to desire against reason," as the *Gloss* of Augustine
on that text says.

Reply Objection 2. Those words of the Apostle are not to be taken as
though man does not wish or does not run of his free choice, but because
free choice is not sufficient for this unless it be moved and helped by God.

Reply Objection 3. Free choice is the cause of its own movement, because by his free choice man moves himself to act. But liberty does not
necessarily require that what is free should be the *first* cause of itself, as
neither for one thing to be the cause of another need it be the first cause.
God, then, is the first cause, Who moves causes both natural and voluntary. And just as by moving natural causes He does not prevent their
actions from being natural, so by moving voluntary causes He does not
deprive their actions of being voluntary; on the contrary, He is the cause
of this very thing in them, for He operates in each thing according to
its own proper character.

Reply Objection 4. "Man's way" is said "not to be his" as regards the
carrying out of his choices, wherein he may be impeded, whether he
will or not. The choices themselves, however, are in us, but presuppose
the help of God.

Reply Objection 5. Quality in man is of two kinds: natural and adventitious. Now the natural quality may be in the intellectual part, or in
the body and its powers. From the very fact, therefore, that man is such

3. Question LXXXI, article 3, ad 2.

by virtue of a natural quality which is in the intellectual part, he naturally desires his last end, which is happiness. This desire is, indeed, a natural desire, and is not subject to free choice, as is clear from what was said above.[4] But on the part of the body and its powers, man may be such by virtue of a natural quality, inasmuch as he is of such a temperament or disposition due to any impression whatever produced by bodily causes, which cannot affect the intellectual part, since it is not the act of a bodily organ. And such as a man is by virtue of a bodily quality, such also does his end seem to him, because from such a disposition a man is inclined to choose or reject something. But these inclinations are subject to the judgment of reason, which the lower appetite obeys, as was said.[5] Therefore this is in no way prejudicial to free choice.

The adventitious qualities, however, are habits and passions, by virtue of which a man is inclined to one thing rather than to another. And yet even these inclinations are subject to the judgment of reason. Such qualities also are subject to reason, as it is in our power either to acquire them, whether by causing them or disposing ourselves to them, or to reject them. And so there is nothing in this that is incompatible with free choice.

Second Article

IS FREE CHOICE A POWER?

Objection 1. It seems that free choice is not a power. For free choice is nothing but a free judgment. But "judgment" denominates an act, not a power. Therefore free choice is not a power.

Objection 2. Moreover, free choice is defined as "the faculty of the will and reason." [6] But "faculty" denominates the facility of a power, which is due to a habit, therefore, free choice is a habit. Moreover Bernard says that free choice is "the soul's habit of disposing of itself." [7] Therefore it is not a power.

Objection 3. Again, no natural power is forfeited through sin. But free choice is forfeited through sin, for Augustine says that "man, by abusing free choice, loses both it and himself." [8] Therefore free choice is not a power.

On the contrary: Nothing but a power, seemingly, is the subject of a habit. But free choice is the subject of grace, by the help of which it chooses what is good. Therefore free choice is a power.

---

4. Question LXXXII, articles 1 and 2.
5. Question LXXXI, article 3.
6. Peter Lombard, *Sentences* II, xxiv, 3(I, 421).
7. St. Bernard, *On Grace and Free Will* I. (Not available in English.)
8. *Enchiridion* XXX.

I answer that: Although "free choice," in its proper sense, denotes an act, in the common manner of speaking we call "free choice" that which is the source of the act by which man judges freely. Now in us the source of an act is both power and habit; for we say that we know something both by science and by the intellectual power. Therefore free choice must be either a power, or a habit, or a power with a habit. That it is neither a habit nor a power together with a habit can be clearly proved in two ways. First of all, because, if it is a habit, it must be a natural one; for it is natural to man to have free choice. But there is no natural habit in us with respect to those things which come under free choice, for we are naturally inclined to those things of which we have natural habits e.g., to assent to first principles. Now those things to which we are naturally inclined are not subject to free choice, as was said in the case of the desire of happiness.[9] Therefore it is against the very notion of free choice that it should be a natural habit; and that it should be a non-natural habit is against its nature. Therefore in no sense is it a habit.

Secondly, this is clear because "habits" are defined as that "by reason of which we are well or ill disposed with regard to actions and passions."[10] For by temperance we are well-disposed as regards concupiscences, and by intemperance ill disposed; and by science we are well disposed to the act of the intellect when we know the truth, and by the contrary habit ill disposed. But free choice is indifferent to choosing well or ill, and therefore it is impossible that it be a habit. Therefore it is a power.

Reply Objection 1. It is not unusual for a power to be named from its act. And so from this act, which is a free judgment, is named the power which is the source of this act. Otherwise, if "free choice" denominated an act, it would not always remain in man.

Reply Objection 2. "Faculty" sometimes denominates a power ready for operation, and in this sense faculty is used in the definition of free choice. But Bernard takes habit, not as divided against power, but as signifying any aptitude by which a man is somehow disposed to act. This may be both by a power and by a habit, for by a power man is, as it were, empowered to do the action, and by the habit he is apt to act well or ill.

Reply Objection 3. Man is said to have lost free choice by falling into sin, not as to natural liberty, which is freedom from coercion, but as regards freedom from fault and unhappiness. With this we shall deal later in the treatise on Morals in the second part of this work.

---

9. Question LXXXII, articles 1 and 2.
10. Aristotle, *Nichomachean Ethics*, II, 5(1105b25).

Third Article

IS FREE CHOICE AN APPETITIVE POWER?

Objection 1. It seems that free choice is not an appetitive, but a cognitive power. For Damascene says that "free choice straightway accompanies the rational power." [11] But reason is a cognitive power. Therefore free choice is a cognitive power.

Objection 2. Moreover, the term "free choice" means free judgment. But to judge is an act of a cognitive power. Therefore free choice is a cognitive power.

Objection 3. Again, the principal function of free choice is electing. But electing seems to pertain to knowledge, because it implies a certain relating of one thing to another; which is proper to the cognitive power. Therefore free choice is a cognitive power.

On the contrary: The Philosopher says that electing is the "desiring of those things which are in our power." [12] But desire is an act of the appetitive power. Therefore electing is also. But free choice is that by which we elect. Therefore free choice is an appetitive power.

I answer that: The proper act of free choice is the act of electing, for we say that we have a free choice because we can take one thing while refusing another; and this is to elect. Therefore we must consider the nature of free choice by considering the nature of the act of election. Now two things concur in this act: one on the part of the cognitive power, the other on the part of the appetitive power. On the part of the cognitive power, (1) counsel is required, by which we judge one thing to be preferred to another; on the part of the appetitive power, it is required (2) that the appetite should accept the judgment of counsel. So Aristotle leaves it in doubt whether choice belongs principally to the appetitive or the cognitive power; for he says that choice is either "an appetitive intellect or an intellectual appetite." [13] But he inclines to its being an intellectual appetite when he describes choice as "a desire proceeding from counsel." [14] And the reason for this is that the proper object of choice is the means to the end. Now the means, as such, has the nature of that good which is called "useful"; and since the good, as such, is the object of the appetite, it follows that choice is principally an act of an appetitive power. And thus free choice is an appetitive power.

Reply Objection 1. The appetitive powers accompany the cognitive, and it is in this sense that Damascene says that free choice immediately accompanies the rational power.

---

11. *On the Orthodox Faith*, II, 27. (Not available in English.)
12. *Nichomachean Ethics*, III, 3(1113a11).
13. *op. cit.*, III, (1113a11).
14. *op. cit.*, III, 3(1113a11).

Reply Objection 2. Judgment, as it were, concludes and terminates counsel. Now counsel is terminated, first, by the judgment of reason; secondly by the acceptation of the desire. Accordingly, the Philosopher says: "having formed a judgment by counsel, we desire in accordance with that counsel." [15] And in this way election itself is called a "judgment," from which free choice takes its name.

Reply Objection 3. This relating which is implied in the term "election" belongs to the preceding counsel, which is an act of reason. For though the appetite does not relate things to one another, yet inasmuch as it is moved by the cognitive power, which does so, it has some likeness to this in choosing one thing in preference to another.

Fourth Article

IS FREE CHOICE A POWER DISTINCT FROM THE WILL?

Objection 1. It seems that free choice is a power distinct from the will. For Damascene says that *thelesis* is one thing and *boulesis* another.[16] But *thelesis* is will, while *boulesis* seems to be free choice, because *boulesis,* according to him, is the will as concerning an object by way of comparison between two things. Therefore it seems that free choice is a power distinct from the will.

Objection 2. Moreover, powers are known by their acts. But option, which is the act of free choice, is distinct from the act of willing, for, as is said, "the act of willing regards the end, whereas the act of choosing regards the means to the end." [17] Therefore free choice is a power distinct from the will.

Objection 3. Again, the will is the intellectual appetite. But on the part of the intellect there are two powers—agent and possible. Therefore, also on the part of the intellectual appetite there should be another power besides the will. And this, seemingly, can be only free choice. Therefore free choice is a power distinct from the will.

On the contrary: Damascene says: "free choice is nothing else than the will." [18]

I answer that: The appetitive powers must be proportionate to the cognitive powers, as was said above.[19] Now, as on the part of intellectual apprehension we have intellect and reason, so on the part of the intellectual appetite we have will and free choice, which is nothing else but the power of option. And this is clear from their relations to their respective objects and acts. For the act of understanding implies the simple accepta-

---

15. *ibid.*
16. *On the Orthodox Faith* XXII. (Not available in English.)
17. *Aristotle, Nichomachean Ethics* III, 2(1111b26).
18. *On the Orthodox Faith* XIV. (Not available in English.)
19. Question LXIV, article 2; question LXXX, article 2.

tion of something. Hence principles which are known through themselves without being derived from other knowledge are said properly to be "understood." But to reason, properly speaking, is to come from one thing to the knowledge of another; and so, properly speaking, we reason about conclusions, which are known from the principles. In like manner, on the part of the appetite, to will implies the simple appetite for something, and so the will is said to regard the end, which is desired for itself. But to choose is to desire something for the sake of obtaining something else, and so, properly speaking, it regards the means to the end. Now in appetitive matters, the end is related to the means, which is desired for the end, in the same way as, in knowledge, principles are related to the conclusion to which we assent because of the principles. Therefore it is evident that as intellect is to reason, so will is to the power of option, which is free choice. But it has been shown above that it belongs to the same power both to understand and to reason, even as it belongs to the same power to be at rest and to be in movement.[20] Hence it belongs also to the same power to will and to choose. And on this account will and the free choice are not two powers, but one.

Reply Objection 1. Boulesis is distinct from *thelesis* because of a distinction, not of powers, but of acts.

Reply Objection 2. Choice and will—i.e., the act of willing—are different acts, yet they belong to the same power, as do understanding and reasoning, as was said.

Reply Objection 3. The intellect is compared to the will as *moving* the will.[21] There is, then, no need to distinguish in the will an agent and a possible will.

---

20. Question LXXIX, article 8.
21. And not as being moved by it.

How the Soul While United to the Body Understands Corporeal Things Beneath It

(In Eight Articles)

We now have to consider the acts of the soul in regard to the intellectual and the appetitive powers, for the other powers of the soul do not come directly under the consideration of the theologian. Now the acts of the appetitive part of the soul come under the consideration of the science of morals, and so we shall treat of them in the second part of this work, to which the consideration of moral matters belongs. But of the acts of the intellectual part we shall treat now. In treating of these acts, we shall proceed in the following order. First, we shall inquire how the soul understands when united to the body; secondly, how it understands when separated from the body.[1]

The former of these inquiries will be threefold: (1) how the soul understands bodies, which are beneath it; (2) how it understands itself and things contained in itself;[2] (3) how it understands immaterial substances, which are above it.[3]

In dealing with the knowledge of corporeal things, there are three questions to be considered: (1) through what does the soul know them; (2) how and in what order does it know them;[4] (3) what does it know in them?[5]

First Article

DOES THE SOUL KNOW BODIES THROUGH THE INTELLECT?

Objection 1. It seems that the soul does not know bodies through the intellect. For Augustine says that bodies cannot be understood by the intellect, nor can anything corporeal be seen except by the senses.[6] He says also that intellectual vision is of those things that are in the soul by

1. Question LXXXIX—omitted from this Treatise. See Introduction.
2. Question LXXXVII.
3. Question LXXXVIII.
4. Question LXXV.
5. Question LXXXVI.
6. *Soliloquies* II, 4.

their essence.[7] But such are not bodies. Therefore the soul cannot know bodies through the intellect.

Objection 2. Moreover, as sense is to the intelligible, so is the intellect to the sensible. But the soul can in no way, through the senses, know spiritual things, which are intelligible. Therefore neither can it, through the intellect, know bodies, which are sensible.

Objection 3. Again, the intellect has as its object things that are necessary and unchangeable. But all bodies are movable and changeable. Therefore the soul cannot know bodies through the intellect.

On the contrary: Science is in the intellect. If, therefore, the intellect does not know bodies, it follows that there is no science of bodies; and thus perishes the science of nature, which treats of mutable bodies.

I answer that: In order to elucidate this question, it must be said that the early philosophers, who inquired into the natures of things, thought there was nothing in the world except bodies. And because they observed that all bodies are subject to motion, and considered them to be ever in a state of flux, they were of the opinion that we can have no certain knowledge of the reality of things. For what is in a continual state of flux cannot be grasped with any degree of certitude, for it passes away before the mind can form a judgment on it. So Heraclitus said, "it is not possible to touch the water in a passing stream twice"—as the Philosopher relates.[8]

After these came Plato, who, wishing to save the certitude of our knowledge of truth through the intellect, maintained that, besides these corporeal things, there is another genus of beings, separate from matter and movement, which he called "forms" or "ideas," by participation in which each one of these singular and sensible things is said to be either a man, or a horse, or the like.[9] Accordingly, he maintained that sciences and definitions, and whatever pertains to the act of the intellect, are not referred to these sensible bodies, but to those immaterial and separate beings; so that the soul does not understand these corporeal things, but their separated forms.

Now this is clearly false for two reasons. First, because, since those forms are immaterial and immobile, knowledge of movement and matter (which is proper to natural philosophy) would be excluded from among the sciences, and likewise all demonstration through moving and material causes. Secondly, because it seems silly, when we seek for knowledge of things which we meet in experience, to introduce other beings, which cannot be the substances of the things with which we began, since they differ from them in being. Hence, even if we had a knowledge of those

---

7. *A Literal Commentary on "Genesis"* XII, 24.
8. *Metaphysics* III, 5(1010a14).
9. cf. *Theaetetus* 156a.

separate substances, we could not for that reason claim to form judgments concerning these sensible things.

Now it seems that in this Plato strayed from the truth because, having observed that all knowledge takes place through some kind of likeness, he thought that the form of the thing known must of necessity be in the knower in the same manner as in the thing known itself. Now he considered that the form of the thing understood is in the intellect under conditions of universality, immateriality, and immobility; that this is apparent from the very operation of the intellect, whose act of understanding is universal, and characterized by a certain necessity. For the mode of action corresponds to the mode of the agent's form. Therefore he concluded that the things which we understand must subsist in themselves under the same conditions of immateriality and immobility.

But there is no necessity for this. For even in sensible things we observe that the form is otherwise in one of them than in another. Thus, whiteness may be of great intensity in one, and of a less intensity in another; in one we find whiteness with sweetness, in another without sweetness. In the same way, the sensible form is in one way in the thing which is external to the soul, and in another way in the senses, which receive the forms of sensible things without receiving matter, such as the color of gold without receiving gold. So, too, the intellect, according to its own mode, receives under conditions of immateriality and immobility the forms of material and mutable bodies; for the received is in the receiver according to the mode of the receiver. It must be said, therefore, that the soul knows bodies through the intellect by a knowledge which is immaterial, universal, and necessary.

Reply Objection 1. These words of Augustine are to be understood as referring to the medium of intellectual knowledge, and not to its object. For the intellect knows bodies by understanding them, not indeed through bodies, nor through material and corporeal likenesses, but through immaterial and intelligible forms, which can be in the soul by their own essence.

Reply Objection 2. As Augustine states, it is not correct to say that as the sense knows only bodies so the intellect knows only spiritual things;[10] for it would follow that God and the angels would not know bodies. The reason for this diversity is that the lower power does not extend to those things that belong to the higher power; whereas the higher power accomplishes in a more excellent manner what belongs to the lower power.

Reply Objection 3. Every movement presupposes something immobile. For when a change of quality occurs, the substance remains unchanged; and when there is a change of substantial form, matter remains un-

---

10. *The City of God* XXII, 29.

changed. Moreover, mutable things have immutable dispositions; e.g., though Socrates be not always sitting, yet it is an immutable truth that whenever he does sit he remains in one place. For this reason there is nothing to hinder our having an immutable science of movable things.

Second Article

DOES THE SOUL UNDERSTAND
CORPOREAL THINGS THROUGH ITS ESSENCE?

Objection 1. It seems that the soul understands corporeal things through its essence. For Augustine says[11] that the soul "collects and lays hold of the images of bodies which are formed in the soul and of the soul; for in forming them it gives them something of its own substance." But the soul understands bodies through the likenesses of bodies. Therefore the soul knows bodies through its essence, which it employs for the formation of such likenesses, and from which it forms them.

Objection 2. Moreover, the Philosopher says that "the soul, after a fashion, is everything."[12] Since, therefore, like is known by like, it seems that the soul knows corporeal things through itself.

Objection 3. Again, the soul is superior to corporeal creatures. Now lower things are in higher things in a higher way than in themselves, as Dionysius points out. Therefore all corporeal creatures exist in a higher way in the essence of the soul than in themselves. Therefore the soul can know corporeal creatures through its essence.

On the contrary: Augustine says: "the mind gathers the knowledge of corporeal things through the bodily senses."[13] But the soul itself cannot be known through the bodily senses. Therefore it does not know corporeal things through itself.

I answer that: The ancient philosophers held that the soul knows bodies through its essence. For it was universally admitted that like is known by like. But they thought that the form of the thing known is in the knower in the same way as in the thing known. The Platonists however were of a contrary opinion. For since Plato perceived that the intellectual soul has an immaterial existence and an immaterial mode of knowing, he held that the forms of things known subsist immaterially. But since the earlier natural philosophers[14] considered that things known are corporeal and material, they held that these things must exist materially even in

11. *On the Trinity* X, 5.
12. *On the Soul* III, 8(431b21).
13. *On the Trinity* IX, 3.
14. i.e., the pre-Socratics.

the soul that knows them. And therefore, in order to attribute to the soul a knowledge of all things, they held that it has the same nature in common with them all. And because the nature of an effect is determined by its principles, they attributed to the soul the nature of a principle; so that those who thought fire to be the principle of all, held that the soul had the nature of fire, and in like manner as to air and water. Now Empedocles, who held the existence of four material elements and two principles of movement, said that the soul was composed of these. Consequently, since they held that things existed in the soul materially, they maintained that all the soul's knowledge is material, thus failing to distinguish intellect from sense.[15]

But this opinion will not hold. *First,* because in the material principle of which they were speaking, effects do not exist except potentially. But a thing is not known according as it is in potency, but only according as it is in act, as is shown.[16] Therefore neither is a power known except through its act. It was therefore insufficient to attribute to the soul the nature of the principles of things in order to guarantee to the soul a knowledge of all things; it was further necessary to admit in the soul the natures and forms of each individual effect, such as bone, flesh, and the like—as Aristotle argues against Empedocles.[17] *Secondly,* because if it were necessary for the thing known to exist materially in the knower, there would be no reason why things which have a material existence outside the soul should be devoid of knowledge. Thus if by fire the soul knows fire, that fire which exists extra-mentally should also have knowledge of fire.

It therefore remains that the material things known must exist in the knower, not materially, but rather immaterially. The reason for this is that the act of knowledge extends to things outside the knower; for we know even the things that are outside us. Now by matter the form of a thing is determined to some one thing. Therefore it is clear that the nature of knowledge is directly opposed to that of materiality. Consequently things that are not receptive of forms, except materially, have no power of knowledge whatever, as in the case of plants—as it is said.[18] But the more immaterially a being receives the form of the thing known, the more perfect is its knowledge. Therefore the intellect, which abstracts the form not only from matter, but also from the individuating conditions of matter, knows more perfectly than the senses, which receive the form of the thing known, without matter indeed, but subject to material conditions. Moreover, among the senses themselves, sight has

---

15. As Aristotle points out, cf. *On the Soul* III, 3(427a21).
16. Aristotle, *Metaphysics* VIII, 9(1051a29).
17. *On the Soul* I, 5(409b23).
18. *op. cit.,* II, 12(424a32).

the most perfect knowledge, because it is the least material, as was said above.[19] So, too, among intellects, the more perfect is the more immaterial.

It is therefore clear from the foregoing that if there be an intellect which knows all things by its essence, then its essence must have all things in itself immaterially; even as the ancient natural philosophers held that the essence of the soul must be composed actually of the principles of all material things in order to know all things. Now it is proper to God that His essence comprise all things immaterially, as effects pre-exist virtually in their cause. God alone, therefore, understands all things through His essence; but neither the human soul nor the angels can do so.

Reply Objection 1. Augustine in that passage is speaking of an imaginary vision, which takes place through the images of bodies. To the formation of such images the soul gives something of its substance, just as a subject is given in order to be informed by some form. In this way the soul makes such images from itself; not that the soul or some part of the soul be converted into this or that image, but in the sense that a body is said to be made into something colored because of its being informed with color. That this is the meaning is clear from the sequel. For he says that the soul "keeps something"—i.e., something not informed with such an image—"which is able freely to judge of the species of these images," and that this is the "mind or the intellect." [20] And he says that the part which is informed with these images—viz., the imagination—is "common to us and beasts."

Reply Objection 2. Aristotle did not hold that the soul was actually composed of all things, as did the ancient natural philosophers; he said that "the soul is all things, *after a fashion*," in that it is in potency to all—through the senses, to all sensible things; through the intellect, to all intelligible things.

Reply Objection 3. Every creature has a finite and determinate being. Therefore, although the essence of a higher creature has a certain likeness to a lower creature, in that they share in a common genus, yet it has not a complete likeness to it, because it is determined to a certain species other than the species of the lower creature. But the divine essence is the perfect likeness of all that may be found to exist in things created, being the universal principle of all.

---

19. Question LXXVIII, article 3.
20. *On the Trinity* X, 5.

Third Article

DOES THE SOUL UNDERSTAND
ALL THINGS THROUGH INNATE IDEAS? [21]

Objection 1. It seems that the soul understands all things through innate ideas. For Gregory says, in a homily for the Ascension, that "man has understanding in common with the angels." But angels understand all things through innate ideas; so that it is said that "every intelligence is full of forms." [22] Therefore the soul also has innate ideas of things, by means of which it understands corporeal things.

Objection 2. Moreover, the intellectual soul is more excellent than corporeal primary matter. But primary matter was created by God under the forms to which it is in potency. Therefore much more is the intellectual soul created by God with intelligible ideas. And so the soul understands corporeal things through innate ideas.

Objection 3. Again, no one can answer the truth except concerning what he knows. But even a person untaught, and devoid of acquired knowledge, answers the truth to every question if put to him in orderly fashion, as we find related in the *Meno* of Plato concerning a certain individual.[23] Therefore we have some knowledge of things even before we acquire knowledge; which would not be the case unless the soul were endowed with innate ideas. Therefore the soul understands corporeal things through innate ideas.

On the contrary: The Philosopher, speaking of the intellect, says that it is like "a tablet on which nothing is written." [24]

I answer that: Since form is the source of action, a thing must be related to the form which is the source of an action in the same way as it is to that action. Thus, if upward motion is from lightness, then that which moves upwards only potentially must be only potentially light, but that which actually moves upwards must be actually light. Now we observe that man sometimes is only a potential knower, both as to sense and as to intellect. And from such potency he is reduced to act: through the action of sensible objects on his senses, he is reduced to the act of sensation; by instruction or discovery, to the act of understanding. Therefore it must be said that the cognitive soul is in potency both to the likenesses which are the sources of sensing, and to the likenesses which are the sources of understanding. For this reason Aristotle held that the intellect

---

21. Literally, "species"—i.e., here, intelligible likenesses or forms in the mind.

22. *The Book On Causes* (*Liber De Causis*) prop. X, p. 170 (R. Steele, ed., Oxford University Press, 1935). (Not available in English.)

23. *Meno* 82 B.

24. *On the Soul* III, 4(430a1).

by which the soul understands has no innate ideas, but is at first in potency to all such species.[25]

But since that which actually has a form is sometimes unable to act according to that form because of some impediment (as a light thing may be hindered from moving upwards), Plato on this account held that man's intellect is naturally filled with all intelligible species, but that, by being united to the body, it is hindered from the realization of its act. But this seems incongruous. *First,* because, if the soul has a natural knowledge of all things, it seems impossible for the soul so far to forget the existence of such knowledge as not to know itself to be possessed of it. For no man forgets what he knows naturally, e.g., that every whole is greater than its part, and the like. And this appears especially incongruous if we suppose that it is natural to the soul to be united to the body, as was established above;[26] for it is absurd that the natural operation of a thing should be totally impeded by that which belongs to it naturally. *Secondly,* the falseness of this opinion is clearly proved from the fact that if a sense be wanting, the knowledge[27] of what is apprehended through that sense is also wanting. Thus, a man who is born blind can have no awareness of colors. This would not be the case if the soul had innate likenesses of all intelligible things. It must therefore be said that the soul does not know corporeal things through innate ideas.

Reply Objection 1. Man indeed has understanding in common with the angels, but not in the same degree of perfection; just as the lower grades of bodies, which merely exist, according to Gregory, have not the same degree of perfection as the higher bodies. For the matter of the lower bodies is not totally actualized by its form, but is in potency to forms which it has not; whereas the matter of the heavenly bodies is totally actualized by its form, so that it is not in potency to any other form, as was pointed out above.[28] Similarly, the angelic intellect is perfected by intelligible forms, in accordance with its nature; whereas the human intellect is in potency to such forms.

Reply Objection 2. Primary matter has substantial being through form, and so it had to be created under some form; otherwise it would not be in act. But when once it exists under one form it is in potency to others. On the other hand, the intellect does not receive substantial being through the intelligible species; and therefore there is no comparison.

Reply Objection 3. If questions be put in an orderly fashion, they proceed from universal self-evident principles to what is particular. Now

---

25. *ibid.,* (429b30).
26. Question LXXVI, article 1.
27. Literally, "science"—which here is a direct cognitive awareness based on induction through *sense* experience.
28. Question LXVI, Article 2.

by such a process knowledge is produced in the soul of the learner. There-fore, when he answer the truth to a subsequent question, this is not be-cause he had knowledge previously, but because he then acquires such knowledge for the first time. For it matters not whether the teacher proceed from universal principles to conclusions by questioning or by asserting; for in either case the intellect of the listener is assured of what follows by that which preceded.

Fourth Article

ARE THE INTELLIGIBLE FORMS DERIVED

BY THE SOUL FROM CERTAIN SEPARATE FORMS?

Objection 1. It seems that the intelligible forms are derived by the soul from some separate forms. For whatever is such by participation is caused by what is such essentially; e.g., that which is on fire is referred back to fire as its cause. But the intellectual soul, so far as it is actually understanding, participates in the intelligibles themselves. For the in-tellect in act is, in a way, the thing understood in act. Therefore those things which in themselves and by their essence are understood in act are the causes of the intellectual soul's actually understanding. Now that which in its essence is actually understood are forms existing without mat-ter. Therefore the intelligible forms, by which the soul understands, are caused by some separate forms.

Objection 2. Moreover, the intelligible is to the intellect as the sensible is to the sense. But the sensible forms which are in the senses, and by which we sense, are caused by the sensible things which exist actually outside the soul. Therefore the intelligible forms, by which our intellect understands, are caused by some actually intelligible things existing outside the soul. But these can be nothing else than forms separate from matter. Therefore the intelligible forms of our intellect are derived from some separate substances.

Objection 3. Again, the potential is in every case made to be actual by that which is actual. If, therefore, our intellect, previously in potency, afterwards actually understands, this must be caused by some intellect which is always in act. But this is a separate intellect. Therefore the in-telligible forms, by which we actually understand, are caused by some separate substances.

On the contrary: If this were true, we should not need the senses in order to understand. And this is proved to be false especially from the fact that if a man be wanting in a sense, he can in no way have knowl-edge[29] of the sensibles corresponding to that sense.

---

29. See above, note 27.

I answer that: Some have held that the intelligible forms present in our intellect are derived from certain separate Forms or substances. And this in two ways. For Plato, as we have noted, held that the forms of sensible things subsist by themselves without matter: e.g., the Form of a man, which he called "man-in-himself," and the Form or Idea of a horse, which he called "horse-in-itself," and so forth.[30] He therefore maintained that these Forms are participated in both by our soul and by corporeal matter: by our soul, for the knowledge of them, and by corporeal matter for their being; so that, just as corporeal matter, by participating in the Idea of a stone, becomes an individual stone, so our intellect, by participating in the Idea of a stone, is made to understand a stone. Now the participation of an Idea takes place by some likeness of the Idea in the participator, in the way that a model is participated in by a copy. So just as he held that the sensible forms, which are in corporeal matter, are derived from the Ideas as certain likenesses of them, so he held that the intelligible forms of our intellect are likenesses of the Ideas, derived therefrom. And for this reason, as was said above, he referred sciences and definitions to those Ideas.

But since it is contrary to the nature of sensible things that their forms should subsist without matter, as Aristotle proves[31] in many ways, Avicenna, rejecting this opinion, held that the intelligible forms of all sensible things, instead of subsisting in themselves without matter, pre-exist immaterially in separate intellects.[32] From the first of these intellects, said he, such forms are derived by a second, and so on to the last separate intellect, which he called the "agent intellect." From the agent intellect, according to him, intelligible forms flow into our souls, and sensible forms into corporeal matter. And so Avicenna agrees with Plato in holding that the intelligible forms of our intellect are derived from certain separate Forms; but these Plato held to subsist of themselves, while Avicenna placed them in the agent intellect. They differ, too, in this respect, that Avicenna held that the intelligible forms do not remain in our intellect after it has ceased actually to understand, and that it needs to turn [to the agent intellect] in order to receive them anew.[33] Consequently, he does not hold that the soul has innate knowledge, as does Plato, who held that the participations of the Ideas remain immutably in the soul.

But in terms of Avicenna's position no sufficient reason can be assigned for the soul being united to the body. For it cannot be said that the intellectual soul is united to the body for the sake of the body, since neither is form for the sake of matter, nor is the mover for the sake of

---

30. See above, Article 1. Also, for this whole paragraph, cf. Plato, *Phaedo* 100D, and *Timaeus* 28A and 30C.

31. *Metaphysics* VI, 14(1039a24).

32. *On the Soul (De Anima)* V, 5(251b); *Metaphysics* IX, 4(105ra). (Neither of these available in English.)

33. St. Thomas Aquinas, *Summa Contra Gentiles*, II, ch. 74.

the thing moved, but rather the reverse. Especially does the body seem necessary to the intellectual soul for the latter's proper operation, which is understanding; since as to its being, the soul does not depend on the body. But if the soul by its very nature had an inborn aptitude for receiving intelligible forms only through the influence of certain separate sources, and were not to receive them from the senses, it would not need the body in order to understand. Hence it would be united to the body to no purpose.

If, however, it be said that our soul needs the senses in order to understand, in that it is in some way awakened by them to the consideration of those things whose intelligible forms it receives from the separate sources, even this seems an insufficient explanation. For this awakening does not seem necessary to the soul, except in so far as it is somehow "overcome by sleep," as the Platonists put it, and by "forgetfulness," because of its union with the body; and thus the senses would be of no use to the intellectual soul except in removing the obstacle which the soul encounters through its union with the body. Consequently the reason for the union of the soul with the body still remains unexplained.

And if it be said, with Avicenna,[34] that the senses are necessary to the soul because by them it is aroused to turn to agent intellect from which it receives the species, neither is this a sufficient explanation. Because if it is natural for the soul to understand through forms derived from the agent intellect, it would follow that the soul can turn to the agent intellect from the inclination of its very nature, or through being aroused by another sense to turn to the agent intellect, and receive the forms of those sensible things for which we are missing a sense. And thus a man born blind could have knowledge[35] of colors; which is clearly untrue. It must therefore be said that the intelligible forms, by which our soul understands, are not derived from separate forms.

Reply Objection 1. The intelligible forms which are participated in by our intellect are traced back, as to their first cause, to a primary source which is by its essence intelligible—viz., God. But they proceed from that source by way of the forms of sensible and material things, from which we gather knowledge, as Dionysius says.[36]

Reply Objection 2. Material things, in their extra-mental existence, can be actually sensible, but not actually intelligible. Therefore there is no comparison between sense and intellect.

Reply Objection 3. Our possible intellect *is* brought from potency to act by an actually existing being, i.e., by the agent intellect, which is a power of the soul, as was said;[37] and not by any separate intellect, as a proper proximate cause, although perhaps as a remote cause.

---

34. *On the Soul* V, 5(25rb). (Not available in English.)
35. See above, note 27.
36. *The Divine Names* VII, 2.
37. Question LXXIX, article 4.

Fifth Article

DOES THE INTELLECTUAL SOUL KNOW
MATERIAL THINGS IN THE ETERNAL EXEMPLARS?

Objection 1. It seems that the intellectual soul does not know material things in the external exemplars. For that in which anything is known must itself be known more and antecedently. But the intellectual soul of man, in the present state of life, does not know the eternal exemplars, for it does not know God in Whom the eternal exemplars exist, but is "united to God as to the unknown," as Dionysius says.[38] Therefore the soul does not know all in the eternal exemplars.

Objection 2. Moreover, it is written (*Romans I, 20*) that "the invisible things of God are clearly seen . . . by the things that are made." But among the invisible things of God are the eternal examplars. Therefore the eternal exemplars are known through creatures, and not conversely.

Objection 3. Again, the eternal exemplars are nothing else but Ideas. For Augustine says that "Ideas are permanent exemplars existing in the divine mind." [39] If therefore we say that the intellectual soul knows all things in the eternal examplars, we come back to the opinion of Plato who said that all knowledge is derived from Ideas.

On the contrary: Augustine says: "If we both see that what you say is true, and if we both see that what I say is true, where do we see this, I pray? Neither do I see it in you, nor do you see it in me; but we both see it in the unchangeable truth which is above our minds." [40] Now the unchangeable truth is contained in the eternal exemplars. Therefore the intellectual soul knows all truths in the eternal exemplars.

I answer that: As Augustine says: "If those who are called philosophers said by chance anything that was true and consistent with our faith, we must claim it from them as from unjust possessors. For some of the doctrines of the pagans are spurious imitations or superstitious inventions, which we must be careful to avoid when we renounce the society of the pagans." [41] Consequently, whenever Augustine, who was imbued with the doctrines of the Platonists, found in their teaching anything consistent with faith, he adopted it; and those things which he found contrary to faith he amended. Now Plato held, as was noted previously, that the forms of things subsist of themselves apart from matter. These he called "Ideas," and he said that our intellect knows all things by participation in them; so that just as corporeal matter, by participating in

---

38. *The Mystical Theology* I, 3.
39. *Book of Eighty-Three Questions,* question 46.
40. *Confessions* XII, 25.
41. *On Christian Doctrine* II, 40.

the Idea of a stone, becomes a stone, so our intellect, by participating in the same Idea, has knowledge of a stone. But it seems contrary to faith that the forms of things should subsist of themselves without matter outside the things themselves, as the Platonists held, asserting that life-in-itself and wisdom-in-itself are certain creative substances, as Dionysius relates.[42] That is why in the place of the Ideas posited by Plato, Augustine maintained that the exemplars of all creatures existed in the divine mind, and that it is according to these that all things are formed, as well as that the human soul knows all things.[43]

When, therefore, the question is asked: Does the human soul know all things in the eternal exemplars? We must reply that one thing is said to be known "in another" in two ways. *First,* as in an object itself known; as one may see in a mirror the images of the things reflected in it. In this way the soul, in the present state of life, cannot see all things in the eternal exemplars; but thus the blessed, who see God and all things in Him, know all things in the eternal exemplars. *Secondly,* one thing is said to be known "in another" as in a source of knowledge; e.g., we might say that we see in the sun what we see by the sun. And in this sense it must be said that the human soul knows all things in the eternal exemplars, since by participation in these exemplars we know all things. For the intellectual light itself, which is in us, is nothing else than a participated likeness of the uncreated light, in which are contained the eternal examplars. Whence it is written (*Psalms 4:6, 7*), "Many say: who showeth us good things?"—to which the Psalmist replies: "The light of Thy countenance, O Lord, is signed upon us"—as though to say: By the very seal of the divine light in us, all things are made known to us.

But, besides the intellectual light which is in us, intelligible forms abstracted from things are required in order that we may have knowledge of material entities. This cognition, therefore, is not due solely to a participation of the eternal examplers, as the Platonists held, maintaining that the mere participation in the Ideas sufficed for knowledge.[44] Accordingly Augustine says: "Although the philosophers prove by convincing arguments that all things occur in time according to the eternal exemplars, were they able to see in the eternal exemplars or to find out from them how many kinds of animals there are and the origin of each? Did they not seek for this information from the story of times and places?" [45]

Now that Augustine did not understand all things to be known in their eternal exemplars or in the unchangeable truth, as though the eternal exemplars themselves were sin, is clear from his remark that "not

---

42. *The Divine Names* XI, 6.
43. *Book of Eighty-Three Questions,* question 46.
44. See below, question LXXXVII, article 1.
45. *The Trinity* IV, 16.

each and every rational soul can be said to be worthy of that vision," viz., of the eternal exemplars, "but only those that are holy and pure" —as are the souls of the blessed.[46]

The solution of the objections is clear from what has been said.

Sixth Article

IS INTELLECTUAL KNOWLEDGE
DERIVED FROM SENSIBLE THINGS?

Objection 1. It seems that intellectual knowledge is not derived from sensible things. For Augustine says that we cannot expect to acquire the pure truth from the senses of the body";[47] and he proves this in two ways: *first,* from the fact that whatever the bodily senses reach is continually being changed; and what is never the same cannot be perceived; *secondly,* from the fact that whatever we perceive by the body, even when not present to the senses, may be present in their images, as when we are asleep or angry; yet we cannot discern by the senses whether what we perceive be the sensible things themselves of their deceptive images. Now nothing can be perceived which cannot be distinguished from its counterfeit. And so he concludes that "we cannot expect to learn the truth from the senses." But intellectual knowledge apprehends the truth. Therefore intellectual knowledge cannot be conveyed by the senses.

Objection 2. Moreover, Augustine says: "It must not be thought that the body can make any impression on the spirit, as though the spirit were to subject itself like matter to the body's action; for that which acts is in every way more excellent than that which it acts on." [48] From this he concludes that "the body does not cause its image in the spirit, but the spirit itself causes it in itself." Therefore intellectual knowledge is not derived from sensible things.

Objection 3. Again, an effect does not surpass the power of its cause. But intellectual knowledge extends beyond sensible things; for we understand some things which cannot be perceived by the senses. Therefore intellectual knowledge is not derived from sensible things.

On the contrary: The Philosopher proves that the origin of knowledge is from the senses.[49]

I answer that: On this point the philosophers held three opinions. For (1) *Democritus* held that all knowledge is caused by images issuing from the bodies we think of and entering into our souls, as Augustine

---

46. *Book of Eighty-Three Questions*, question 46.
47. *op. cit.*, q. 9.
48. *A Literal Commentary on "Genesis"* XII, 16.
49. *Metaphysics* I, 1(981a2), and elsewhere.

remarks. And Aristotle says that Democritus held that knowledge is caused by a discharge of images.[50] And the reason for this opinion was that both Democritus and the other early philosophers did not distinguish between intellect and sense, as Aristotle points out.[51] Consequently, since the sense is activated by the sensible, they thought that all our knowledge is caused merely by an activation deriving from sensible things. This activation Democritus held to be caused by a discharge of images.

(2) *Plato,* on the other hand, held that the intellect differs from sense, and that it is an immaterial power not making use of a bodily organ for its action. And since the incorporeal cannot be affected by the corporeal, he held that intellectual knowledge is not brought about by sensible things activating the intellect, but by the intellect's participation in separate intelligible forms, as we have already said. Moreover, he held that sense is a power operating through itself. Consequently not even the sense itself, since it is a spiritual power, is affected by sensible things; but the sensible organs are affected by them, with the result that the soul is in a way aroused to form within itself the species of such things. Augustine seems to touch on this opinion in saying that the "body does not feel, but the soul feels through the body, which it makes use of as a kind of messenger, for reproducing within itself what is announced from without." [52] Thus according to Plato, neither does intellectual knowledge proceed from sensible knowledge, nor does sensible knowledge itself come entirely from sensible things; but these arouse the sensible soul to sensation, and the senses likewise arouse the intellect to the act of understanding.

(3) *Aristotle* took a middle course. For with Plato he agreed that intellect and sense are different.[53] But he held that the sense has not its proper operation without the cooperation of the body; so that sensation is not an act of the soul alone, but of the composite. And he held the same in regard to all operations of the sensory part of the soul. Since, therefore, it is not incongruous that the sensible things which are outside the soul should produce some effect in the composite, Aristotle agreed with Democritus in this, that the operations of the soul's sensory part are caused by the impression of the sensible on the sense; not indeed in the manner of a discharge, as Democritus held, but through some kind of operation. (For Democritus, it is clear, maintained that every action is effected through a discharge of atoms.) Aristotle, however, held that the intellect has an operation in which the body does not share.[54] Now nothing corporeal can cause an impression upon the incorporeal. And therefore, in order to cause intellectual operation, according to Aristotle,

---

50. *On Divination* II (464a5).
51. *On the Soul* III, 3(427a17).
52. *A Literal Commentary on "Genesis"* XII, 24.
53. *On the Soul* III, 3(427b6).
54. *On the Soul* III, 4(429a24).

the impression produced by sensible bodies does not suffice, but something superior is required; "for the agent is more noble than the patient," as he says.[55] This does not mean that intellectual operation is effected in us by the mere impression of some superior beings, as Plato held. Rather, the "higher" and "nobler" agent, which Aristotle calls the "agent intellect" (of which we have spoken above) [56] causes the phantasms received from the senses to be actually intelligible, by a certain kind of abstraction.

According to this teaching then, intellectual knowledge is caused by the senses, viz., the sense representations [phantasms]. However, since the sense representations cannot of themselves activate the possible intellect but must be made actually intelligible by the agent intellect, it cannot be said that sense cognition is the total and perfect cause of intellectual cognition, but rather is in a way the matter of the cause.

Reply Objection 1. These words of Augustine mean that truth is not entirely from the senses. For the light of the agent intellect is needed, through which we know the truth of changeable things unchangeably, and discern things themselves from their likenesses.

Reply Objection 2. In this passage Augustine speaks not of intellectual knowledge but of the imagination. And since, according to Plato's theory, the imagination has an operation which belongs to the soul only, Augustine, in order to show that corporeal images are impressed on the imagination, not by bodies but by the soul, uses the same argument as Aristotle does in proving that the agent intellect is something separate, because "the agent is more noble than the patient." [57] And without doubt, according to the above theory, in the imagination there must be not only a passive but also an active power. But if we hold, with Aristotle, that the action of the imaginative power is an action of the composite, no difficulty ensues; because the sensible body is more noble than the organ of the animal, in that its relation to it is that of a being in act to a being in potency; like the relation of an object actually colored to the pupil, which is potentially colored. True enough, the first activation of the imagination is effected through the agency of sensible things; for, as it is said, "the phantasm is a movement produced in accordance with sensation." [58] Nevertheless, there is in man an operation which by division and composition forms images of various things, even of things not perceived by the senses. And Augustine's words may be taken in this context.

Reply Objection 3. Sense cognition is not the entire cause of intellectual knowledge. And therefore it is not strange that intellectual knowledge should extend beyond sense knowledge.

---

55. *op. cit.*, III, 5(430a18).
56. Question LXXIX, articles 3 and 4.
57. *On the Soul* III, 3(429a1).
58. *op. cit.*, III, 7(431a16).

Seventh Article

CAN THE INTELLECT UNDERSTAND ACTUALLY THROUGH THE INTELLIGIBLE FORMS WHICH IT POSSESSES, WITHOUT TURNING TO SENSE REPRESENTATIONS?

Objection 1. It seems that the intellect can understand actually through the intelligible forms which it possesses, without turning to sense representations [phantasms]. For the intellect is actuated by the intelligible form whereby it is informed. But if the intellect is in act, it understands. Therefore the intelligible forms suffice for the intellect to understand actually without turning to sense representations.

Objection 2. Moreover, the imagination is more dependent on the senses[59] than the intellect on the imagination. But the imagination can actually imagine in the absence of the sensible. Therefore much more can the intellect understand actually without turning to sense representations.

Objection 3. Again, there are no phantasms of incorporeal things, for the imagination does not transcend time and space. If, therefore, our intellect cannot understand anything actually without turning to sense representations, it follows that it cannot understand anything incorporeal —which is clearly false, for we understand truth, and God and the angels.

On the contrary: The Philosopher says that "the soul understands nothing without a phantasm." [60]

I answer that: In the state of the present life, in which the soul is united to a perishable body, it is impossible for our intellect to understand anything actually, except by turning to sense representations. And of this there are two indications. *First,* because the intellect, being a power that does not make use of a bodily organ, would in no way be impeded in its act through the lesion of a bodily organ if there were not required for its act the operation of some power that does not make use of such an organ. Now sense, imagination, and the powers belonging to the soul's sensory part make use of a bodily organ. Therefore it is clear that for the intellect to understand actually, not only when it acquires new knowledge, but also when it uses knowledge already acquired, there is need for the act of the imagination and of the other powers. For when the act of the imagination is hindered by an organic lesion, as in cases of frenzy, or when the act of the memory is impeded, as in cases of lethargy, we see that a man is hindered from understanding actually even those things of which he had a previous knowledge. *Secondly,* anyone can experience this of himself: when he tries to understand some-

---

59. i.e., the external senses. The imagination is an internal sense power.
60. *op. cit.,* III, 7(431a16).

thing he forms certain sense representations to serve him by way of examples, in which as it were he observes what he is desirous of understanding. So it is that when we wish to help someone to understand something, we lay examples before him, from which he can form phantasms for the purpose of understanding.

Now the reason for this is that the knowing power is proportioned to the knowable thing. That is why the proper object of the angelic intellect, which is entirely separate from a body, is an intelligible substance separate from a body. On the other hand, the proper object of the human intellect, which is united to a body, is a quiddity or nature existing in corporeal matter; and it is through these natures of visible things that it rises up even to some knowledge of things invisible. Now it belongs to such a nature to exist in some individual, and this cannot be apart from corporeal matter; even as it belongs to the nature of a stone to be in an individual stone and to the nature of a horse to be in an individual horse, and so with the rest. Therefore the nature of a stone or any material thing cannot be known completely and truly except by being known as existing in the individual. Now we apprehend the individual through sense and imagination. That is why the intellect, in order to understand actually its proper object, must of necessity turn to sense representations so as to perceive the universal nature existing in the individual. But if the proper object of our intellect were a separate form, or if, as the Platonists say, the forms of sensible things subsisted apart from the individual, there would be no need for the intellect to turn to sense representations whenever it understands.

Reply Objection 1. The forms preserved in the possible intellect exist there habitually when it is not actually knowing them, as was said above.[61] Hence for actual understanding on our part, the fact that the forms are preserved does not suffice; we need further to make use of them in a manner befitting the things of which they are the forms, which things are natures existing in individuals.

Reply Objection 2. Even the sense representation itself is the likeness of an individual thing; and so the imagination does not need any further likeness of the individual, whereas the intellect does.

Reply Objection 3. Incorporeal beings, of which there are no sense representations, are known to us by reference to sensible bodies, of which there are sense representations. Thus we understand truth by considering a thing in which we see the truth; and God, as Dionysius says, we know as cause, by way of excess and by way of remotion.[62] Other incorporeal substances we know, in the state of the present life, only by way of remotion or through some relationship to corporeal things. Hence, when we understand something about such substances, we need to turn to the

61. Question LXXIX, article 6.
62. *The Divine Names* I, 5.

sensible representations of bodies, although there are no such representations of those substances themselves.

Eighth Article

IS THE JUDGMENT OF THE INTELLECT
HINDERED THROUGH SUSPENSION OF THE SENSE POWERS?

Objection 1. It seems that the judgment of the intellect is not hindered by suspension of the sense powers. For the superior does not depend on the inferior. But the judgment of the intellect is higher than the senses. Therefore the judgment of the intellect is not hindered through suspension of the senses.

Objection 2. Moreover, to syllogize is an act of the intellect. But during sleep the senses are suspended, as is said.[63] And yet it sometimes happens to us to syllogize while asleep. Therefore the judgment of the intellect is not hindered through suspension of the senses.

On the contrary: "What a man while asleep does against the moral law is not imputed to him as a sin," as Augustine says.[64] But this would not be the case if man, while asleep, had free use of his reason and intellect. Therefore the use of reason is hindered by suspension of the senses.

I answer that: As was said above, our intellects' proper and proportionate object is the nature of a sensible thing.[65] Now a perfect judgment concerning anything cannot be formed unless all that pertains to that thing be known; especially if one be ignorant of the term and end of the judgment. For the Philosopher says that "as the end of productive science is a work, so the end of the science of nature is that which is perceived principally through the senses." [66] Thus the metalworker does not seek to know what a knife is except for the purpose of making this particular knife; and likewise the natural philosopher does not seek to know the nature of a stone or a horse, except for the purpose of knowing the essential properties of those things which he perceives with his senses. Now it is clear that a metalworker cannot judge perfectly of a knife unless he knows what making this particular knife involves. Even so, the natural philosopher cannot judge perfectly of natural things unless he knows sensible things. But in the present state of life whatever we understand is through relationship with natural sensible things. Consequently it is impossible for our intellect to form a perfect judgment while the senses, through which we grasp sensible things, are suspended.

---

63. Aristotle, *On Sleep and Waking* I, (454b13).
64. *A Literal Commentary on "Genesis"* XII, 15.
65. Preceding article.
66. *On the Heavens* III, 7(306a16).

Reply Objection 1. Although the intellect is superior to the senses, nevertheless in a manner it receives from the senses, and its first and principal objects are founded in sensible things. That is why suspension of the senses necessarily impedes the judgment of the intellect.

Reply Objection 2. The senses are suspended in the sleeper through certain evaporations and the escape of certain exhalations, it is said;[67] and, therefore, it is according to the disposition of such evaporations that the senses are more or less suspended. For when the movement of the vapors is very agitated, not only are the senses suspended, but also the imagination, so that there are no phantasms; as happens especially when a man falls asleep after much eating and drinking. If, however, the movement of the vapors be somewhat less violent, phantasms appear, but distorted and without sequence; as happens in cases of fever. And if the movement be still more quieted, the phantasms will have a certain sequence; as happens especially toward the end of sleep, and in men who are sober and those who have a strong imagination. If the movement be very slight, not only does the imagination retain its freedom, but even the common sense[68] is partly freed; so that sometimes while asleep a man judges that what he sees is a dream, discerning, as it were, between things and their images. Nevertheless the common sense remains partly suspended; and therefore, although it distinguishes some images from reality, yet it is always deceived in some particular. Therefore, while a man is asleep, to the extent that sense and imagination are free, so is the judgment of his intellect unfettered, though not entirely. That is why those who syllogize while asleep invariably recognize, upon awakening, some flaw in their thinking.

---

67. Aristotle, *On Sleep and Waking* (*De Somno et Vigilia*), III (456b17).
68. The central, unifying, internal sense power.

The Mode and Order of Understanding

(In Eight Articles)

First Article

DOES OUR INTELLECT UNDERSTAND
CORPOREAL AND MATERIAL THINGS BY
ABSTRACTION FROM SENSE REPRESENTATIONS?

Objection 1. It seems that our intellect does not understand corporeal and material things by abstraction from sense representations [phantasms]. For the intellect is false if it understands a thing otherwise than as it is. Now the forms of material things do not exist in abstraction from the particular things represented by sensible likenesses. Therefore, if we understand material things by the abstraction of intelligible forms from sense representations, there will be error in the intellect.

Objection 2. Moreover, material things are those natural things which include matter in their definition. But nothing can be understood apart from that which enters into its definition. Therefore material things cannot be understood apart from matter. Now matter is the principle of individuation. Therefore material things cannot be understood by the abstraction of the universal from the particular; and this is to abstract intelligible forms from sense representations.

Objection 3. Again, the Philosopher says that "the phantasm is to the intellectual soul what color is to the sense of sight." [1] But seeing is not caused by abstraction of forms from colors, but by colors impressing themselves on the sense of sight. Therefore neither does the act of understanding occur through the abstraction of something from sense representations, but by the latter impressing themselves on the intellect.

Objection 4. And again, two things are said to be in the intellectual soul—the possible intellect and the agent intellect. [2] But it does not belong to the possible intellect to abstract intelligible forms from sense representations, but to receive them already abstracted. Neither does this seem to be the function of the agent intellect, which is related to sensible likenesses as light is to colors; since light does not abstract anything from

---

1. *On the Soul* III, 7(431a14) .
2. *op. cit.*, III, 5(430a14).

colors, but rather acts on them. Therefore in no way do we understand by abstraction from sense representations.

Objection 5. Then, too, the Philosopher says that "the intellect understands the species in the phantasms"; and not, therefore, by abstraction.[3]

On the contrary: There is the dictum: "things are intelligible in proportion as they are separable from matter." [4] Therefore material things must be understood according as they are abstracted from matter and from material likenesses, viz., sense representations.

I answer that: As stated above, the object of knowledge is proportionate to the power of knowledge.[5] Now there are three grades of the cognitive powers. (1) One cognitive power, viz., the *sense,* is the act of a bodily organ. That is why the object of every sense power is a form as existing in corporeal matter; and since such matter is the principle of individuation, every power of the soul's sensory part can have knowledge only of particulars. (2) There is another grade of cognitive power which is neither the act of a bodily organ, nor in any way connected with corporeal matter; and this is the *angelic intellect,* the object of whose cognitive power is therefore a form existing apart from matter. For though angels know material things, they do not know them except in something immaterial, viz., either in themselves or in God. (3) The *human intellect,* however, holds a middle place; for it is not the act of an organ, and yet it is a power of the soul, which is the form of the body, as is clear from what was said above.[6] That is why it is proper to the human intellect to know a form existing individually in corporeal matter, but not as existing in this individual matter. But to know what is in individual matter, yet not as existing in such matter, is to abstract the form from individual matter, which is represented by the sensible likenesses. Therefore it must be said that our intellect understands material things by abstracting from such likenesses; and that through material things thus considered we attain to some knowledge of immaterial things, just as, on the contrary, angels know material things through the immaterial.

But Plato, considering only the immateriality of the human intellect, and not that it is somehow united to the body, held that the objects of the intellect are separate Ideas, and that we understand, not by abstraction, but rather (as Aristotle points out) by participating in abstractions, as was noted above.[7]

Reply Objection 1. Abstraction may occur in two ways. *First,* by way of composition and division, as when we understand one thing not to be

---

3. *op. cit.,* III, 7(431b2).
4. *op. cit.,* III, 4(429b21).
5. Question LXXXIV, article 7.
6. Question LXXVI, article 1.
7. Question LXXXIV, article 1.

in another, or to be separate from it. *Secondly,* by way of a simple and absolute consideration, as when we understand one thing alone, without considering anything pertaining to something else. Thus, for the intellect to abstract one from another things which are not really abstract from one another, does, in the first mode of abstraction, imply falsehood. But, in the second mode of abstraction, for the intellect to abstract things which are not really abstract from one another, does not involve falsehood, as clearly appears in the case of the senses. For if we thought or said that color is not in a colored body, or that it is separate from it, there would be error in what we thought or said. But if we consider color and its properties, without reference to the apple which is colored, or if we express in word what we thus understand, there is no error in such an opinion or assertion; for apple is not essential to color, and therefore color can be understood independently of apple. In like manner, I say that the things which belong to the specific nature of a material thing, such as a stone, or a man, or a horse, can be thought without the individual factors, which do not belong to it. This is what is meant by abstracting the universal from the particular, or the intelligible form from the sense representation, viz., the consideration of the nature of the species apart from the individual factors involved, which are represented by sensible likenesses. If, therefore, the intellect is said to be "false" when it understands a thing otherwise than as it is, that is so if the word "otherwise" refers to the thing understood; for there is falsity in the intellect when a thing is understood to be otherwise than as it is. Such would be the case if the intellect abstracted the specific nature of a stone from its matter in such a way as to think that it did not exist in matter, as Plato held.[8] But it is not so if the word "otherwise" be taken to refer to the one who understands. For it is true that the way the knower exists in knowing is not the same as the way in which a thing exists in its own being: the thing known as immaterially in the knower, in a manner appropriate to intellect, and not materially, after the fashion of a material thing.

Reply Objection 2. Some have thought that the specific essence of a natural thing is a form only, and that matter is not part of the specific essence. If that were so, matter would not enter into the definition of natural things. Therefore it must be said against this that matter is twofold, *common* and *signate,* or individual: common, such as flesh and bone; individual, such as this flesh and these bones. The intellect therefore abstracts the specific essence of a natural thing from the individual sensible matter, but not from the common sensible matter. Thus, as is said,[9] it abstracts the specific essence of *man* from *this flesh* and *these bones,* which do not belong to the essence as such, but to the individual,

---

8. See above, question LXXXIV, article 4.
9. Aristotle, *Metaphysics* VI, 10(1035b28).

and hence need not be considered in the essence. But the specific essence of man cannot be abstracted by the intellect from *flesh* and *bones*.[10]

Mathematical essences, however, can be abstracted by the intellect not only from individual sensible matter, but also from common sensible matter. But they cannot be abstracted from common intelligible matter, but only from individual intelligible matter. For sensible matter is corporeal matter as subject to sensible qualities, such as being cold or hot, hard or soft, and the like; while intelligible matter is substance as subject to quantity. Now it is manifest that quantity has a prior being in substance to that of sensible qualities. Hence quantities, such as number, dimension, and figures, which are the terminations of quantity, can be considered apart from sensible qualities; and this is to abstract them from sensible matter. But they cannot be considered apart from the concept of substance as subject to quantity; for that would be to abstract them from common intelligible matter. Yet they can be considered apart from this or that substance; and this is to abstract them from individual intelligible matter.

There are some things, however, which can be abstracted even from common intelligible matter. Such are being, unity, potency, act, and the like—all of which can exist without matter, as is evident in the case of immaterial substances. And because Plato failed to consider the twofold kind of abstraction, as above explained,[11] he held that all those things which we have stated to be abstracted by the intellect are abstract in reality.

Reply Objection 3. Colors, as being in individual corporeal matter, have the same mode of existence as the power of sight; and therefore they can impress their own image on the eye. But phantasms, since they are likenesses of individuals, and exist in corporeal organs, have not the same mode of being as the human intellect, as is clear from what has just been said, and therefore they have not the power of themselves to cause an impression upon the possible intellect. But through the power of the agent intellect, there results in the possible intellect a certain likeness produced by the turning of the agent intellect toward the phantasms. This likeness represents what is in the phantasms, but only as to the nature of the species. It is thus that the intelligible species is said to be abstracted from the phantasms; not that the identical form which previously was in the phantasms is subsequently in the possible intellect, as a body transferred from one place to another.

Reply Objection 4. Not only does the agent intellect illumine phantasms, but also by its power intelligible species are abstracted from sensible likenesses. It illumines the latter because, just as the soul's sensory part acquires a greater power through its conjunction with the intellect,

---

10. i.e., man is *specifically* endowed with an organic, living body of a certain *type*.
11. Question LXXXIV, article 1.

so through the power of the agent intellect sense representations are made more fit for the abstraction of intelligible notions from them. Now the agent intellect abstracts intelligible species from sense representations, in that through its power we are enabled to take into our consideration specific natures apart from individual conditions. It is in accord with the likenesses of such natures that the possible intellect is informed.

Reply Objection 5. Our intellect both abstracts the intelligible essences *from* phantasms, in that it considers the natures of things universally, and yet it grasps these natures *in* the sense representations. For it cannot understand the things whose essences it abstracts without turning to sense representations, as was said above.[12]

Second Article

ARE THE INTELLIGIBLE FORMS [13]

ABSTRACTED FROM SENSE REPRESENTATIONS RELATED

TO OUR INTELLECT AS THAT WHICH IS UNDERSTOOD?

Objection 1. It seems that the intelligible forms abstracted from sense representations are related to our intellect as that which is understood. For that which is actually being understood is in the one understanding, because the former *is* the intellect itself in act of understanding. But nothing of what is understood is in the actually understanding intellect except the abstracted intelligible form. Therefore this form is what is actually understood.

Objection 2. Moreover, what is actually known must be in something; otherwise it would be nothing. But it is not in something outside the soul; for, since what is outside the soul is material, nothing therein can be actually known. Therefore what is actually known is in the intellect. Consequently it can be nothing else than the aforesaid intelligible form.

Objection 3. Again, the Philosopher says that "words are signs of the passions in the soul." [14] But words signify the things known, for we express by word what we understand. Therefore these "passions of the soul," viz., the intelligible forms, are what is actually known.

On the contrary: The intelligible form is to the intellect what the sensible form is to the sense. But the sensible form is not what is perceived, but rather that by which the sense perceives. Therefore the intelligible form is not *what* is actually known, but that *by which* the intellect knows.

I answer that: Some have asserted that our powers of knowing attain

---

12. Question LXXXIV, article 7.
13. Literally, "intelligible species."
14. *On Interpretation (Perih.),* I, 1(16a3).

only the impressions made on them; e.g., that sense is cognizant only of the impression made on its own organ. According to this theory, the intellect grasps only its own impression, viz., the intelligible form received in it, and its knowing is in terms of this form.

This opinion, however, is manifestly false for two reasons. *First*, because the things we know are also the objects of science. Therefore, if what we know is merely the intelligible form in the soul, it would follow that every science would be concerned, not with things outside the soul, but only with the intelligible forms within the soul; just as, according to the Platonists, all sciences are about Ideas, which they held to be that which is actually known. *Secondly*, it is untrue, because it would lead to the error of the ancient natural philosophers who maintained that "whatever seems, is true," [15] and that consequently contradictories are true simultaneously. For if a power knows only its own impressions, it can judge only of them. Now a thing *seems* according to the impression made on the cognitive power. Consequently the cognitive power will always judge of its own impression as such; and so every judgment will be true. Thus, if taste perceived only its own impression, when anyone with a healthy taste perceives that honey is sweet, he would judge truly, and if anyone with an unhealthy taste perceives that honey is bitter, this would be equally true: for each would judge according to the impression on his taste. So that every opinion—indeed, every sort of apprehension—would be equally true.

It must therefore be said that the intelligible form is related to the intellect as that *by which* it knows. Which is proved thus. Now, as it is said,[16] action is twofold: *one* which remains in the agent (e.g., seeing and knowing), and another which passes into an external object (e.g., heating and cutting).[17] Each of these actions proceeds in virtue of some form. And just as the form from which proceeds an act tending to something external is the likeness of the object of the action, as heat in the heater is a likeness of the thing heated, so the form from which proceeds an action remaining in the agent is a likeness of the object. Hence that by which the sight sees is the likeness of the visible thing; and the likeness of the thing known, i.e., intelligible form, is the form by which the intellect knows. But since the intellect reflects upon itself, by such reflection it knows both its own act of knowing, and the form by which it knows. Thus the intelligible form is secondarily that which is known; but that which is primarily known is the thing of which that form is the likeness.

This also appears from the opinion of the ancient philosophers of

---

15. cf. Aristotle, *Metaphysics* III, 5(1009a8).
16. *op. cit.,* VIII, 8(1050a23).
17. Hence these are called, respectively, "immanent" and "transitive."

nature who held that "like is known by like." [18] For they supposed that the soul knows the earth outside itself by the earth within itself; and so of other things. If, therefore, we take the intelligible form of the earth instead of the earth itself, in accord with Aristotle who says that "a stone is not in the soul, but only the likeness of the stone," [19] it follows that by means of its intelligible form the soul knows the things which are outside it.

Reply Objection 1. The thing known is in the knower by its own likeness. It is in this sense that we say that the thing actually being known is the intellect in act, because the likeness of the thing understood is the form of the intellect, just as the likeness of a sensible thing is the form of the sense actually sensing. Hence it does not follow that the abstracted intelligible form is what is actually known; but rather that it is the likeness thereof.

Reply Objection 2. This expression, "the thing actually known," has a double meaning: (1) the thing which is known, and (2) the fact that it is known. Similarly, the words, "abstract universal," mean two things: (1) the nature of a thing, and (2) its abstraction or universality. Therefore the nature itself which is subject to being understood, or to being abstracted, or the intention of universality, exists only in individuals; but that it is understood, abstracted, or considered as universal, is in the intellect. We see something similar to this in the senses. For sight perceives the color of the apple apart from its smell. If therefore it be asked where is the color which is seen apart from the small, it is clear that the color which is seen is only in the apple; but that it be perceived apart from the smell is owed to the sense of sight, in that sight receives the likeness of color and not of smell. In like manner, the human nature which is understood exists only in this or that man. But that human nature be apprehended without the conditions of individuality, i.e, that it be abstracted and consequently considered as universal, is due to its being perceived by the intellect, in which there is a likeness of the specific nature, but not of the individual principles.

Reply Objection 3. There are two operations in the sensory part of the soul. *One* is limited to impressing, and thus the operation of the senses takes place when the senses are impressed by sensible things. The *other* is formation, according to which the imagination forms for itself an image of an absent thing, or even of something never seen. Both of these operations are found in the intellect. For first there is the impression of the possible intellect through its being informed by the intelligible form. Then the possible intellect, as thus informed, fashions a definition, or a division, or a composition, which is expressed by language. And so, the

18. cf. Aristotle, *On the Soul* I, 5(409b26).
19. *op. cit.*, III, 8(431b29).

notion signified by a term is a definition; and a proposition signifies the intellect's division or composition. Words do not therefore signify the intelligible forms themselves; but that which the intellect fashions for itself for the purpose of judging of external things.

Third Article

IS THE MORE UNIVERSAL

PRIMARY IN OUR INTELLECTUAL COGNITION?

Objection 1. It seems that the more universal is not primary in our intellectual cognition. For what is primary and more known in its own nature is secondarily and less known in relation to ourselves. But universals come first as regards their nature, because that is prior which does not imply the existence of its consequent.[20] Therefore universals are secondarily known by our intellect.

Objection 2. Moreover, the composite precedes the simple in relation to us. But universals are the more simple. Therefore they are known secondarily by us.

Objection 3. Again, the Philosopher says that "the object defined comes in our knowledge before the parts of its definition." [21] But the more universal is part of the definition of the less universal, as "animal" is part of the definition of "man." Therefore universals are secondarily known by us.

Objection 4. And again, we come to a knowledge of causes and principles through their effects. But universals are principles. Therefore universals are secondarily known by us.

On the contrary: There is the dictum that "we must proceed from the universal to the singular." [22]

I answer that: In our knowledge there are two things to be considered. *First,* that intellectual knowledge in some measure arises from sense knowledge. Now because sense has singular and individual things for its object, and intellect has the universal for its object, it follows necessarily that our knowledge of the former precedes our knowledge of the latter. *Secondly,* we must consider that our intellect proceeds from a state of potency to a state of act and that every power thus proceeding from potency to act attains first to an incomplete actuation, intermediate between potency and act, before attaining to perfect actuation. The perfect actuation of the intellect is complete knowledge, when the object

20. cf. Aristotle, *Categories* XII, 14a30; e.g., one is prior to two; for if there are two, there must be one. But not conversely.

21. *Physics* I, 1(184b11).

22. *ibid.,* (184a23).

is distinctly and determinately known; whereas the incomplete actuation is imperfect knowledge, when the object is known indistinctly, in a certain *con-fused mode*.[23] A thing thus imperfectly known is known partly in act and partly in potency. That is why the Philosopher says: "What is manifest and certain is known to us at first confusedly; afterwards we know it by distinguishing its principles and elements." [24] Now it is evident that to know something that comprises many things, without a proper knowledge of each thing contained in it, is to know that thing *confusedly*. In this way we can have knowledge not only of the universal whole, which contains parts potentially, but also of the integral whole; for each whole can be known con-fusedly, without its parts being known distinctly. But to know distinctly what is contained in the universal whole it to know the less common; e.g., to know animal indistinctly is to know it as animal, whereas to know animal distinctly is to know it as rational or irrational animal, i.e., to know a man or a lion. So in our intellect the concept of animal is prior to that of man; and the same holds true in comparing any more universal concept with the less universal.

Moreover, as sense, like intellect, proceeds from potency to act, the same order of cognition applies to the senses. For by sense we judge of the more common before the less common, in reference both to place and time. In reference to place, when a thing is perceived afar off it is seen to be a body before it is seen to be an animal, and to be an animal before it is seen to be a man, and to be a man before it is seen to be Socrates or Plato. The same is true as regards time; a child distinguishes man from not-man before he distinguishes this man from that, and that is why it is said that "children at first call all men fathers, and later on distinguish each one from the others." [25] The reason for this is clear: he who knows a thing indistinctly is in a state of potency as regards its principle of distinction; just as he who knows the genus is in a state of potency as regards knowledge of the difference. Thus it is evident that indistinct knowledge is midway between potency and act.

It must therefore be said that knowledge of the singular and individual is prior, as regards us, to the knowledge of the universal, just as sense knowledge is prior to intellectual knowledge. But in both sense and intellect the knowledge of the more common precedes the knowledge of the less common.

Reply Objection 1. The *universal* can be considered in two ways. *First,* the universal nature may be considered together with the form[26] of

---

23. i.e., indeterminately: this *"con-fusion,"* then, is purely formal or intellectual, not psychological in the modern sense.

24. *ibid.* (184a21).

25. *ibid.* (184b12).

26. Literally, "intention"; i.e., the mental form, or formal concept.

universality. And since the form of universality—viz., the relation of one and the same to many—is due to intellectual abstraction, the universal thus considered is subsequent in our knowledge. Hence the dictum: "the universal animal is either nothing or something subsequent." [27] But according to Plato, who held that universals are subsistent, the universal would be prior to the particular, for to him the latter are mere participations in the subsistent universals, which he called "Ideas."

Secondly, the universal can be considered according to the nature itself (e.g., the nature of animality or humanity) as existing in the individual. Hence we must distinguish two orders of nature: *one,* by way of generation and time; and thus the imperfect and the potential are prior. In this way the more common is prior in the order of nature. This appears clearly in the engendering of man and animal; for "the animal is generated before man," as is said.[28] The *other order* is that of perfection or of the intention of nature. In this order, act considered in itself is naturally prior to potency, and the perfect to the imperfect; and thus the less common is naturally prior to the more common, as man to animal. For the intention of nature does not stop at the engendering of animal, but aims at the engendering of man.

Reply Objection 2. The more common universal is compared to the less common as a whole, and as a part. As a whole, in that under the more universal there is potentially contained not only the less universal, but also other things; as under *animal* is contained not only *man* but also *horse.* As a part, in that the less common universal contains in its notion not only the more common, but also other factors; as *man* contains not only *animal* but also *rational.* So it is that *animal* considered in itself is in our knowledge prior to *man;* but *man* is prior to *animal* considered as a part of the notion of man.

Reply Objection 3. A part can be known in two ways. *First,* absolutely, as it is in itself; and thus nothing prevents the parts from being known before the whole, as stones are known before a house is known. *Secondly,* as belonging to a certain whole; and thus we must know the whole before its parts. For we know a house in a certain con-fused manner before we know its different parts. So, likewise, that which defines is as such known before the thing defined is known; otherwise the thing defined would not be made known by the definition; and yet as parts of the definition they are known after. For we know man confusedly as man before we know how to distinguish all that belongs to human nature.

Reply Objection 4. The universal, considered under the form of universality, is, in a certain manner, a principle of knowledge, in so far as the form of universality follows upon the mode of understanding, which is by way of abstraction. But that which is a principle of knowledge need

27. Aristotle, *On the Soul* I, 1(402b7).
28. Aristotle, *On the Generation of Animals* II, 3(736b2).

not be a principle of being, as Plato thought, since at times we know a cause through its effect, and the substance through accidents. Therefore the universal thus considered is for Aristotle neither a principle of being, nor a substance, as he makes clear.[29] But if we consider the generic or specific nature itself as existing in the singular, then in a way it has the character of a formal principle in regard to singulars; for it is matter which accounts for the singular, whereas the nature of the species is derived from the form. But the generic nature is compared to the specific nature rather in the manner of a material principle, because the generic nature is taken from that which is material in a thing, while the nature of the species is taken from that which is formal. Thus the notion of animal is taken from the sensory factor, whereas the notion of man is taken from the intellectual factor. So it is that the ultimate intention of nature is toward the species, and not the individual, nor the genus; because the form is the end of the genetic process, while matter is for the sake of the form. Neither need the cognition of any cause or principle be posterior in regard to us, since through sensible causes we sometimes acquire knowledge of unknown effects, and sometimes conversely.

Fourth Article

CAN WE UNDERSTAND MANY THINGS SIMULTANEOUSLY?

Objection 1. It seems that we can understand many things simultaneously. For intellect is above time, whereas the succession of *before* and *after* belongs to time. Therefore the intellect does not understand different things in succession, but at the same time.

Objection 2. Moreover, there is nothing to prevent forms not opposed to each other from actually being in the same subject, as color and smell in the apple. But intelligible forms are not opposed to each other. Therefore there is nothing to prevent the same intellect from being in act as regards different intelligible forms. Thus it can understand many things at the same time.

Objection 3. Again, the intellect understands some wholes simultaneously, such as a man or a house. But every whole contains many parts. Therefore the intellect understands many things at the same time.

Objection 4. And again, it is impossible to know the difference between two things unless both be known at the same time, as it is said.[30] and the same applies in any similar case. But our intellect knows the difference between one thing and another. Therefore it knows many things simultaneously.

---

29. *Metaphysics* VI, 13(1038b8).
30. Aristotle, *On the Soul* III, 2(426b22).

On the contrary: There is the dictum: "Understanding is of one thing only, science is of many." [31]

I answer that: The intellect can, indeed, understand many things as one, but not as many, that is to say, through one but not through many intelligible forms. For the mode of every action follows upon the form which is the source of that action. Therefore whatever things the intellect can understand under one intelligible form, it can understand together. So it is that God sees all things simultaneously, because He sees all in one, i.e., in His essence. But whatever things the intellect understands under different intelligible forms, it does not understand simultaneously. The reason for this is that it is impossible for one and the same subject to be perfected at the same time by many forms of one genus and diverse species, just as it is impossible for one and the same body at the same time and in the same respect to have different colors or different shapes. Now all intelligible forms belong to one genus, because they are the perfections of one intellectual power even though the things which the forms represent belong to different genera. Therefore it is impossible for one and the same intellect to be perfected at the same time by different intelligible forms so as actually to understand different things.

Reply Objection 1. The intellect is above that time which is the measure of the movement of corporeal things. But the multitude itself of intelligible forms causes a certain succession of intelligible operations, according as one operation is prior to another. And this succession is called "time" by Augustine, who says that "God moves the spiritual creature through time." [32]

Reply Objection 2. Not only is it impossible for opposite forms to exist at the same time in the same subject, but neither can any forms belonging to the same genus, although they be not opposed to one another, as is clear from the example of colors and shapes.

Reply Objection 3. Parts can be understood in two ways. *First,* in a con-fused way, as existing in the whole; and thus they are known through the one form of the whole, and so are grasped simultaneously. *In another way,* they are known distinctly; and thus each is known through its specific form, and hence they are not grasped simultaneously.

Reply Objection 4. When the intellect grasps the difference or comparison between one thing and another, it knows both under the aspect of their difference or comparison; just as it knows the parts under the whole, as was said above.

---

31. Aristotle, *Topics* II, 10(114b34).
32. *A Literal Commentary on "Genesis"* VIII, 20; 22.

Fifth Article

DOES OUR INTELLECT UNDERSTAND BY SYNTHESIS AND ANALYSIS? [33]

Objection 1. It seems that our intellect does not understand by synthesis and analysis. For these deal only with a multiplicity, whereas the intellect cannot apprehend many things simultaneously. Therefore it cannot understand by synthesis and analysis.

Objection 2. Moreover, every synthesis and analysis implies past, present, or future time. But the intellect abstracts from time, as well as from other particular conditions. Therefore the intellect does not understand by synthesis and analysis.

Objection 3. Again, the intellect understands things by an assimilation to them. But synthesis and analysis are not in things; for nothing is in things except the reality which is signified by the predicate and the subject, and which is one and the same reality, provided that the composition be true. (Thus man is truly what animal is.) Therefore the intellect does not act by synthesis and analysis.

On the contrary: Words signify conceptions of the intellect, as the Philosopher says.[34] But in language there is synthesis and analysis, as we see in affirmative and negative propositions. Therefore the intellect acts by synthesis and analysis.

I answer that: The human intellect must of necessity understand by synthesis and analysis. For since the intellect passes from potency to act, it has a likeness to generated things, which do not attain to perfection all at once but acquire it by degrees. In the same way, the human intellect does not acquire full knowledge of a thing in its initial act of knowing; but it first apprehends something of the thing, such as its quiddity, which is the primary and proper object of the intellect; and then proceeds to a knowledge of properties, accidents, and various factors affecting the thing's essence. Thus it necessarily relates one thing with another by synthesis or analysis; and from one synthesis and analysis it necessarily proceeds to another, and this is reasoning

But the angelic and the divine intellects, like all imperishable realities, have their perfection at once from the beginning. Hence the angelic and the divine intellect have the entire knowledge of a thing at once and perfectly; so that, in knowing the quiddity of a thing, they know at once whatever we can know by synthesis, analysis, and reasoning. So it is that the human intellect knows by synthesis, analysis, and reasoning. But the divine and the angelic intellects indeed have a knowledge of these intel-

---

33. Literally, "composing" and "dividing."
34. *On Interpretation (Perih.)* I, 1(16a3).

lectual processes, not by the processes themselves, but through immediately grasping the simple essence.

Reply Objection 1. Synthesis and analysis of the intellect are made by differentiating and comparing. Hence the intellect knows many things through synthesizing and analyzing, by knowing the difference and comparison of things.

Reply Objection 2. Although the intellect abstracts from sense representations, it does not understand actually without turning to them, as has been said.[35] And in so far as it does this, time is obviously involved in the processes of synthesis and analysis.

Reply Objection 3. The likeness of a thing is received into the intellect according to the intellect's own mode of being, not according to that of the thing. Hence, although something on the part of the thing corresponds to the intellect's synthesis [*compositio*] and analysis, it does not however exist in the same way in the intellect and in the thing. For the proper object of the human intellect is the quiddity of a material thing, which is apprehended by the senses and the imagination. Now in a material thing there is a twofold synthesis. *First,* there is the synthesis of form with matter. To this corresponds that synthesizing[36] of the intellect whereby the universal whole is predicated of its part: for the genus is derived from common matter, while the difference that completes the species is derived from the form, and the particular from individual matter. *The second synthesis* is of accident with subject; and to this corresponds that synthesizing of the intellect whereby accident is predicated of subject, as when we say "the man is white." Nevertheless, the synthesizing [*compositio*] found in the intellect differs from that in things. For the components in the thing are diverse, whereas the intellectual synthesis is a sign of the identity of the things synthesized. Thus the above instance of intellectual synthesis was not such as to assert that "man is whiteness"; rather, the assertion, "the man is white," means that "the man is something having whiteness." In other words, man is identical in subject with the being having whiteness. It is the same with the synthesis of form and matter. For "animal" signifies that which has a sensory nature; "rational," that which has an intellectual nature; "man," that which has both; and "Socrates," that which has all these things, together with individual matter. And so, according to this kind of identity our intellect synthesizes one thing with another by means of predication.

---

35. Article 1; Question LXXX 14, article 7.
36. Literally, "composition."

Sixth Article

CAN THE INTELLECT BE SUBJECT TO FALSITY?

Objection 1. It seems that intellect can be subject to falsity, for the Philosopher says that "truth and falsity are in the mind." [37] But the mind and intellect are the same, as was said above.[38] Therefore falsity may be in the intellect.

Objection 2. Moreover, opinion and reasoning belong to the intellect. But falsehood exists in both. Therefore falsity can be in the intellect.

Objection 3. Again, sin is in the intellectual part. But sin involves falsity, for "those err that work evil" (*Proverbs 14:22*). Therefore falsity can be in the intellect.

On the contrary: Augustine says that "everyone who is deceived, does not rightly understand that wherein he is deceived." [39] And the Philosopher says that "the intellect is always true." [40]

I answer that: The Philosopher compares intellect with sense on this point. For the sense faculty is not deceived in its proper object (as sight in regard to color), except accidentally, through some hindrance to the sensible organ. Thus, the taste of a fever-stricken person judges a sweet thing to be bitter, because his tongue is vitiated by ill humors. The sense faculty, however, may be deceived as regards common sensible objects, such as size or figure; as when it judges the sun to be only a foot in diameter, whereas in reality it exceeds the earth in size. Much more is the sense faculty deceived concerning accidental sensible objects; as when it judges that vinegar is honey because the color is similar. The reason for this is evident. Every power, as such, is essentially directed to its proper object; and things of this kind are always uniform. Hence, so long as the power exists, its judgment concerning its own proper object does not fail. Now the proper object of the intellect is the quiddity in a thing. Hence, properly speaking, the intellect is not in error concerning this quiddity; whereas it may go astray as regards the accompaniments of the essence or quiddity in a thing, either in referring one thing to another, in what concerns synthesis or analysis, or also in the process of reasoning. That is why it is also true that the intellect cannot err in regard to those propositions which are understood as soon as their terms are understood. Such is the case with first principles, from which there also arises infallible truth in the certitude of scientific knowledge with respect to conclusions.

The intellect, however, may be accidentally deceived in the quiddity

---

37. *Metaphysics* V, 4(1027b27).
38. Question LXXIX, article 1.
39. *Book of Eighty-Three Questions,* question 32.
40. *On the Soul* III, 10(433a26).

of composite things, not by the defect of its organ, for the intellect is not a power which makes use of an organ, but on the part of the intellectual synthesis involved in definition. This may happen, for instance, when the definition of a thing is false in relation to something else, as the definition of a circle attributed to a triangle; or when a definition is false in itself as involving the composition of things incompatible, such as the definition of anything as a "rational winged animal." Hence as regards simple things, in whose definitions there is no composition, we cannot be deceived; but if we fail, we fail completely in understanding them, as it is said.[41]

Reply Objection 1. Falsity is said to be "in the mind" as regards the act of judgment by which it affirms and denies.[42] The same answer applies to the second objection concerning opinion and reasoning; as well as to the third objection, concerning the error of the sinner, who errs in the practical judgment of the appetible object. But in the absolute[43] consideration of the quiddity of a thing, and of those factors which are known thereby, the intellect is never deceived. In this sense are to be understood the authorities quoted in proof of the opposite conclusions.

Seventh Article

CAN ONE PERSON UNDERSTAND ONE AND

THE SAME THING BETTER THAN ANOTHER PERSON?

Objection 1. It seems that one person cannot understand one and the same thing better than another can. For Augustine says: "Whoever understands a thing otherwise than as it is, does not understand it at all. Hence it is clear that there is a perfect understanding, than which none other is more perfect; and therefore there are not infinite degrees of understanding a thing, nor can one person understand a thing better than another can." [44]

Objection 2. Moreover, the intellect is true in its act of understanding. But truth, being a certain equality between thought and thing, is not subject to *more* or *less;* for a thing cannot be said to be "more or less" equal. Therefore a thing cannot be *more* or *less* understood.

Objection 3. Again, the intellect is that which most pertains to the form in man. But different forms cause different species. Therefore if one man understands better than another, it would seem that they do not belong to the same species.

---

41. Aristotle, *Metaphysics* VIII, 10(1052a1).
42. Literally: "according to composition and division."
43. i.e., pure and simple.
44. *Book of Eighty-Three Questions,* question 32.

On the contrary: Experience shows that some understand more pro-
foundly than do others; as one who carries a conclusion to its first principles and ultimate causes understands it better than the one who reduces
it only to its proximate causes.

I answer that: To say that a thing is understood "more" by one than
by another may be taken in two senses. *First,* so that the word "more"
be taken as determining the act of understanding as regards the thing
understood; and thus, one cannot understand the same thing *more* than
another, because to understand it otherwise than as it is, either better
or worse, would be to be deceived rather than to understand, as Augustine
argues. *In another sense,* the word "more" can be taken as determining
the act of understanding on the part of the one who understands. In this
way, one may understand the same thing better than someone else,
through having a greater power of understanding; just as a man may see
a thing better with his bodily sight, whose power is greater, and whose
sight is more perfect. The same applies to the intellect in two ways.
First, as regards the intellect itself, which is more perfect. For it is plain
that the better the disposition of a body, the better the soul allotted to it;
which clearly appears in things of different species. The reason for this
is that act and form are received into matter according to the capacity
of matter; and thus because some men have bodies of better disposition,
their souls have a greater power of understanding. Hence it is said that
"those who have soft flesh are of apt mind." [45] Secondly, this occurs in
regard to the lower powers which the intellect needs for its operation; for
those in whom the imaginative, cogitative, and memorative powers are
in better condition, are more apt for understanding.

The reply to the *first* objection is clear from the above; and likewise
the reply to the *second,* for truth in the intellect consists in its understanding a thing as it is.

Reply Objection 3. The difference of form, which is due only to the
different disposition of matter, does not cause a specific but only a nu-
merical difference: for different individuals have different forms, diversified according to the diversity of matter.

Eighth Article

DOES THE INTELLECT UNDERSTAND

THE INDIVISIBLE BEFORE THE DIVISIBLE?

Objection 1. It seems that the intellect understands the indivisible before the divisible. For the Philosopher says that "we understand and
know from the knowledge of principles and elements." [46] But indivisibles

---

45. Aristotle, *On the Soul* II, 9(421a25).
46. *Physics* I, 1(184a12).

are the principles and elements of divisible things. Therefore the indivisible is known to us before the divisible.

Objection 2. Moreover, the definition of a thing contains what is known antecedently, for a definition "proceeds from the first and more known," as it is said.[47] But the indivisible is included in the definition of the divisible, as a point in the definition of a line; for, as Euclid says,[48] "a line is length without breadth, the extremities of which are two points." So, too, unity comes into the definition of number, for "number," as it is said "is multitude measured by one." [49] Therefore our intellect understands the indivisible before the divisible.

Objection 3. Again, like is known by like. But the indivisible is more like the intellect than is the divisible, because "the intellect is simple," as it is said.[50] Therefore our intellect first knows the indivisible.

On the contrary: It is said that "the indivisible is made known as a privation." [51] But privation is known secondarily. Therefore so is the indivisible.

I answer that: The object of our intellect in its present state is the quiddity of a material thing, which it abstracts from sense representations, as was stated above.[52] And since that which is known first and of itself by our cognitive power is its proper object, we must consider its relationship to that quiddity in order to discover in what order the indivisible is known. Now the indivisible is threefold, as it is said.[53] *First,* the continuous is indivisible, since it is actually undivided, although potentially divisible. This indivisible is known to us before its division, which is a division into parts, because con-fused knowledge is prior to distinct knowledge, as was said above.[54] *Secondly,* there is the indivisible in species, as man's nature is something indivisible. This way, too, the indivisible is understood before its division into the parts of nature, as was also said there; and again before the intellect composes and divides by affirmation and negation. The reason of this priority is that both these kinds of indivisible are understood by the intellect of itself as its proper object. The *third* kind of indivisible is what is altogether indivisible, as a point and unity, which cannot be divided either actually or potentially. And this indivisible is known secondarily, through the privation of divisibility. Therefore a point is defined by way of privation "as that which has no parts"; and in like manner the notion of *one* is that it is *indivisible,*

---

47. Aristotle, *Topics* VI, 4(141a32).
48. *Elements,* Book I.
49. Aristotle, *Metaphysics* IX, 6(1057a3).
50. Aristotle, *On the Soul* III, 4(429a18; b23).
51. *op. cit.,* III, 6(430b21).
52. Question LXXXIV, article 7.
53. *op. cit.,* III, 6(430b6).
54. Article 3, ad 3.

as it is said.[55] And the reason for this posteriority is that this indivisible has a certain opposition to a corporeal being, the quiddity of which is the primary and proper object of the intellect.

But if our intellect understood by participation in certain separate indivisibles, as the Platonists maintained, it would follow that such an indivisible is prior in the understanding, for, according to the Platonists, the prior are first in being participated by things.

Reply Objection 1. In the acquisition of knowledge, principles and elements are not always first; for sometimes from sensible effects we arrive at the knowledge of principles and intelligible causes. But in perfect knowledge, the knowledge of effects always depends on the knowledge of principles and elements; for, as the Philosopher says in the same passage, "Then do we consider that we know, when we can resolve principles into their causes." [56]

Reply Objection 2. A point is not included in the definition of a line in general; for it is manifest that in a line of indefinite length, and also in a circular line, there is no point, except potentially. Euclid defines a straight line of definite length, and therefore he includes a point in the definition of the line, as the limit in the definition of that which is limited. Unity, however, is the measure of number; and thus it is included in the definition of a measured number, but it is not included in the definition of the divisible, but rather conversely.

Reply Objection 3. The likeness through which we understand is the form of the thing known in the knower. Hence a thing is prior in knowledge, not with respect to the likeness of its nature to the knowing power, but according to its agreement with the proper object of that power. Otherwise, sight would perceive hearing rather than color.

---

55. Aristotle, *Metaphysics* IX, 1(1052b16).
56. *Physics* I, 1(184a12).

What Our Intellect Knows in Material Things

(In Four Articles)

DOES OUR INTELLECT KNOW SINGULARS?

Objection 1. It seems that our intellect knows singulars. For whoever knows a composition, knows the terms of composition. But our intellect knows this composition: "Socrates is a man"; for the intellect can form a proposition to this effect. Therefore our intellect knows this singular, Socrates.

Objection 2. Moreover, the practical intellect directs to action. But action has relation to singular things. Therefore the intellect knows the singular.

Objection 3. Again, our intellect understands itself. But in itself it is a singular; otherwise it would have no action of its own; for actions have to do with singulars. Therefore our intellect knows the singular.

Objection 4. And again, a superior power can do whatever is done by an inferior power. But sense knows the singular. Much more, therefore, can the intellect know it.

On the contrary: There is the Philosopher's dictum: "the universal is known by reason, and the singular is known by sense." [1]

I answer that: Our intellect cannot know the singular in material things directly and primarily. The reason for this is that the principle of singularity in material things is individual matter; whereas our intellect, as was said above, understands by abstracting the intelligible forms from such matter. [2] Now what is abstracted from individual matter is universal. Hence our intellect knows directly only universals. Indirectly, however, and as it were by a kind of reflexion, it can know the singular, because, as was said above, [3] even after abstracting the intelligible form, the intellect, in order to understand actually, needs to turn to sense representations in which it grasps such forms, as is said. [4] Therefore it understands the universal directly through the intelligible form, and indirectly the

---

1. *Physics* I, 5(189a5).
2. Question LXXXV, article 1.
3. Question LXXXIV, article 7.
4. Aristotle, *On the Soul* III, 7(431b2).

singular represented by the sense images. And thus it forms the proposition, *Socrates is a man.*

Therefore the reply to the first objection is clear.

Reply Objection 2. The choice of a particular thing to be done is, as it is said, like the conclusion of a syllogism formed by the practical intellect.[5] But a singular proposition cannot be directly inferred from a universal proposition, except through the medium of a singular proposition. Therefore the universal reasoning power of the practical intellect does not operate except through the medium of the particular apprehension of the sensory part of the soul.

Reply Objection 3. Intelligibility is incompatible with the singular, not as such, but as material; for nothing is understood otherwise than immaterially. Therefore if there be an immaterial singular such as the intellect, there is no reason why it should not be intelligible.

Reply Objection 4. The higher power can do what the lower power can, but in a higher mode. And so, what the sense knows materially and concretely—and this is to grasp the singular directly—the intellect knows immaterially and in the abstract—and this is to know the universal.

Second Article

CAN OUR INTELLECT KNOW AN INFINITE NUMBER OF THINGS?

Objection 1. It seems that our intellect can know an infinite number of things. For God excels all infinite things. But our intellect can know God, as was said above.[6] Much more, therefore, can our intellect know all other infinite things.

Objection 2. Moreover, our intellect can naturally know genera and species. But there is an infinity of species of some genera, as of number, proportion and figure. Therefore our intellect can know an infinite number of things.

Objection 3. Again, if one body can coexist with another in the same place, there is nothing to prevent an infinite number of bodies being in one place. But one intelligible form can exist simultaneously with another in the same intellect, for many things can be habitually known at the same time. Therefore our intellect can have a habitual knowledge of an infinite number of things.

Objection 4. And again, since the intellect is not a corporeal power, as was said, it appears to be an infinite power.[7] But an infinite power has a capacity for an infinite number of things. Therefore our intellect can know an infinite number of things.

---

5. Aristotle, *Nichomachean Ethics* VII, 3(1147a28).
6. Question XII, article 1.
7. Question LXXVI, article 1.

On the contrary: It is said that the "infinite, considered as such, is unknown." [8]

I answer that: Since a power is proportioned to its object, the intellect must be related to the infinite in the same way as its object, which is the quiddity of a material thing. Now in material things the infinite does not exist actually, but only potentially, which is to say, successively, as it is noted.[9] Therefore infinity is potentially in our intellect through its considering successively one thing after another; because never does our intellect understand so many things that it cannot understand more.

On the other hand, our intellect cannot know the infinite either actually or habitually. Not actually, for our intellect can know actually at the same time only what it knows through one intelligible form. But the infinite is not represented by one intelligible form; since if it were it would be something whole and complete. Consequently it cannot be apprehended except by a successive consideration of one part after another, as is clear from its definition. For the infinite is "that from which, however much we may take, there always remains something to be taken." [10] Thus the infinite could not be known actually, unless all its parts were counted; which is impossible.

For the same reason we cannot have habitual knowledge of an infinite number of things: because our habitual knowledge results from actual consideration; since by understanding we become knowers, as it is said.[11] Hence it would not be possible for us to have a *habitus* of an infinity of things distinctly known unless we had already considered the entire infinity, enumerating them according to the succession of our knowledge; which is impossible. And so our intellect can not know an infinite number of things either actually or habitually, but only potentially, as was explained above.

Reply Objection 1. As was said above, God is called "infinite" because He is a form unlimited by matter;[12] whereas in material things the term "infinite" is applied to that which is deprived of any formal termination. And since form is known in itself, whereas matter cannot be known without form, hence it is that the material infinite is in itself unknown. But the formal infinite, God, is of Himself known; yet He is unknown to us because of the weakness of our intellect, which in its present state has a natural aptitude only for the knowledge of material things. That is why we cannot know God in our present life except through material effects. In the future life this defect of our intellect will be removed by the state of glory, when we shall be able to see the essence of God Himself, but not in a comprehensive mode.

---

8. Aristotle, *Physics* I, 4(187b7).

9. *op. cit.,* III, 6(204a20).

10. *ibid.,* (207a7).

11. Aristotle, *Nichomachean Ethics* I, 1(1103a33).

12. Question VII, article 1.

Reply Objection 2. It is the nature of our intellect to know *species* by abstraction from sense images; and therefore it cannot know either actually or habitually *species* of numbers or figures which have not been imagined—except perhaps in a generic way and in universal principles; and this is to know them potentially and indeterminately.

Reply Objection 3. If two or more bodies were in the same place, there would be no need for them to occupy the place successively, in order for the things placed to be enumerated according to this succession of occupation. On the other hand, intelligible forms enter our intellect successively, because a plurality of things cannot be actually apprehended simultaneously; and therefore there must be a definite and not an infinite number of forms in our intellect.

Reply Objection 4. In the way in which our intellect is infinite in power, so does it know the infinite. Now its power is infinite in that it is not terminated by corporeal matter. Moreover, it can know the universal, which is abstracted from individual matter, and which consequently is not limited to one individual, but, considered in itself, extends to an infinite number of individuals.

Third Article

CAN OUR INTELLECT KNOW CONTINGENT THINGS?

Objection 1. It seems that the intellect cannot know contingent things. For, as it is said, "the objects of understanding, wisdom and science are not contingent, but necessary things." [13]

Objection 2. Moreover, there is the dictum: "What sometimes is and sometimes is not, is measured by time." [14] Now the intellect abstracts from time, and from other material conditions. Therefore, since it is proper to a contingent thing sometime to be and sometime not to be, it seems that contingent things are not known by the intellect.

On the contrary: Every science is in the intellect. But some sciences are of contingent things, as the moral sciences, which consider human actions subject to free choice; and, again, the sciences of nature in as far as they consider things generable and corruptible. Therefore the intellect knows contingent things.

I answer that: Contingent things can be considered in two ways: either as contingent, or as containing some element of necessity. For every contingent thing has in it something necessary. For example, that Socrates runs is in itself contingent; but the relation of running to motion is necessary, for it is necessary that Socrates move if he runs. Now contingency arises from matter, for contingency is a potentiality to be or not

---

13. Aristotle, *Nichomachean Ethics* VI, 6(1040b31).
14. Aristotle, *Physics* IV, 12(221b29).

to be, and potentiality belongs to matter; whereas necessity results from form, because whatever is consequent on form is of necessity in the subject. But matter is the principle of individuation, whereas the universal comes from the abstraction of the form from particular matter. Moreover, it was said above that the intellect of itself and directly has the universal for its object;[15] while the object of sense is the singular, which in a certain way is the indirect object of the intellect, as was pointed out. Therefore the contingent, considered as such, is known directly by the sense and indirectly by the intellect; while the universal and necessary aspects of contingent things are known by the intellect. Hence if we consider knowable things in their universal intelligibilities, then all sciences are of necessary objects. But if we consider the things themselves, some sciences are thus of necessary things, some of contingent things.

From which the solution of the objections is clear.

Fourth Article

DOES OUR INTELLECT KNOW FUTURE THINGS?

Objection 1. It seems that our intellect knows future things. For it knows by means of intelligible forms, which abstract from the *here* and *now,* and are thus related indifferently to all time. But it can know present things. Therefore it can know future things.

Objection 2. Moreover, man, while his senses are in abeyance, can know some future things, as in sleep and in frenzy. But the intellect is more vigorous when freed from the senses. Therefore the intellect of its own nature can know future things.

Objection 3. Again, man's intellectual knowledge is superior to any knowledge in brutes. But some animals know certain future things; e.g., crows by their frequent cawing foretell rain. Therefore much more can the intellect know future things.

On the contrary: It is written (*Ecclesiastes 8:6,7*): "There is great affliction for man, because he is ignorant of things past; and things to come he cannot know by any messenger."

I answer that: We must apply the same distinction to future things as we applied above to contingent things. For future things considered as subject to time are singular, and the human intellect knows them by reflexion only, as was noted previously. But the reasons of future things can be universal; and thus they may enter the domain of the intellect and become the objects of scientific knowledge.

Speaking, however, of the knowledge of future things in a general way, it must be said that such things may be known in two ways: either in themselves, or in their causes. They cannot be known in themselves ex-

---

15. Article 1.

cept by God alone, to Whom even that is present which in the course of events is future, since from eternity His glance embraces the whole course of time, as was said above when treating of God's knowledge.[16] But in so far as they exist in their causes, future things can be known also by us. Now if the causes be such as to have a necessary connection with their future results, then the latter are known with scientific certitude, just as the astronomer foresees the future eclipse. If, however, the causes be such as to produce certain results more frequently than not, then the future can be known more or less conjecturally, according as the causes are more or less inclined to produce the effects.

Reply Objection 1. This argument holds of that knowledge which is drawn from universal causal reasons; from these the future may be known, according to the order of the effects to the cause.

Reply Objection 2. As Augustine says, the soul has a certain power of forecasting, so that by its nature it can know future things.[17] Thus the soul, when withdrawn from the bodily senses and, as it were, concentrated on itself, shares in the knowledge of things future. This opinion indeed would be reasonable if we were to admit that the soul receives knowledge by participating in the Ideas, as the Platonists maintained, because in that case the soul by its nature would know the universal causes of all effects, and would only be impeded in its knowledge by the body; and hence when withdrawn from the bodily senses it would know future things.

But since it is connatural to our intellect to know things, not thus, but by receiving its knowledge from the senses, it is not natural for the soul to know future things when withdrawn from the senses. Rather, it knows such things through the agency of higher spiritual and corporeal causes: of spiritual causes, when by divine power the human intellect is enlightened through the ministry of angels, and the sense images are referred to the knowledge of future events; or when the demons work on the imagination to foretell some future events known to them, as was noted above.[18] The soul is naturally more inclined to receive these impressions of spiritual causes when it is withdrawn from the senses, as it is then nearer to the world of spiritual substances and freer from external distractions. The knowledge of future things may also derive from higher corporeal causes. For it is clear that higher bodies influence lower bodies. Hence, since sense powers are the 'acts' of corporeal organs, the influence of the heavenly bodies causes the imagination to be affected; and so, as the heavenly bodies cause many future events, the imagination receives certain signs of some such events. These signs are perceived more at night and while we sleep than in the daytime while we are awake, for as it is

---

16. Question XIV, article 13.
17. *Confessions*, VII, 6.
18. Question LVII, article 3.

said, "impressions made by day are evanescent. The night air is calmer, when silence reigns; and hence bodily impressions are made in sleep, when slight internal movements are felt more than in wakefulness, and such movements produce in the imagination images from which the future may be foreseen." [19]

Reply Objection 3. Brute animals have no power above the imagination to regulate their images, as man has his reason, and therefore their imagination follows entirely the influence of the heavenly bodies. Thus from such animals' movements some future things, such as rain and the like, may be known rather than from human movements directed by reason. That is why the Philosopher says that "some who are most imprudent are most far-seeing; for their intelligence is not burdened with cares, but is as it were barren and bare of all anxiety, moving at the caprice of whatever is brought to bear on it." [20]

---

19. Aristotle, *On Divination* II (464a12)
20. *ibid.,* (464a18).

QUESTION LXXXVII

How the Intellectual Soul Knows Itself
and All That Is Within Itself

(In Four Articles)

First Article

DOES THE INTELLECTUAL SOUL

KNOW ITSELF BY ITS ESSENCE?

Objection 1. It seems that the intellectual soul knows itself by its own essence. For Augustine says; "the mind knows itself by itself, because it is incorporeal." [1]

Objection 2. Moreover, both angels and human souls belong to the genus of intellectual substance. But an angel understands himself by his own essence. Therefore so does the human soul.

Objection 3. Again, as it is said, "in things without matter, the intellect and that which is known are the same." [2] But the human mind is without matter, not being the act of a body, as was remarked above.[3] Therefore the intellect and its object are the same in the human mind; and therefore the human mind understands itself by its own essence.

On the contrary: It is said that the "intellect understands itself in the same way as it understands other things." [4] But it understands other things, not by their essence, but by their likenesses. Therefore it does not understand itself by its own essence.

I answer that: As it is pointed out, everything is knowable so far as it is in act, and not so far as it is in potency;[5] for a thing is a being, and is true, and therefore knowable, according as it is actual. This is evident as regards sensible things; for the eye does not see what is potentially, but what is actually, colored. In like manner, it is clear that the intellect, so far as it knows material things, does not know except what is in act. That is why it is said not to know primary matter except as related to

---

1. *On the Trinity* IX, 3.
2. Aristotle, *On the Soul* III, 4(430a3).
3. Question LXXV, article 2.
4. Aristotle, *op. cit.*, III, 4(430a2).
5. Aristotle, *Metaphysics* VIII, 9(1051a29).

163

form.[6] Consequently immaterial substances are intelligible by their own essence, according as each one is actual by its own essence.

So it is that the essence of God, the pure and perfect act, is absolutely and perfectly in itself intelligible; and hence God by His own essence knows Himself, and all other things also. The angelic essence belongs, indeed, to the genus of intelligible things as act, but not as pure act, nor as a complete act; and hence the angel's act of intelligence is not completed by his essence. For, although an angel understands himself by his own essence, still he cannot understand all other things by his own essence; he rather knows things other than himself by their likenesses. Now the human intellect is only potential in the genus of intelligible beings, just as primary matter is potential in the genus of sensible being; and hence it is called "possible." Therefore in its essence the human intellect is potentially understanding. Hence it has in itself the power to understand, but not to be understood, except as it is made actual. For even the Platonists asserted that an order of intelligible beings existed above the order of intellects, since the intellect understands only by participation in the intelligible. But that which participates is according to them below what it participates.

If, therefore, the human intellect, as the Platonists held, became actual by participating in separate intelligible Forms, it would understand itself by such a participation in incorporeal beings. But since in this life our intellect has material and sensible things for its proper object, as was stated above,[7] it understands itself according as it is made actual by the forms abstracted from sensible things, through the light of the agent intellect, which not only actualizes the intelligibles themselves, but also, by their instrumentality, actualizes the possible intellect. Therefore the intellect knows itself, not by its essence, but by its act. This happens in two ways: *In one way,* singularly, as when Socrates or Plato perceives that he has an intellectual soul because he perceives that he understands. *In another way,* universally, as when we consider the nature of the human mind from a knowledge of the intellectual act. It is true, however, that the judgment and power of this knowledge, by which we know the nature of the soul, is ours through the derivation of our intellectual light from the divine truth which contains the exemplars of all things, as was stated previously.[8] Hence Augustine says: "We gaze on the inviolable truth whence we can as perfectly as possible define, not what each man's mind is, but what it ought to be in the light of the eternal exemplars." [9] There is, however, a difference between these two kinds of knowledge, and it consists in this, that the mere presence of the mind suffices for the first; since

---

6. Aristotle, *Physics* I, 7(191a8).
7. Question LXXXIV, article 7.
8. Question LXXXIV, article 5.
9. *On the Trinity* IX, 6.

the mind itself is the principle of action whereby it perceives itself, and hence it is said to know itself by its own presence. But as regards the second kind of knowledge, the mere presence of the mind does not suffice, but there is further required a careful and subtle inquiry. That is why many are ignorant of the soul's nature, and many have erred about it. So Augustine says concerning such mental inquiry: "Let the mind strive not to see itself as if it were absent, but to discern itself as present"—i.e., to know how it differs from other things;[10] which is to know its quiddity and nature.

Reply Objection 1. The mind knows itself by means of itself, because at length it arrives at a knowledge of itself, though led thereto by its own act: because it is itself that it knows, since it loves itself, as Augustine says in the same passage. Now a thing can be called "self-evident" in two ways: either because we can know it by nothing else except itself, as first principles are called "self-evident"; or because it is not accidentally knowable, as color is visible of itself, whereas substance is visible accidentally.

Reply Objection 2. The essence of an angel is an actuality in the genus of intellectual things, and therefore it is both knower and thing known. Hence an angel apprehends his own essence through himself. Not so the human intellect, which is either altogether in potency to intelligible things, as is the possible intellect, or is the 'act' of the intelligible forms abstracted from sense images, as is the agent intellect.

Reply Objection 3. This saying of the Philosopher is universally true for every kind of intellect. For as the sense actually sensing is the sensible actually being sensed, by reason of the sensible likeness which is the form of the sense actually sensing, so likewise the intellect actually knowing is the object actually being known, by reason of the likeness of the thing known, which is the form of the intellect actually knowing. So the human intellect, which is actuated by the form of the thing known, is itself known by the same form as by its own. Now to say that in "things without matter the intellect and what is known are the same," is equal to saying that "as regards things actually being known the intellect and what is being known are the same." For a thing is actually known in that it is immaterial. But a distinction must be drawn, since the essences of some things are immaterial, as the separate substances called "angels," each of which is both knower and known; whereas there are other things whose essences are not without matter but only their abstract likenesses. Hence the Commentator says that the proposition quoted is true only of separate substances;[11] because in a sense it is verified in their regard, and not in regard to other substances, as was already stated.

---

10. *op. cit.,* X, 9.

11. Averroes, *On Aristotle's "On the Soul"* III, comm. 15(VI 169r). (Not available in English.)

Second Article

DOES OUR INTELLECT KNOW THE
HABITS OF THE SOUL BY THEIR ESSENCE?

Objection 1. It seems that our intellect knows the habits [*habitus*] of the soul by their essence. For Augustine says: "Faith is not seen in the heart wherein it abides in the same way as the soul of a man may be seen by another from the movement of the body; but we know most certainly that it is there, and conscience proclaims its existence." [12] The same applies to the other habits of the soul. Therefore the habits of the soul are not known by their acts, but by themselves.

Objection 2. Moreover, material things outside the soul are known because their likenesses are present in the soul, and are said therefore to be known by their likenesses. But the soul's habits are present by their essence in the soul. Therefore the habits of the soul are known by their essence.

Objection 3. Again, the cause of the formal perfection of each thing has that perfection in a higher degree. But habits and intelligible forms cause things to be known by the soul. Therefore they are still more known by the soul in themselves.

On the contrary: Habits, like powers, are the principles of acts. But, as it is said, "Acts and operations are logically prior to powers." [13] Therefore in the same way they are prior to habits; and so the latter, like the powers, are known by their acts.

I answer that: A habit is intermediate between pure potency and pure act. Now it has been said that nothing is known but as it is actual; and therefore so far as a habit falls short of being a perfect act, it falls short in being of itself knowable, and can be known only by its act. So anyone knows he has a habit from the fact that he can produce the act proper to that habit; or he may inquire into the nature and character of the habit by considering the act. The first kind of knowledge of the habit arises from its being present, for the very fact of its presence causes the act whereby it is known. The second kind of knowledge of the habit arises from a careful inquiry, as was explained above concerning the mind.[14]

Reply Objection 1. Although faith is not known by external movements of the body, it is perceived by the subject wherein it resides by the interior act of the heart. For no one knows that he has faith except because he knows that he believes.

Reply Objection 2. Habits are present in our intellect, not as its object (since in the present state of life our intellect's object is the nature of a

12. *On the Trinity* XIII, 1.
13. Aristotle, *On the Soul* II, 4(415a18).
14. Preceding article.

material thing, as was stated above),[15] but as that by which it understands.

Reply Objection 3. The axiom, "Whatever is the cause that a thing is such, is still more so," is true of things that are of the same order, e.g., those in the same causal genus. Thus we may say that health is desirable *because* of life, and therefore that life is more desirable still. But in regard to things of different orders, the axiom is not true. For we may say that health is caused by medicine, but it does not follow that medicine is more desirable than health, since health belongs to the order of final causes, whereas medicine belongs to the order of efficient causes. So to two things belonging essentially to the order of the objects of knowledge, the one which causes the other to be known will be the more known, as principles are more known than conclusions. But a habit as such does not belong to the order of objects of knowledge; nor are things known by reason of the habit as by reason of an object known, but rather as by reason of a disposition or form *whereby* the subject knows. Therefore the argument does not hold.

Third Article

DOES OUR INTELLECT KNOW ITS OWN ACT?

Objection 1. It seems that our intellect does not know its own act. For what is known is the object of the knowing power. But the act differs from the object. Therefore the intellect does not know its own act.

Objection 2. Moreover, whatever is known is known by some act. If, then, the intellect knows its own act, it knows it by some act, and again it knows that act by some other act. This is to proceed indefinitely—which seems impossible.

Objection 3. Again, the intellect has the same relation to its act as sense has to its act. But the proper sense does not perceive its own act, for this belongs to the common sense, as it is pointed out.[16] Therefore neither does the intellect understand its own act.

On the contrary: Augustine says: "I understand that I understand." [17]

I answer that: As was already remarked, a thing is known according as it is in act. Now the ultimate fulfillment of the intellect consists in its own operation. For this is not an act tending to something else in which lies the fulfillment of the work accomplished, as building is the fulfillment of the thing built; but it remains in the agent as its fulfillment and 'act,' as it is said.[18] Therefore the first thing concerning the intellect

---

15. Question LXXXIV, article 7, and elsewhere.
16. Aristotle, *On the Soul* III, 2(425b12).
17. *On the Trinity* X, 11.
18. Aristotle, *Metaphysics* VIII, 8(1050a36).

that is known is its own act of knowing. This occurs in different ways with different intellects. For there is an intellect, viz., the divine, which is its own act of knowing, so that in God the knowing of His knowing and the knowing of His essence are one and the same act, because His essence is His act of knowing. But there is another intellect, the angelic, which is not its own act of knowing, as was said above;[19] and yet the first object of that act is the angelic essence. Therefore, although there is a logical distinction between the act whereby the angel knows that he knows, and that whereby he knows his essence, yet he knows both by one and the same act; because to know his own essence is the proper fulfillment of his essence, and by one and the same act is a thing, together with its fulfillment, known. And there is yet another, viz., the human intellect, which is not its own act of knowing, nor is its own essence the first object of its act of knowing, for this object is the nature of a material thing. And therefore that which is first known by the human intellect is an object of this kind, and that which is known secondarily is the act by which that object is known; and through the act the intellect itself is known, whose fulfillment is the act itself of knowing. That is why the Philosopher said that objects are known before acts, and acts before powers.[20]

Reply Objection 1. The object of the intellect is something universal, viz., being and the true, under which the act of knowing is itself included. Therefore the intellect can know its own act; but not primarily, since the first object of our intellect, in this state of life, is not every being and everything true, but being and truth as found in material things, as was said above, from which it acquires knowledge of all other things.[21]

Reply Objection 2. The act of the human intellect is not the act and perfection of the nature understood, as if the nature of the material thing and the act of the intellect could be understood by one act; just as a thing and its perfection are understood by one act. Hence the act whereby the intellect understands a stone is distinct from the act whereby it understands that it understands a stone; and so on. Nor is it incongruous for the intellect to be infinite potentially, as was explained above.[22]

Reply Objection 3. The proper sense perceives by reason of the change effected in the material organ by the external sensible object. A material thing, however, cannot affect itself, but one is affected by another; and therefore the act of the proper essence is perceived by the common sense. The intellect, on the contrary, does not have understanding through the material alteration of an organ; and so there is no comparison.

---

19. Question LXXIX, article 1.
20. *On the Soul* II, 4(415a16).
21. Question LXXXIV, article 7.
22. Question LXXXVI, article 2.

Fourth Article

DOES THE INTELLECT UNDERSTAND THE ACT OF THE WILL?

Objection 1. It seems that the intellect does not understand the act of the will. For nothing is known by the intellect unless it be in some way present in the intellect. But the act of the will is not in the intellect, since the will and the intellect are distinct powers. Therefore the act of the will is not known by the intellect.

Objection 2. Moreover, the act is specified by the object. But the object of the will is not the same as the object of the intellect. Therefore the act of the will also is specifically distinct from the object of the intellect. Therefore the act of the will is not known by the intellect.

Objection 3. Augustine says of the soul's affections that "they are known neither by images, as bodies are known; nor by their presence, like the arts; but by certain notions." [23] Now it does not seem that there can be in the soul any other notions of things except either the essences of the things known or their likenesses. Therefore it seems impossible for the intellect to know the affections of the soul, which are the acts of the will.

On the contrary: Augustine says: "I understand that I will." [24]

I answer that: As was stated above, the act of the will is nothing but an inclination consequent on the form understood;[25] just as natural appetite is an inclination consequent on the natural form. Now the inclination of a thing resides in it according to its mode of being; and hence natural inclination resides in a natural thing naturally, and the inclination called the "sense appetite" is in the sentient being sensibly; and likewise the intellectual inclination, which is the act of the will, is in the intelligent being intelligibly, as in its primary source and proper subject. That is why the Philosopher says that "the will is in the reason." [26] Now whatever is intelligibly in an intelligent subject is understood by that subject. Therefore the act of the will is understood by the intellect, both in that one perceives that one wills, and in that one knows the nature of this act, and consequently, the nature of its source, which is a habit or a power.

Reply Objection 1. This argument would hold good if the will and the intellect were in different subjects, in addition to being distinct powers; for then whatever was in the will would not be in the intellect. But since both are rooted in the same substance of the soul, and since one is in a

---

23. *Confessions* X, 17.
24. *On the Trinity* X, 11.
25. Question LIX, article 1.
26. *On the Soul* III, 9(432b5).

way the source of the other, it follows that what is in the will is, in a way, also in the intellect.

Reply Objection 2. The good and the true, which are the objects of the will and of the intellect, differ logically, but one is contained in the other, as was said above;[27] for the true is a certain good, and the good is a certain true. Therefore the objects of the will fall under the intellect, and those of the intellect can fall under the will.

Reply Objection 3. The affections of the soul are in the intellect, not by likeness only, as are bodies, nor as being present in their subject, as are the arts; but as the thing caused is in its source, which contains the notion of the thing caused. And so Augustine says that the soul's affections are in the memory by certain notions.

27. Question LXXXII, article 4, ad 1; question XVI, article 4, ad 1.

How the Human Soul Knows What Is Above Itself

(In Three Articles)

First Article

DOES THE HUMAN SOUL IN THE PRESENT STATE OF LIFE UNDERSTAND IMMATERIAL SUBSTANCES IN THEMSELVES?

Objection 1. It seems that the human soul in the present state of life can know immaterial substances in themselves. For Augustine says: "As the mind itself acquires the knowledge of corporeal things by means of the corporeal senses, so it gains through itself the knowledge of incorporeal things." [1] But these are the immaterial substances. Therefore the human mind knows immaterial substances.

Objection 2. Moreover, like is known by like. But the human mind is more akin to immaterial than to material things; since its own nature is immaterial, as is clear from what was said above.[2] Since then our mind knows material things, much more is it able to know immaterial things.

Objection 3. Again, the fact that objects which are in themselves most eminently sensible are not most perceived by us, comes from the fact that the sense is overwhelmed by their very pre-eminence. But the intellect is not subject to such a disorganizing influence from the superiority of its object, as is said.[3] Therefore things which are in themselves in the highest degree of intelligibility are likewise to us most intelligible. Since material things, however, are intelligible only so far as we make them actually so, by abstracting them from material conditions, it is clear that those substances are more intelligible in themselves whose nature is immaterial. Therefore they are much more known to us than are material things.

Objection 4. And again, the Commentator says that, "nature would be frustrated in its end were we unable to know abstract substances, because it would have made what in itself is naturally intelligible not to be known

---

1. *On the Trinity* IX, 3.
2. Question LXXVI, article 1.
3. Aristotle, *On the Soul* III, 4(429b2).

at all." [4] But in nature nothing is idle or purposeless. Therefore imma terial substances can be known by us.

Objection 5. Also, as the sense is to the sensible, so is the intellect to the intelligible. But our sight can see all things corporeal, whether superior and incorruptible, or sublunary and corruptible. Therefore our intellect can know all intelligible substances, including the superior and immaterial.

On the contrary: It is written (*Wisdom 9:16*): "The things that are in heaven, who shall search out?" But these substances are said to be in heaven, according to *Matthew 18:10,* "their angels in heaven," etc. Therefore immaterial substances cannot be known by human investigation.

I answer that: In the opinion of Plato, immaterial substances are not only known by us, but are also the objects we know first of all. For Plato taught that immaterial subsisting Forms, which he called "Ideas," are the proper objects of our intellect, and are thus first and essentially known by us. Furthermore, material things are known by the soul in so far as imagination and sense are joined to the intellect. Hence the purer the intellect is, so much the more clearly does it perceive the intelligible truth of immaterial things.[5]

But in Aristotle's judgment, which experience corroborates, our intellect in its present state of life has a natural relation to the natures of material things; and therefore it can know only by turning to sense images, as was said above.[6] Thus it clearly appears that immaterial substances, which do not fall under sense and imagination, cannot be known by us first and essentially, according to the mode of knowledge of which we have experience.

Nevertheless Averroes teaches that in this present life man can in the end arrive at the knowledge of separate substances by being joined or united to a certain separate substance, which he calls the "agent intellect," and which, being a separate substance itself, can naturally know separate substances.[7] Hence, when it is united to us so that we are enabled to know perfectly through it, we too shall be able to know separate substances; just as in the present life, through the possible intellect united to us, we can understand material things.

Now he held that the agent intellect is united to us as follows.[8] For since we understand by means of both the agent intellect and intelligible objects (as, for instance, we grasp conclusions through principles already known), the agent intellect must be compared to the objects known, either

4. Averroes, *Commentary on Aristotle's "Metaphysics"* II, comm. 1(VIII, 14v). (Not available in English.)

5. cf. Plato, *Phaedo* 80A-B.

6. Question LXXXIV, article 7.

7. *Commentary on Aristotle's "On the Soul"* III, comm. 36, pt. 5 (VI, 1780). (Not available in English.)

8. *ibid.,* (VI, 179rv).

as the principle agent is to the instrument, or as form to matter. For an action is attributed to two principles in one of these two ways: (1) to a principal agent and to an instrument, as cutting to the workman and the saw; (2) to a form and its subject, as heating to heat and fire. In both these ways the agent intellect can be compared to the intelligible object as perfection is to the perfectible, and as act is to potency. Now a subject is made perfect and receives its perfection at one and the same time, as the reception of what is actually visible synchronizes with the reception of light in the eye. Therefore the possible intellect receives the intelligible object and the agent intellect at the same time. And the more numerous the intelligible objects received, so much the nearer do we come to the point of perfect union between ourselves and the agent intellect; so much so, that when we shall have understood all the intelligible objects, the agent intellect will become perfectly united to us, and through it we shall understand all things material and immaterial. In this he makes the ultimate happiness of man to consist. Nor, as regards the present inquiry, does it matter whether the possible intellect in that state of happiness understands separate substances through the agent intellect, as he himself maintains, or whether (as he imputes to Alexander) the possible intellect can never understand separate substances (because according to him it is corruptible), but man understands separate substances through the agent intellect.

All this, however, is untrue. *First*, because, supposing the agent intellect to be a separate substance, we could not formally know through it; for the formal medium of an agent's action is its own form and act, since every agent acts according as it is in act, as was said of the possible intellect.[9] *Secondly*, this opinion is untrue because the agent intellect, supposing it to be a separate substance, would not be joined to us in its substance, but only in its light, as participated in the objects known by us. But this would not extend to the other acts of the agent intellect so as to enable us to know immaterial substances; just as when we see colors illuminated by the sun, we are not united to the substance of the sun so as to act like the sun, but only its light is united to us, that we may see the colors.

Thirdly, this opinion is untrue because, even supposing that the agent intellect were united to us in substance in the aforesaid manner, still it is not said that it is wholly united to us according to one intelligible object, or two; but rather according to all intelligible objects. But all such objects together do not equal the power of the agent intellect, as it is a much greater thing to know separate substances than to know all material things. Hence it clearly follows that the knowledge of all material things would not make the agent intellect to be so united to us as to enable us to understand separate substances through it.

---

9. Question LXXVI, article 1.

Fourthly, this opinion is untrue because it is hardly possible for anyone in this world to understand all material things; and thus no one, or very few, would reach perfect felicity. This is against the Philosopher's dictum that happiness is a "kind of common good, communicable to all capable of virtue." [10] Further, it is against reason that only the few of any species attain to the end of the species.

Fifthly, the Philosopher expressly says that happiness is "an operation according to perfect virtue";[11] and after enumerating many virtues he concludes that ultimate happiness, consisting in the knowledge of the highest things intelligible, is attained through the virtue of wisdom,[12] which he had named as the chief of the speculative sciences.[13] Hence Aristotle clearly placed the ultimate felicity of man in that knowledge of separate substances which is obtainable by speculative science; and not in any union with the agent intellect, as some have imagined.

Sixthly, as was shown above, the agent intellect is not a separate substance, but a power of the soul, extending itself actively to the same objects to which the possible intellect extends receptively;[14] because, as Aristotle states, the possible intellect is "all things potentially," and the agent intellect is "all things in act." [15] Therefore both intellects, according to the present state of life, extend only to material things, which are made actually intelligible by the agent intellect, and are received in the possible intellect. Hence, in the present state of life, we cannot know immaterial substances in themselves, either by the possible or by the agent intellect.

Reply Objection 1. Augustine may be taken to mean that the knowledge of incorporeal things in the mind can be gained through the mind itself. This is so true that Aristotle also remarks that the knowledge concerning the soul is a kind of source for the knowledge of separate substances. For by knowing itself, the soul attains to some knowledge of incorporeal realities such as is within its compass; not that the knowledge of itself gives it a perfect and absolute knowledge of them.

Reply Objection 2. The likeness of nature is not a sufficient principle of knowledge. Otherwise, one would have to say with Empedocles that the soul needs to have the nature of all in order to know all.[16] But knowledge requires that the likeness of the thing known be in the knower, as a kind of form in the knower. Now our possible intellect, in the present state of life, is such that it can be informed with the likenesses

---

10. *Nichomachean Ethics* I, 9(1099b18).
11. *op. cit.,* I, 10(1101a14).
12. *op. cit.,* X, 7(1177a21); 8(1179a30).
13. *op. cit.,* VI, 7(1141a20).
14. Question LXXIX, article 4.
15. *On the Soul* III, 5(430a14).
16. cf. *Fragment* 333, Book II, and Aristotle, *On the Soul* I, 2(404b11).

abstracted from sense images: and therefore it knows material things rather than immaterial substances.

Reply Objection 3. There must be a certain commensuration between the object and the power of knowledge; as between the active and the passive, between the perfection and the perfectible. Hence that sensible objects of the highest order are not grasped by the senses is due not merely to the fact that they overwhelm the organ, but also to their being disproportionate to the sensory powers. And it is thus that immaterial substances are not proportionate to our intellect, in our present state of life; so that it cannot know them.

Reply Objection 4. This argument of the Commentator fails in several ways. *First,* because if separate substances are not known by us, it does not follow that they are not known by any intellect; for they are known by themselves, and by one another.

Secondly, to be known by us is not the end of separate substances; and only that is vain and purposeless which fails to attain its end. It does not follow, therefore, that immaterial substances are purposeless, even if they are not at all known by us.

Reply Objection 5. The sense power knows bodies, whether higher or lower, in the same way, i.e., by the sensible thing acting on the organ. But we do not know material and immaterial substances in the same way. The former we know by abstraction, which is impossible in the case of the latter, for there are no sense representations of what is immaterial.

Second Article

CAN OUR INTELLECT COME

TO KNOW IMMATERIAL SUBSTANCES

THROUGH ITS KNOWLEDGE OF MATERIAL THINGS?

Objection 1. It seems that our intellect can come to know immaterial substances through the knowledge of material things. For Dionysius says that "the human mind cannot be raised up to immaterial contemplation of the heavenly hierarchies, unless it uses thereto material guidance according to its own nature." [17] Therefore we can be led by material things to know immaterial substances.

Objection 2. Moreover, science resides in the intellect. But there are sciences and definitions of immaterial substances; for Damascene defines an angel,[18] and we find angels discussed both in theology and in philosophy. Therefore immaterial substances can be understood by us.

17. *On the Celestial Hierarchy* I, 3. (Not available in English.)
18. *On the Orthodox Faith* II, 3. (Not available in English.)

Objection 3. Again, the human soul belongs to the genus of immaterial substances. But it can be understood by us through its act, by which it knows material things. Therefore other immaterial substances also can be known by us, through their effects in material things.

Objection 4. And again, the only cause which cannot be comprehended through its effects is that which infinitely transcends them, and this belongs to God alone. Therefore other created immaterial substances can be understood by us through material things.

On the contrary: Dionysius says that "intelligible things cannot be known through sensible things, nor composite things through simple, nor incorporeal things through corporeal." [19]

I answer that: Averroes says that a philosopher named Avempace taught that by the understanding of material substances we can be led, according to true philosophical principles, to the knowledge of immaterial substances.[20] For since it is the nature of our intellect to abstract the quiddity of material things from matter, anything material residing in that abstracted quiddity can again be made subject to abstraction. And as the process of abstraction cannot go on forever, it must finally arrive at the knowledge of a quiddity which is absolutely without matter—to wit, the knowledge of an immaterial substance.

Now this opinion would be true, were immaterial substances the forms and natures of these material things, as the Platonists thought. But supposing, on the contrary, that immaterial substances differ altogether from the quiddity of material things, it follows that, however much our intellect may abstract the quiddity of a material thing from matter, it could never arrive at anything like an immaterial substance. Therefore we are not able to know immaterial substances perfectly[21] through material substances.

Reply Objection 1. From material things we can rise to some sort of knowledge of immaterial things, but not to a perfect knowledge; for there is no proper and adequate proportion between material and immaterial things, and the likenesses drawn from material things for the understanding of immaterial things are very unlike them, as Dionysius says.[22]

Reply Objection 2. Science treats of higher things principally by way of remotion. Thus Aristotle explains the heavenly bodies by denying to them the properties of sublunary bodies.[23] Hence it follows that much less can immaterial substances be known by us in such a way as to make

---

19. *The Divine Names* I, 1.

20. *Commentary on Aristotle's "On the Soul"* III, comm. 36, pt. 3(VI, 177v-178v). (Not available in English.)

21. i.e., directly, affirmatively, quidditatively, as contrasted with indirectly, negatively, analogically.

22. *On the Celestial Hierarchy* II, 2. (Not available in English.)

23. *On the Heavens,* I, 3(269b18).

us know their quiddity; but we may have a knowledge of them from the sciences by way of negation and through their relation to material things.

Reply Objection 3. The human soul knows itself through its own act of knowing, which is proper to it, showing perfectly its power and nature. But the power and nature of immaterial substances cannot be perfectly known through such an act, nor through any other and material thing, because there is no proportion between the latter and the power of the former.

Reply Objection 4. Created immaterial substances are not in the same natural genus as material substances, for they do not agree in power or in matter; but they belong to the same logical genus, because even immaterial substances are in the category of substance, since their essence is distinct from their act of being. But God has nothing in common with material things either according to a natural genus or a logical one; because God is not in any genus whatever, as was stated above.[24] Hence through the likenesses derived from material things we can know something positive concerning the angels, according to some common notion, though not according to their specific nature; whereas we cannot acquire any such knowledge at all about God.

Third Article

IS GOD THE FIRST OBJECT KNOWN BY THE HUMAN MIND?

Objection 1. It seems that God is the first object known by the human mind. For that object in which all others are known, and by which we judge others, is the first thing known to us; as light is to the eye, and first principles to the intellect. But "we know all things in the light of the first truth, and thereby judge of all things," as Augustine says.[25] Therefore God is the first object known to us.

Objection 2. Moreover, there is the axiom: The cause of the formal perfection of each thing has that perfection in a higher degree. But God is the cause of all our knowledge; for "He is the true light which enlighteneth every man that cometh into this world" (*John 1:9*). Therefore God is our first and most known object.

Objection 3. Again, what is first known in an image is the exemplar to which the image is formed. But in our mind is "the image of God," as Augustine says.[26] Therefore God is the first object known to our mind.

On the contrary: "No man hath seen God at any time" (*John 1:18*).

I answer that: Since the human intellect in the present state of life cannot know immaterial created substances, much less can it know the

---

24. Question III, article 5.
25. *On the Trinity* XII, 2.
26. *op. cit.,* XII, 4.

essence of the uncreated substance. Hence it must be said unqualifiedly that God is not the first object of our knowledge. Rather, we come to know God through creatures, according to the Apostle (*Romans 1:20*): "the invisible things of God are clearly seen, being understood through the things that are made." Now the first object of our knowledge in this life is the quiddity of a material thing, which is the proper object of our intellect, as was repeatedly noted above.[27]

Reply Objection 1. We see and judge of all things in the light of the first truth, insofar as the light itself of our intellect, whether natural or gratuitous, is nothing else than an impression of the first truth upon it, as was said above.[28] Hence, since the light itself of our intellect is not that which the intellect knows, but the medium whereby it knows, much less can it be said that God is the first thing known by our intellect.

Reply Objection 2. The axiom, "Whatever causes a thing to be such, is more so," must be understood of things belonging to one and the same order, as was explained above.[29] Other things than God are known because of God, not as if He were the first known object, but because He is the first cause of our power of knowledge.

Reply Objection 3. If there existed in our souls a perfect image of God, as the Son is the perfect image of the Father, our mind would know God at once. But the image in our mind is imperfect;[30] and hence the argument does not hold.

---

27. Question LXXXIV, article 7; question LXXXV, article 8; question LXXXVII, article 2, ad 2.

28. Question XII, article 11, ad 3; question LXXXIV, article 5.

29. Question LXXXVII, article 2, ad 3.

30. ". . . in man there is some likeness to God, copied from God as from an exemplar; yet this likeness is not one of equality, for such an exemplar infinitely excells its copy." —St. Thomas Aquinas *Summa Theologiae* I, q. 93, a. 1.